CW01647961

The Quiet Revolutionary

Errata:
Brandler's co-founder of the KPO was August Thalheimer, not Thalmann (page 147, line 9); the last democratic elections to the Reichstag were in 1933, not 1934 (page 157, line 1).

Bookmarks
London, Chicago and Melbourne

The Quiet Revolutionary

The Autobiography of Margaret Dewar

The Quiet Revolutionary
by Margaret Dewar

Published March 1989
Bookmarks, 265 Seven Sisters Road, London N4 2DE, England
Bookmarks, PO Box 16085, Chicago, IL 60616, USA
Bookmarks, GPO Box 1473N, Melbourne 3001, Australia
Copyright © Bookmarks and Margaret Dewar

ISBN 0 906224 50 0

Printed by Biddles Limited, Guildford, England
Cover design by Roger Huddle

Bookmarks is linked to an international grouping of socialist organisations:

Australia: *International Socialists*, GPO Box 1473N, Melbourne 3001
Belgium: *Socialisme International*, 9 rue Marexhe, 4400 Herstal, Liege
Britain: *Socialist Workers Party*, PO Box 82, London E3
Canada: *International Socialists*, PO Box 339, Station E, Toronto, Ontario M6H 4E3
Denmark: *Internationale Socialister*, Morten Borupsgade 18, kld, 8000 Arhus C
France: *Socialisme International*, BP 189, 75926 Paris Cedex 19
Ireland: *Socialist Workers Movement*, PO Box 1648, Dublin 8
Norway: *Internasjonale Sosialister*, Postboks 5370, Majorstua, 0304 Oslo 3
United States: *International Socialist Organization*, PO Box 16085, Chicago, IL 60622
West Germany: *Sozialistische Arbeiter Gruppe*, Wolfgangstrasse 81, D-6000 Frankfurt 1

This book is published with the aid of the Bookmarks Publishing Co-operative . Many socialists have some savings put aside, probably in a bank or savings bank. While it is there, this money is being loaned out by the bank to some business or other to further the capitalist search for profit. We believe it is better loaned to a socialist venture to further the struggle for socialism. That's how the co-operative works: in return for a loan, repayable at a month's notice, members receive free copies of books published by Boookmarks. At the time this book was published, the co-operative had more than 250 members, from as far apart as London and Malaysia, Canada and Norway.

Like to know more? Write to the Bookmarks Publishing Co-operative, 265 Seven Sisters Road, Finsbury Park, London N4 2DE, England.

Dedication

To the memory of those who taught me to see the world as it is and as it should be.
Above all to the memory of Hugo, to whom I owe so much and who first urged me to write down these pages.
My special thanks are due to Margaret Renn and Peter Marsden for their encouragement and patient help.

Contents

Part One:
Life in Russia

CHAPTER 1

Earliest Memories

THE YEAR was 1904. We were travelling in a *kibitka* through the snow. Sitting snugly on straw in the depth of the sleigh, wrapped up to the tips of our noses in rugs, our nanny, my sister Helga and I were following the *kibitka* carrying my parents, on our way from the port of Arkhangelsk to Ust-Tsylma, some 300 miles further north-east, less than a hundred miles from the Arctic Circle. Suddenly our *kibitka* turned over and we all tumbled into the deep snow. No harm was done, except for the shock to our parents. My sister was just over a year old, I was three. These are my very first memories.

Why were we travelling so far north? My father had been manager of a pencil factory in Riga, the capital of Latvia, which was at that time part of Russia. In a desire to branch out on his own, he had decided, in partnership with a Polish civil engineer, to explore the slate deposits near Ust-Tsylma. The slate proved to be of inferior quality, the venture came to nothing and we returned to Riga about a year and a half later.

In spite of some difficulties, life there was not unpleasant according to my mother. Ust-Tsylma was the district town of the region, a glorified village where the rivers Tsylma and Pechora meet. It consisted of one-storey log-houses for the local people and larger two-storey houses for the doctor, the judge, the teacher, the paymaster, and for us. This was the sum total of the élite—all Russians, except my family who were a mixture. The rest of the population were the *Samoyedy*, a slightly Mongolian type of people—now called by their ethnic name *Nentsy*, the inhabitants of the Nenetski and two neighbouring districts. They were breeders of reindeer, fishermen, and some worked at the nearby sawmill (which provided Helga and me with sawdust, in place of sand, to play with).

As I look at the map I see that even now there is no railway line running through those parts, though oil has been discovered on the Yamal Peninsula. Reindeer were the only means of transport in winter, as horses were unable to stand the temperatures down to minus 40 degrees Centigrade. Large stretches of the tundra were permanently frozen to a considerable depth. In the short but quite warm summer the surface of the tundra turned into marshes and bogs. Vegetation was poor, but there were coniferous virgin forests and I remember a picnic in the summer on the edge of a forest by a small stream and my father standing on the top of a hill on the other side. I insisted on following him, promptly slipped on the flat stones and had to be rescued, wet and howling.

The people of the region were friendly, and were hardy workers, if rather primitive and mostly illiterate. A young woman who helped my mother in the house, a young wife of six months' standing, sobbed bitterly, complaining that her husband did not love her. Proof of this was, as she explained to my mother, that he had never yet beaten her, a custom which he had apparently shed after working for a time in a larger town. The log houses were primitive, as were most peasant houses in Russia before the Revolution. Ust-Tsylma had one common bath house, a sort of sauna where the locals all used to go together; there they sweated on hot bricks, slashing each other with birch branches to massage themselves, pouring hot water over themselves from wooden buckets. Then, stark naked, they hopped out into the cold air, rolled themselves in the freezing snow, and then repeated the process of steaming and cooling off. I imagine we and the rest of the 'élite' had some sort of wash tubs in our houses, which had to be filled and emptied by hand.

In winter everybody—men, women and children—wore *malitzas*, a kind of reindeer-skin coat, hand-sewn together in one piece, which had to be pulled on and off over the head. On our feet we wore high, soft, fur boots, called *pimy*, beautifully made from long strips of reindeer fur, dyed in different colours. For winter entertainment the five families got together for parties and dances, and sometimes a fancy-dress ball. I remember a photograph of my parents dressed in native wedding attire: the bridegroom in a long reindeer-skin tunic, the bride in a similar coat-dress, made of some thick, luxurious, golden material, which my mother had borrowed from somebody.

Sometimes some of the men would organise excursions to surrounding areas. My father, who was very keen on collecting and pressing plants, was astonished to find Forget-me-nots beyond the Arctic circle.

On the whole life was quite bearable. In the short summer,

when the rivers and the Barents Sea were free of ice, huge barges would arrive, selling household goods, fabrics, clothing, tools, and all sorts of luxury food. The paymaster had taken a fancy to us children, especially me, as I could already walk around and talk. He used to take me to the barges and treat me to delicious sweets, lovely toys and dolls, as well as the traditional carved and painted Russian bowls and spoons.

When we returned to Riga, We went by ship to Arkhangelsk. One morning my mother called me to the port-hole of the cabin and I saw with astonishment huge ice blocks, almost mountains, floating in the water, lit up in pink and pale yellow in the early morning sun.

This was 1905. At about the time of our return the Revolution broke out. The defeat of the Russian navy in the war against Japan and growing unrest among workers and peasants throughout the summer, had led in October to the setting up of the workers' councils (*soviets*) in St Petersburg, under Leon Trotsky's leadership. Later, my mother told us about shooting, dead bodies in the streets of Riga, and her anxiety every time my father had to leave the house. I don't think she knew what it was all about, and at the time, of course, I knew nothing. All I remember of that winter was that an ice rink was made for me in the back garden of our house and on my fifth birthday I was given my first pair of skates.

I was born early in 1901 and named Margarete. But Rita was the name I became known by, from the Russian Margarita. My sister Helga was born next, in 1902. Our brother Hardy was born in 1906. During the First World War we Russified her name to Olga, or Olya, and called Hardy by his second name, Andreas—or Andryusha for short. When Hardy was born we were kept in the garden all day while my mother was in labour. She was disappointed as she would have liked only daughters. But she loved him dearly all the same, especially as he was a frail child during the first years of his life. The doctors diagnosed haemophilia and he was frequently 'at death's door'. His condition improved in later years and disappeared altogether when he grew up. Perhaps it was a false diagnosis.

My mother Ella had rather delicate health, probably because she worried about my brother. She had married at eighteen or nineteen; my father, Leonard Watz, was twelve years older. But my mother must have been pretty tough, having to withstand all our moves and see us through most of the children's diseases that were rampant in those days: measles, scarlet fever, whooping cough, diphtheria and the like. Our family doctor was a familiar figure in our house.

During that time in Riga I became more aware of our extended family. My mother's father had died early, leaving his widow to bring up five daughters and two sons on his civil service pension. I have a photograph in which our stately and handsome grandmother sits with an air of quiet and slightly amused authority, surrounded by all her children, a daughter-in-law and a son in-law.

After 1940, when the Baltic states were occupied by the Russians, and later incorporated into the USSR as federal republics, these aunts emigrated to Germany together with their husbands and children. Only one cousin, a forester, and our uncle Arthur stayed on.

We saw far less of the relatives on my father's side, yet I remember more of their way of life—perhaps because it was so very different. They had a farm at a place called Rujen, with fields, horses, cows and other animals. The one-storey timber house was spacious, and I particularly remember a large, light room with colourful home-made rugs on the white-washed wooden floor, and my grandmother's bedroom with numerous pillows of varying sizes piled up in pyramid-fashion, and a large, high chest of drawers. There was also a separate building, a kitchen with two large, built-in cauldrons where something was always simmering and being stirred.

There was another room where the family sat together in the evening. It was darkly lit with candles or paraffin lamps, and my baby sister lay in an old cradle which hung from the ceiling. Once, when I was rocking the cradle, the spring near the ceiling suddenly snapped and hit my sister on the forehead very near her eyes. The scar remained for many years. I was petrified and, though it was obviously not my fault, went round the room saying, 'I am sorry', to every single person. I seem to have been obsessed by feelings of guilt when very small.

They too were a large family. My father had ten or eleven brothers and sisters, but the only ones we knew well were my father's youngest sister Victoria—Aunt Tori—who subsequently lived with us for several years, and Uncle Oskar, who stayed with us in Riga during his vacations while a medical student. He later became a very successful gynaecologist with a house in Riga and a summer house at the seaside. He too emigrated in 1940 with his wife, daughter and son-in-law, to Eastern Germany—where he worked at a hospital, had his private practice and was called upon for his opinion as a forensic consultant. He died at a very ripe old age.

My father's family were Latvian. Our grandmother spoke hardly any Russian or German. The daughters knew more Russian than German, and all except Aunt Tori married locally and stayed on the land. As children we were not really conscious of our partly Latvian ancestry, or at any rate it did not mean anything to us. Latvian was never spoken at home, except when our mother and Aunt Tori wanted to talk about something that we were not supposed to know (when, with a kind of sixth sense, I always vaguely guessed what it was about). It was the language of the lower classes, the workers and peasants, the artisans and servants. When Latvian parents were in a position to afford a secondary education and perhaps university for their sons (hardly ever for daughters), many of them no longer considered themselves Latvians, but merged with the native German middle class, all of whom spoke Russian owing (or thanks) to the Russification policy of the Tsarist government.

Latvia was one of the Baltic states. Together with Estonia, it came under Russian rule in the 18th century; Lithuania followed after one of the partitions of Poland. They were all to become independent Republics for the first time after the 1917 Revolution. At the beginning of the century the population of Latvia was 65 per cent Latvians and about 15 per cent each Germans and Russians. The Germans, possibly because of their generally better education and standard of living, played a significant role in the running of the country. Even before 1917 there must have been a national liberation movement among the younger generation of middle-class Latvians, and some Latvians joined the Red Army and the state political administration which later became the KGB, the secret police.

Aunt Tori became our main contact with our Latvian background. She came to live with us for a number of years after we had moved to St Petersburg in 1907. She must have been around twenty then, cheerful and a good companion for us children. She used to sing Latvian folk-songs and tell us about country customs. In those years we went to the farm for holidays, and were once allowed to watch the mid-summer's night festival, when young girls and boys dressed in their attractive national costumes, the girls with embroidered white blouses, swinging skirts, wreaths of flowers and long multi-coloured ribbons on their heads; the boys in embroidered shirts. They danced their national dances and sang. At midnight fires were lit and the boys and girls jumped through the flames.

In later years, even after we had moved to St Petersburg, we went to the seaside instead. The Baltic coast is ideal for summer holidays with its fine, white sand, long, almost melancholy, dunes, and, behind them, high and slender pine trees. The scent of the pines combined with the smell of the sea was wonderful. Sometimes a whiff of smoke would drift across from the huts and the shacks where freshly caught fish was smoked or cured. There was no tide, but to a small child the waves in windy weather seemed enormously high. The bathing costumes of the women would bulge out in the wind like red or blue balloons with white patterns. They looked rather funny, their sleeves with frills and ribbons right down to the elbow, the legs reaching down to the knees. With the bathing suits went a bonnet adorned with lace and ribbons. That must have been for mixed bathing, because a little further along the beach there was also nude bathing, at different times for women and for men. I don't remember what kind of bathing suits we children wore. I only remember our play-suits, which my mother had made for us herself: bright red with white; bulging knickers with braces and elastic around the waist, to be worn with or without a blouse. I found them ridiculous and hated wearing them, but had to all the same.

There was a footpath of long planks of wood, separating the houses and villas from the beach, but no real promenade. There were larger, more fashionable seaside resorts, with a proper promenade, cafés and other places of amusement, but our parents seemed content with the more modest one. And the sea and sand did my little brother no end of good. One year, somebody suggested 'sand baths' for him because of his poor health, so we buried him in the sand regularly, right up to his neck. When we returned to town our family doctor could hardly believe he was the same child, so good and almost unexpected was his recovery.

In St Petersburg we lived in a flat in a large house on the corner of two wide streets. Our walks were now mainly in the Botanical Gardens nearby. My most vivid memory is of one of the hot-houses, which contained a pond and on it a most unusual plant, a *Victoria Regis*, completely flat with an upturned rim, which looked like a gigantic green frying pan. We were told by one of the attendants that the plant was strong enough to hold my five-year-old sister. Sometimes in winter we were taken for walks through the streets, our little brother sitting in a pram (there were no push-chairs in those days) or carried by my mother or Aunt Tori. He would be wrapped up in a long white coat with a cape reaching over his shoulders and arms, a blue gauze veil protecting his face from the cold wind and his eyes from the glare of the sun.

St Petersburg was built at the beginning of the 18th century by Peter the Great. He had travelled abroad, had studied West European industrial and technical methods and had himself worked for a time as a ship's carpenter in Holland. He was determined to introduce these methods in backward Russia which still lived in the Dark Ages, with harsh and rigorous measures against those who dared to oppose the will of the Tsars. He made the Boyars, the ruling clique, shave off their long beards and exchange their tunic-like kaftans for European clothes, much to their disgust and opposition. But he persisted. And he could also swing an axe and a hammer. He first built the port and fortress of Kronstadt in the gulf of Finland as a protection for the future town of St Petersburg, and as a base for the Baltic Fleet which was to play such a victorious role in the revolution of 1917, and such a disputed role in the uprising of 1921 against the policy of the Bolsheviks. Peter the great built himself a tiny house right by the river Neva, rolled up his sleeves and got down to building this fleet, directing and supervising, earning himself the title 'the carpenter-Tsar'. That tiny house, full of tools and drawings plus a bed, is probably still there, unless it has been transferred somewhere else since my childhood days.

He then started on the construction of St Petersburg, on land reclaimed in the estuary of the Neva. He engaged French and Italian architects, who planned a spacious city of classical beauty, with numerous outstanding buildings. Later the resplendent Isaac Cathedral was built, with its huge cupola covered with gold leaf, and many splendid palaces for the aristocracy alongside the canals. On one of the squares a bronze memorial was erected on a granite block: Peter the Great sitting on a rearing horse with one arm outstretched over the city he had built. In time, St Petersburg became the capital city, an international cultural and social centre, and also the chief industrial centre of Russia with its large armament plants, the workers of which played such a decisive role in 1905 and 1917.

On 9 January 1905 some 200,000 workers, led by the priest Gapon, a police stooge, gathered on the vast parade ground in front of the Winter Palace to petition Tsar Nicholas II for better working conditions, an easing of the autocratic regime and a constitutional government. In reply thousands of workers on the parade ground, as well as in other parts of the city, were mowed down by artillery fire, thus unleashing the first Russian Revolution—the dress rehearsal for 1917.

I remember some of the more prominent buildings and streets in St Petersburg, but my most vivid memory is of the Peter and Paul Fortress, with its sharp golden needle glistening in the sun and stretching high into the sky. Many revolutionaries, men and women, languished there for years, some till they died, others till they were banished to Siberia. Many made the long trek into exile on foot with chains around their ankles. Their plight had been described in the Russian literature of the 19th century, as had the compassion shown to them in the countryside.

The fortress is situated on the banks of the Neva by a bridge which we had to cross over whenever we went to the centre of the town. I knew what it was, but, of course, at the age of seven or eight I knew next to nothing of history or politics. For me, as for many others, it just happened to be near where the great event of the year took place: the breaking of the ice on the Neva in spring. It was an impressive spectacle. A few days before the ice got going there was a roar and a rumbling, and sounds as if from an explosion. Then the people knew: *'Lyod poshol!'*—'The ice is on the move'. The first real cracks were then announced by cannon shots from the Peter and Paul Fortress, and everybody who could would rush to the embankments or on to the bridge. It was a tremendous sight: the masses of ice split, small and large cracks appeared, lumps of ice of all sizes and shapes would pile one upon the other, crushing into each other with crunching and grinding sounds, and all this mass moving in a steady, rapid stream towards the estuary and the sea. I was allowed to watch this spectacle from the bridge with Aunt Tori. Then summer came with its white nights. What a bore it was to have to go to bed in daylight!

I regret never having revisited what is now Leningrad—St Petersburg became Petrograd during the First World War, and Leningrad after the October Revolution; it also ceased to be the capital, which moved to Moscow. I had an opportunity to go back in 1931, but I didn't have the time—of this more in due course.

But I did visit Moscow again, in 1961, working as an interpreter at the British Industrial Trade Fair which was held in the huge Sokolniki Park on the outskirts. The delegates and interpreters were able to book theatre and concert tickets through Intourist, the state travel agency, and most of the businessmen and their secretaries went to the ballet at the Bolshoi Theatre. I went to the opera, for old times' sake, and to a play at the Maly Theatre (the equivalent of London's National Theatre).

But what I wanted to see was a new play, **The Emperor's**

New Clothes, at the small Sokolniki Theatre. All the tickets were sold out, Intourist assured me. This may have been true, but I knew the play was about Stalin and his disastrous personality cult, which had been denounced by Khrushchev in 1956. A period of relaxation had followed, reflected in changes in the economy, in politics and in the arts—the ice was on the move. So I went to the theatre's director, explained that I and a colleague were anxious to see the play, and he kindly gave us tickets. It was an amazing play, full of allusions to Stalin while keeping strictly to the original story. There was an unmistakeable stirring in the theatre and two youngish men sitting in front of us kept turning to each other with amazed and delighted expressions on their faces. The 'ice' was indeed on the move!

I started school at the age of seven, which is still customary in Russia, but in those days school was not compulsory. Consequently, the illiteracy rate among the workers and, particularly, the peasants of pre-revolutionary Russia was extremely high. I was sent to the German school, and though I must have attended the preparatory forms for two years, I remember nothing at all of those school days. All I recollect are the tram rides to school with my father, who usually sat reading the paper. I tried to imitate him—with some difficulty, since the paper was too large for a small child to handle. But I could read—my mother taught me when I was five—and I was trying to puzzle out what could be interesting in a newspaper. I asked my father whether everything printed in it was true. With slight amusement, perhaps mixed with cynicism, my father replied: 'Some of it is.'

I wish I could recollect something of my first school years, but there is a complete blank. However, I clearly remember homework sessions under the strict supervision of my mother, who aimed at near perfection for her first-born, and many times I had to copy and recopy the work. Apart from that my mother spent a great deal of time playing with us and teaching us to do things. Among the games I disliked intensely was a singing and miming game, 'the washerwomen', where we had to imitate their movements during the whole process of washing.

There were no washing machines or launderettes in those days. Whoever could afford it, and did not have sufficient permanent maids to live in, hired a woman for the whole day to rub the washing—everything from handkerchiefs to sheets—over a washing board in the kitchen sink, after boiling the whites in a big container on the wood-burning kitchen stove. The sheets were pulled straight by two people, folded and put through the mangle.

Ironing was done with big clumsy irons filled with glowing charcoal, which had to be renewed as soon as the coal had burnt out. A laborious process, the whole business.

To our great delight on these days, and occasionally on Saturdays when there was a lot of baking going on, we often just had boiled potatoes with marinated herring and onions for lunch or, better still, slices of very fresh black bread, thickly spread with butter and tomatoes—much better than the usual two or even three-course midday meal.

I was not very fond of dolls. I much preferred to play with small tin soldiers, of which I had quite a collection. (Yet military music in the streets always made me cry.) But one day sticks in my memory: rebuked by my mother for not playing often enough with Helga, I got conscience-stricken and spent a whole day with her, trundling our dolls' prams up and down the corridor, in and out of the rooms, dressing and undressing them. That night I felt very virtuous when I went to bed.

Much more fun than dolls and miming games were the various handicraft skills our mother taught us. Fretwork was fascinating, and painting on cloth, and burning various designs with specially heated needles on wooden objects—boxes, trays, napkin rings and so on. We loved modelling with plasticine, and I was particularly fond of making tiny objects from aluminium foil. Our parents themselves took pleasure in making things for us, especially at Christmas: dolls' houses, furniture, dolls' dresses and similar things.

What a delight Christmas was in my childhood. There was nothing commercialised about the festival. Simply mystery and anticipation were in the air: the carrying and hiding of parcels by our parents; their inexplicable activities, which stopped in a pointedly casual way the moment we entered the room. Of course, we always knew that all this concerned Christmas and we desperately tried to discover what exactly was planned. The last few days before Christmas Eve the flat was full of cooking and baking smells: the traditional *Pfefferkuchen*—brown, spiced treacle biscuits, sand-biscuits that melted in your mouth, cakes and tarts. On Christmas Eve itself there was always clear soup with small savouries, shaped like half moons, filled with chopped bacon and onions; home-made brawn and other Baltic delicacies. For Christmas dinner the Russian tradition was to have a stuffed, roasted, suckling pig. There was a big market in the centre of Moscow, where row upon row of stiff, pink piglets were laid out for the inspection of prospective customers.

The living room with the tall Christmas tree reaching from the floor to ceiling was out of bounds for us during the day on Christmas Eve. So was practically the entire flat, since we were considered to be in the way almost everywhere. The midday meal was scrappy and hurried. We could hardly contain our impatience and curiosity whilst our parents were decorating the tree in the afternoon with dozens of colourful candles and glittering and sparkling decorations.

Sometimes we were taken to the Protestant church for the Christmas service in the early evening. This was both a solemn and joyful experience: the two huge lit-up trees, the hearty singing of the congregation, the generally festive mood.

Then, at home again, we sat in semi-darkness in a last, expectant hush. The little bell finally tinkled, the double doors were flung open, and the candlelight blinded us for a moment as we faced the gloriously bright and sparkling tree. But we had to pay for the surprise, the delight and the presents. For weeks beforehand we had to practise Christmas carols and learn to recite special Christmas verses with good wishes and promises to be good in the New Year. I had to copy out these poems on large Christmas cards under the supervision of my mother (for whom it was thus no surprise). Only then were we let loose to rush to inspect all the wonderful things we had been given. We were rarely disappointed. One thing, though, marred my joy: I was never very demonstrative, and my mother often interpreted this as ingratitude.

On the following two or three days there was a round of visits from or to relatives and friends. But the most enjoyable moments for me were waking up in the morning, not to be rushed out of bed, to take in all the Christmas smells—the tree, the candles, the cooking and baking—that pervaded the house and to read one of my new books. I particularly remember one Christmas morning when, having for some reason or other slept in the living room right under the Christmas tree, I avidly began to read Goethe's **Faust** in a version with useful annotations. I don't know how much I understood of it at the age of twelve or thirteen, but I found it fascinating.

Next were the New Year's Eve amusements with the traditional pastime of 'looking into the future'. Together with the grown-ups we stuck labels with different inscriptions on the inside of a large bowl of water and used the halves of empty walnut shells as boats, into which we stuck small lighted candles. They floated on the water, which we agitated, and we waited until the boats came to rest at one of the labels: journey, surprise, good school reports, marriage, and so on. Or we placed different objects under upturned saucers—keys, rings, coins, a picture of a house —which were discovered and interpreted when the saucers were lifted. Among the Russian peasant customs were staring into a mirror alone in a darkly lit room just on midnight, when a young girl would see the face of her future sweetheart or husband next to hers in the mirror. Or they (and we) sat on the floor with their backs to an open door and flung a shoe over their heads. If the toe of the shoe came to rest towards the door, it meant the person would leave the house that year.

The greatest fun was perhaps the melting of lead, usually in an old spoon, over a small flame. When it became liquid, it was quickly tipped into cold water, where it acquired most intriguing shapes, which then had to be interpreted by holding the transformed lead against a wall on to which it threw its shadow. Sometimes one could see a sailing boat, sometimes trees, or a house. New Year's Day was always a holiday and I, among other people, always started the day with good resolutions, and tried not to do anything all day long that I disliked doing, lest I would have to do them all through the year.

Since then, Father Christmas has been pensioned off in the Soviet Union and replaced by Grandad Frost, who visits the children with presents for New Year, which is celebrated in no less sumptuous and lively style than the old-fashioned Christmas.

There have been a great many New Year's Eves for me since then. Some gay and merry in the midst of friends, some quiet and contemplative, nostalgic or hopeful. But I particularly remember one in Prague, where I lived as a refugee from Nazi Germany. I had quite a few friends there among the other refugees, but that winter had been a troublesome time for me and I did not feel like celebrating. I chose to stay in my furnished room. There I saw in the year 1937 quietly and peacefully all by myself, with a glass of blackcurrant juice. That year I left for England and—apart from the war years—the least troubled and happiest period of my grown-up life.

The Russian winters could be really severe, not only in Siberia but in Moscow too, where the temperature at Christmas usually fell to minus 25 degrees Centrigrade or lower. Whilst the summer clothes of the townspeople varied little from that of the middle class in western Europe, winter clothing was a different story. People wore thickly padded or fur-lined coats, or—depending on circumstances—fur coats, Persian lamb or other rare skins. All coats had fur collars, and women sometimes wore skins (such as fox-skins) draped over their shoulders. The usual head-dress in winter, especially for children and men, was a fur cap with separate flaps for the forehead, ears and neck; these could be turned down, or folded back and tied on top. I brought one back from my visit to Moscow in 1961. Alas, it was only black cat skin. If it was windy a *bashlyk* was worn on top of the cap, a kind of Seven Dwarves hood, made from some soft, warm material, usually white or light grey, with golden or silver trimming, and long straps to wind around the neck for extra protection. Hands in fur mittens or thick, knitted gloves were tucked into a muff.

In very severe weather we had to protect our faces with vaseline, and if by chance (or out of curiosity) you touched an iron railing with bare fingers, the skin was sure to come off. Fur boots kept our feet warm; and we children also had to put on some woollen leggings, which we took off indoors. So dressing for outdoors, and undressing, was something of a procedure. Peasants and workers wore knee-high, rather shapeless and clumsy-looking felt boots, *valenki*, but they were warm. In early spring when the snow began to melt, or in rainy weather, everybody wore *galoshi*—rubber overshoes to keep one's shoes, boots, and feet dry.

In winter a favourite pastime for the wealthy landed gentry and town-dwellers, and occasionally even for peasants, was to take a ride in a large sleigh drawn by a *troika* of three horses, of which the lead horse in the middle was usually gaily decorated with coloured ribbons. The coachman sat high above them, cracking his whip, with the sleigh gliding over the crisp snow, glittering in the sun or moonlight.

The most important celebration in old Russia was Easter. It usually coincided with the arrival of spring, which made it something special: the intoxicating vapour rising from the earth covered for months with snow and ice, now rapidly melting away in the warm sun. It also melted the snow in the trees, the ice on the roofs, the icicles hanging down. Little rivulets were running everywhere on to the pavement, down into the streets and gutters, hurrying into the gullies. The sky was often blue, with large white clouds floating high above. People would shed their furs, their padded winter coats and heavy boots, and feel light and free. There would be an indefinable longing in the air, an expectation and happiness. There was inevitably an indescribable amount of slush and mud in the streets as the snow and ice was scraped and swept from the pavements on to the streets.

Easter was also the end of Lent, the seven-week fast to which the very orthodox old people adhered rigorously. The less orthodox fasted for only a week, or just for the last two or three days before Easter Sunday, if at all. Then shortly before midnight on Easter Saturday the crowds, dressed up in their best, would flock into the churches—there was one on practically every street corner in old Russia. Some of the churches were very rich and could display precious icons painted in the Middle Ages by well-known artists, such as Andrei Rublyov. The faces and figures were set into golden frames, adorned with pearls and precious stones, and each icon had a big candelabrum in front with innumerable lighted candles.

The Easter mass was rather special: each person would hold a burning candle. The priests and deacons would change their vestments twelve times, each time putting on a more beautiful and festive one, finishing up with a particularly splendid one, white, and richly embroidered with golden thread and pearls. A great procession would then take place with the whole crowd following the priests three times round the outside of the church. The main part of the mass was over and only the most devout remained for the rest until the early hours of the morning. The majority would leave for home, their candles still burning, to light the little oil lamps that hung in front of the icons in the right-hand corner of the main room in every house. These oil lamps had been extinguished the night before, and now, newly lit, they would burn for another year, and people coming into the room would cross themselves, asking for the blessing of whoever was represented on the icon. This was certainly the custom among religious people, particularly in the villages.

When my sister and I were old enough, we both used to attend the Easter mass at one of the Greek Orthodox churches—the official church in Russia. To us it was all rather exciting and mystical: that procession of endless little candles in the dark of the night, protected by paper bags against the wind, men and women carrying small bundles with painted eggs and Easter cakes, which they had brought to the church for the priest's blessing. Afterwards, at home, a great orgy would start in Russian houses and sometimes continue right through the night. The table would almost break under the burden of all the food: a whole cured ham, then a bowl with colourful hand-painted Easter eggs, some in plain bright colours red, blue, yellow, green, others with elaborate designs on them. There was *paskha*, made from curdled milk, cream, butter, eggs, sugar, raisins, finely chopped almonds and spices, mixed together, strained and pressed in the shape of a pyramid and decorated with a red flower on top. It tasted delicious. There was a fairly plain cake, a *Baba*, decorated with a sugar Easter lamb. These were the basics for an Easter meal at midnight. Then there were all sorts of other delicacies: soup, smoked and cured fish, red and black caviar, cold meat and various pickles, served with vodka. There were also desserts and wine.

One of the most fascinating things before the Easter holiday was a market and fair on the huge square in Moscow, now known as Red Square. You could buy almost everything there, but as children we were most interested in the small animals and birds and the toys: small clowns carved from wood, balloons, all kinds of trumpets. My favourite was a glass tube filled with water and tightly covered with a bit of rubber. Inside was a tiny glass devil. As you pressed or released the rubber, he would rise to the top or fall down to the bottom. I also remember smallish pink rubber piglets, round and plump when blown up; but as the air gradually escaped the little pig would slowly collapse. I found that unbearably sad and invariably cried at the sight of the expiring piglets.

Among our Easter, Christmas and birthday presents there were always a few books from our parents and friends. I early discovered the pleasure of reading, no doubt encouraged by my mother. At the age of seven or so, I seem to have been reading indiscriminately everything I could lay my hands on, including scraps of newspapers without beginning or end, which, in the days before rolls of lavatory paper, sometimes found their way into those secluded spots. I also tried to read whilst soaking in the bath, until my mother discovered it, looking through a crack in the door, wondering what I was up to being so long. (This latter habit I still indulge in occasionally on leisurely Sunday mornings.) And I would even lean over the window sill trying to catch the last of the daylight, before it got dark enough for the kerosene lamp to be lit over the large table in the middle of the room, around which we sat in the evening.

Oh those lamps! The smell and the soot from them went all over the room if the wick had accidentally been turned up too high! The airing on cold winter evenings and the cleaning and wiping away of the soot on everything in the vicinity of the lamp! The airing was done by opening the very small casement widows. The rest of the double windows were tightly sealed with putty for the whole winter. But those small windows were quite enough for the cold incoming air to make itself felt. In spring the windows would be flung open—till the onset of the next winter.

As a small child I used surreptitiously to read the bible in bed in the beam of light from the next room, where my parents often sat with the door slightly ajar in order to be able to hear us, just in case. What made me read the bible with its tiny print I don't know; somehow it fascinated me for a while. Religion was not rammed down our throats at home, though we were taught to say our prayers in the evening and we sometimes went to church (the Lutheran one). Religious tuition at school was compulsory and it was probably taken for granted that everybody believed in God. I was to lose my faith literally overnight at the age of thirteen: having said my usual prayer in bed, I added a special request to God for the good health and long life of my parents. Early the following morning my father died of a heart attack, leaving my mother devastated. But that was in September 1914, still some years off.

In my childhood there were no public or school libraries, so the choice of our books depended largely on exchanges with school friends or on my parents. Very occasionally I managed to get hold of my mother's books. I particularly remember one, on which my mother had imposed a strict ban, and which therefore became even more interesting to me. It dealt with Tsar Ivan the Terrible's special army, with which he broke the resistance of the old Boyars and princes against his ever more autocratic rule. Whether it was the description of the cruelties perpetrated by these *Oprichniki* or whether there was also a love story which I was not supposed to read about, I don't remember. However, with an unerring instinct I managed to find the book in its successive hiding places: in drawers, in my mother's sewing basket, behind wardrobes or in the kitchen cupboard. Yet it was a historical novel. Whereas only a little later, when I was eleven or twelve, nobody objected to my reading the most trashy, sentimental novels by a well-known writer, Courts-Mahler. They were love stories *à la* Barbara Cartland, I imagine (not ever having held a book of hers in my hands), where the girls were pure and virtuous, and young men declared their love kneeling before the chosen one, and death threatened when love was unrequited.

But that was later. Until the age of eight or nine I read young girls' books, which served as a base for a fantasy world of my own. At times I imagined myself to be a robust, country girl, enjoying a healthy life on a farm, to which my plump physique and rosy cheeks as well as part of our ancestry seem to have predisposed me. At other times I preferred to be a pale sometimes languid, sometimes wild, creature with large grey eyes (instead of my grey-green, smallish ones), dreaming indefinable dreams. This last fantasy was no doubt inspired by a series of girls' books about Knyazhna Nina Dzhavakha, a Caucasian princess, too unruly to be brought up at home, who was therefore sent to a boarding school. This seemed to me very attractive at the time. She was beautiful with black curls, clever and quite pleasant to her schoolmates when she chose to be. But she was the terror of her teachers and headmistress, forever plotting and organising tricks. She spent her holidays at home in the Caucasian mountains where she donned the *cherkesska*, the traditional black attire of the cossacks and Caucasian mountain people: over a tight-fitting bodice they wore a kind of knee-length coat, slightly flared from the waist down, with breast pockets on the slant for cartridges. Her long hair hidden under a high fur cap, she galloped on fiery horses up and down the mountains and over precipices, with the wild river Terek cascading and foaming down below over its rocky river bed. It took years and several books to tame this princess, but by then I seem to have lost interest in her.

Whether under the pernicious influence of that beautiful but rebellious princess, or due to my own awakening desire for a certain self-determination, I was beginning to get into arguments with my mother. She liked to dress us up, to roll our hair at night over paper curlers, or make it look full with lots of plaits. I hated all this, preferring my hair combed straight back and tied with a plain ribbon. My mother protested that I was making myself look even less pretty than I was. I also liked to wear comfortably large gloves and shoes, whereas my mother was in favour of smaller ones. Luckily my hair began to curl naturally at the age of eleven or twelve, and my hands and feet stopped growing before I did. Then there were perennial arguments about losing the big ribbons we had to wear or letting teasing boys pull them off.

At times I also stood up for my sister when she was scolded by our mother, or apologised on her behalf, if she had done something wrong. She was timid and I felt rather protective towards her. This very timidity and gentleness sometimes irritated my mother, as did the fact that Helga so easily burst into tears. But she was even more infuriated by my refusal to cry when I was scolded, which was sheer stubbornness on my part. So life became somewhat less smooth for a while.

In retrospect our mother's educational methods were practical, direct and unsophisticated. She was not averse to administering a quick slap to assert her authority and to make us behave, but I don't think she was all that strict, and she rarely appealed to my father for stricter measures or greater paternal authority. He was very quick-tempered and perhaps she tried to avoid rousing his wrath for our sake as much as for his. He loved to teach us things, especially those that interested him. He would display his collection of plants, pressed and lightly glued to thin sheets of paper, which he kept in large box-like books, or long tins of the kind used for steaming whole fish. Each plant was carefully marked with its name, the place and the date he had found it. He loved to show them to us, but none of us had more than a superficial interest in his hobby.

He would take us out for walks on clear autumn nights and point out the constellations to Helga and me, holding our hands, so that we could feel the warmth of his own. Unfortunately, I learned little on these walks and, even today, I can recognise only the Great and Small Bears, the Polar Star and Orion. Or he would explain something to us in his study. I liked that room where he sat at his desk behind ledgers and a press—in those days before typewriters, word processors or photocopiers, he used this to make copies of business letters written by hand. A lamp with a green-glass shade threw a soft light on the desk, the bookshelf and, dimly, on to the sofa, where my sister and I sat.

We did not at all enjoy the Sunday afternoon walks with our parents, all dressed up in our Sunday best and made to walk sedately in front of them. This ritual was terribly boring. Sometimes we went to the nearby Tsarskoye Selo, the Tsar's village or summer residence, built in imitation of the Palace of Versailles near Paris, with its ornamental gardens and multitude of unusual fountains. We were hopping along a lovely tree-lined pathway on one of these walks when my mother drew our attention to an apparently still lovelier green pathway down an embankment. So we ran down—and nearly drowned. The 'pathway' was a stream completely overgrown with short, lush pond weed.

While we lived in St Petersburg we were fairly frequently visited by Uncle Arthur, our mother's brother. We particularly enjoyed his visits because he was great fun and always brought us delicious cream and chocolate cakes. I always kept the choicest morsels to the last, but more often than not my little brother would sneak up and snatch them from my plate when I was not looking. Very annoying. Generally I was a great sharer, especially with my sister. If we had been given sweets or chocolates in different wrappings, for example, we shared each piece, in case the fillings were different. And when there were pieces of chocolate of different sizes, I would bite off the surplus until both were the same. It took me years to realise this gave me the largest share!

Uncle Arthur was a colourful person and the black sheep of the family, which nevertheless accepted his unorthodox way of life—especially as he did not live too close to the family home in Riga. He had round, slightly sagging cheeks and cheerful, slightly mocking eyes and he often made us laugh at his jokes. He always had unusual hobbies. At one time it was embroidery and he made a very handsome bedcover for my mother. Then he became fascinated by photography, which was still new at that time for amateurs. It was a complicated procedure as it required a tripod, good lighting and plenty of time. The camera had to be loaded with a large glass plate, then one had to cover it and one's head with a black cloth to cut out the light, check the desired position of the people to be photographed, and press the little balloon linked to the camera.

I still have a faded photograph of our family, for which half the bedroom had to be cleared as it had the best light. There is my mother sitting in the middle, holding Hardy on her lap, and Helga, with cropped hair, sitting in front of her. All three look somewhat weary: the children were just recovering from scarlet fever, and my mother is visibly worn out. I had somehow managed not to fall ill, so there I am by the side of my mother, proudly conscious of my first school uniform and my new boots. On the other side stands my father, very erect, with his high forehead, dark wavy hair and a handlebar moustache. He combed and set his moustache every morning, covering it with a special moustache net while he was dressing until it had set for the day.

Uncle Arthur worked for a tobacco company and often had to travel all over European Russia to contact manufacturers. He invariably brought back small mementoes—ash trays, salt and pepper cellars, spoons, all marked with the names of hotels. During his visits to us, he pulled them out of his pockets looking quite puzzled. When rebuked, he protested, with an innocent expression and a twinkle in his eye, that he had not the slightest idea how this or that object had found its way into his pocket.

From one such trip he brought back not a small memento, but Zina—a strikingly blonde tobacco worker. She was very handsome and very astute, and also quite uneducated. He taught her reading, writing, manners and deportment; he bought her beautiful clothes and jewellery, made her take singing lessons—she had a very good voice—and generally spoiled her. It was not long before she had started to imitate what was at one time called a 'grande dame' and demanded more and more. There was a constant whine: *'Arturkhen,kupi'*, 'Little Arthur, buy this'. I think Arturkhen finally put a stop to this, when she asked him for a horse and carriage since 'she could not possibly rub shoulders in the tram with every Tom, Dick and Harry'.

Years later, during the First World War, when we no longer lived in St Petersburg, I visited them in their comfortable flat on my way to Kronstadt. They both received me very hospitably. But it eventually came to a sad end: Zina abandoned him during the Second World War for an army officer who, presumably, was not only younger, but had some pull to obtain food and other useful things so precious in besieged and starving Leningrad. After the war Uncle Arthur returned to Riga where he died in a municipal old people's home, a lonely, sick and half-blind old man, visited only by a nephew, our forester cousin, who was the only other member of my mother's family not to have emigrated to Germany in 1940.

At the beginning of 1910 we faced another move—this time to Moscow. It was to be the last move for my father.

As a town, Moscow was quite different from St Petersburg, which was built to a plan, with straight, wide streets, elegant houses and Renaissance palaces. Moscow, of the 'white stones and golden cupolas', was not really built: it 'grew' on the hilly side of the river Moskva. It was the seat of the medieval princes and Boyars, and the first Russian Tsars. There was an enclosure, not very far from the Kremlin, with some old streets and the Tsar's small, picturesque medieval house. Inside, it had no doors, only arches cut through the thick walls—and cut so low that whoever passed through had to bend low and thus, willingly or not, show respect to the prince or Tsar. The town and the streets, as I knew them, were mostly quite irregular, with crooked side streets and lanes leading away from the main streets. There were also, of course, straight and wide streets, and a very attractive 'Ring of Boulevards'. Nevertheless, when I visited Moscow in 1961 as one of the interpreters at the British Trade Fair, I had the strong impression that the central part of Moscow was an overgrown village. By then there were a number of high-rise houses, fewer in the centre and more in the outlying districts, particularly along the route from the airport. But in the 1960s they were still interspersed with small timber structures.

In Moscow we had a flat with electric lighting for the first time. What a blessing after the kerosene lamps! We also had a more modern flush toilet, with a bottom which opened up when you pulled a knob; the water came rushing and swirling with a great noise, and I sometimes felt that a witch would appear and pull me down. But though we had graduated to electricity, we had no bathroom. A previous occupier had installed a bath tub (without piping!) in one of the rooms. A most inconvenient arrangement. So we took it out, and instead went every Saturday to the private baths, the Sandunovskiye Bani, which were somewhere between the Bolshoi and Maly Theatres and the Lubyanskaya Ploshchad (later to become notorious as the site of the headquarters of the GPU, later the KGB).

This was quite an expedition: my mother packed a case, or more likely a travel basket after the fashion of those days, with clean underwear, towels and refreshments. My father hired a cab (a sleigh in winter), and the whole family got under way. This particular bath house was a mixture of primitive weekly ablutions and Victorian comfort. On arrival my father bought a ticket for an 'apartment', which had a red carpet, old dusty curtains, and red plush furniture—a settee, chairs and a round table. The door was locked, we undressed and then entered the actual bath room. There may have been a bathtub there, I don't remember. But usually we sat on the wooden benches around the walls, put our feet into wooden buckets of hot water, while our mother, from her bucket, washed or scrubbed us. Finally, we poured cold water over ourselves to cool off before we dressed. Then it was our father's turn. There was a brick stove for a Turkish bath. My father climbed on to it, poured buckets of hot water over the surface to produce steam, and then lashed himself with bundles of fresh birch leaves as a kind of massage. Ablutions finished, we all sat down around the table and rang for the attendant to bring cool drinks, while my mother unpacked the sandwiches, oranges and apples. Then, warmly wrapped up, we returned home fresh and clean, after my father had, as was the custom, suitably bargained with the cabby over the fare.

Our maternal grandmother visited us that year. We brought her home from the railway station in style—in one of the new contraptions, the motor car. It was an open vehicle in those days, driven rather slowly. It was easily followed by the cab horses, which tried to poke their heads over the seats of the car, making my grandmother shriek with fear.

Then there was a visit by our paternal grandmother. She was a small, lively woman, who spoke only Latvian, which we children did not speak or understand. But she patiently played with us, and especially with our little brother. He sat on a small cushion on which she pulled him round and round the dining table to his great delight. She brought us a bale of dark red material, spun and woven by the farm women on those long winter days and evenings. For years this material was never made up. Then, when my father died, it was hurriedly dyed black and made up within a few days. And we wore these heavy and scratchy woollen dresses all through that winter into spring.

Of the more momentous events of that year I remember the consternation of the grown-ups at the news that Lev Tolstoy, author of **War and Peace** and **Anna Karenina**, had died. He was a nobleman, who eventually became a moraliser, a seeker of truth, who preached Christian love, non-resistance to force, and who strove after the simple life and faith of the peasants. He had eventually left his long-suffering wife, and died of pneumonia at a small railway station on the way to somewhere, with only his daughter Alexandra present. Sick as he was, he absolutely refused to allow his wife to come to his bedside.

The summer of 1910 was memorable for me in another respect: I acquired my first 'admirer'! We had rented—as was the custom in Russia for those who could afford it—a summer house, a *dacha*, for about three months, the summers being rather hot in Moscow, and the school holidays very long. The really wealthy people used to spend the summer in the Crimea or the Caucasus. Others, like our family, preferred to be near enough to town for husbands and fathers to join them every night. These *dachas* were usually two-storey timber houses, often built in the old Russian style, with carvings around the gables, window-frames and shutters. They usually had a large terrace and a balcony and were surrounded by a garden, with perhaps an orchard at the back.

Our neighbours were a Russian merchant family. They owned their house, which had a large garden with many rose beds. We had only a nodding acquaintance with them, but there was Kolya, ten years old, a year older than me, who had spied me through a gap in the hedge separating our gardens. So he took to throwing me a red rose over the hedge every morning. One day, when dusk had begun to fall, he crawled through the hedge into our garden and gave me my first kiss. Then... lightning and thunder descended upon my head. My mother had seen us. She came rushing out, chased Kolya away and uttered a flood of angry words at me as if she thought I had just taken my first steps on the road to vice and loose living. It was rather preposterous and I had not the slightest idea what she was talking about. I was puzzled and greatly resented her anger. Even now I cannot quite understand my mother's outburst. She was, on the whole, quite tolerant and not narrow-minded.

Back in Moscow at the end of the summer, I sometimes went sightseeing with Aunt Tori. One day, the Tsar and his family were to make a public appearance, walking the short distance from the Palace within the Kremlin enclosure to the Uspensky Sobor, one of the Kremlin cathedrals. The crowd was enormous. In front were the guards in a thick row. (The Tsar and his family were heavily guarded wherever they went. If they travelled by train, along the route soldiers were lined up every few yards and all the small stations heavily guarded.) The procession moved along a high platform erected between the Palace and the Sobor, so that in spite of the crowd everyone could catch a glimpse of them. Ahead went the Tsar and the Tsarina, followed by their four daughters, all dressed in white (it must have been late spring or early autumn). Behind them followed a big Cossack, carrying the young Tsarevich, who suffered from haemophilia and was at times very weak. He must have been about six years old then, about the same age as my brother.

The excitement among the crowd was enormous. The Tsar was the crowned head of the State and the Church but it is difficult to say why the appearance of the Imperial family always aroused so much interest. I doubt that he was really popular with the people, but neither did they blame him for the misery of the working class and the poverty of the peasants: his officials and servants were to blame. If only he knew what people thought... But how could one get to him?! *'Do Boga Vysoko, a do tsarya dalyoko'*—'God is high up, and the Tsar is far away'.

It was during the winter of 1911-12, after Aunt Tori had left us to get married, that I became dimly aware of tensions between my parents. Among their acquaintances was a couple who used to come to play cards and chat; the lamp with its silk lampshade with long fringes cast a bright light on the group around the table and a soft glow over the rest of the room. The woman was buxom, with a ready, loud laugh. They were telling each other jokes—jokes that I could not understand at all. There was a lot of laughter, especially from that couple. I sensed there was something behind their words that was not quite right, and I resented it. My father seemed to be responding in a lively manner, shedding his usual taciturn ways. Was there some attraction between him and that lively woman, who was so different from our delicately built mother? I never knew. But there were arguments and scenes between my parents around that time, after which my father sank, pale and exhausted, into a chair while my mother took refuge in faints.

Without wanting to do injustice to my mother, she did not always make life easy for my father. She was very much a child of her age—the end of the 19th century—brought up, it seems to me now, in the belief that it was a woman's privilege to indulge in an occasional caprice and be spoilt by her husband. It was not objectionable to suffer from 'nerves' or to get slightly hysterical and faint. So life was probably not always easy for my father. But it was not always a bed of roses for her either: my father's changes of career led to frequent moves from one town to another with all that this entailed, particularly the loss of friends.

As long as he lived my mother was totally dependent on him; she never did any important shopping without him. My father did all he could for her—even putting silver roubles at the bottom of glasses to induce her to take her medicine or tonic! And, on the whole, my parents got on very well together. After my father's sudden and unexpected death a few years later, and my mother's initial despair, she bravely faced the task of bringing up her three children through war and revolution, and trying to make a new life in Germany. I suspect that in the final analysis our delicate mother was the tougher of the two.

When Aunt Tori left, my parents had engaged a Russian governess for us. Margarita Petrovna was blonde and not very pretty. But she was kind and pleasant and I had the feeling, in retrospect, that she was rather lonely. She became very fond of me, probably because I was the eldest and therefore more interesting to her. At any rate, she devoted a great deal of time to me and also tried to curry special favours by feeding me with sweets and chocolates on top of the very generous rations my mother dished out to us. My mother had a special allowance for sweets, and every week bought a supply of the most delectable bonbons and chocolates. We took some to school every day with our sandwiches, and in the evening we had more sweets after supper. I don't think it did our teeth much good.

About Margarita Petrovna: in the summer of 1912 I caught typhoid and for six weeks I had hardly anything to eat except rusks, clear soup and tea without milk—and that at the height of the strawberry season! I felt miserable and Margarita Petrovna entertained me as best she could. When I began to recuperate and was allowed to sit on the large balcony overlooking the garden, she fed me until I could eat no more, then laughed and teased me because I had eaten so much! That made me really furious.

That summer was also remarkable for my fierce fights and

quarrels with my six-year-old brother Hardy, five and a half years my junior! The exact reasons for these quarrels I no longer remember. He may have begun to resent the authority I tried to exert over him. So we quarrelled and fought, and one day at the *dacha* practically went for each other with knives. Our mother was away in town helping my father in his business, and Margarita Petrovna was evidently powerless to control us. Helga stood by, crying, too frightened to interfere. I must have been bossy, because my sister and brother often called me governess. When reading, for example, or absorbed in some interesting occupation, I often called out 'Helga, bring me some water', 'Hardy, open the door', 'Switch the light on', and so on. (The word 'please' is not used half as much in Russian as in English— perhaps because it's such a long word: *pozhaluista*.)

Back in town, Margarita Petrovna continued to spoil me and on cold winter nights she would take me into her bed and talk with me before sending me back to my own. One night she decided to enlighten me about sexual relations between men and women. It did not bother me, and in any case I did not believe her. However, my parents must have noticed something, and probably objected to her taking me into her bed. She had to go, under the pretext that we spoke too much Russian and were forgetting our German. I think it almost broke her heart.

Towards the end of that summer we joined our father on a combined business and holiday journey to the Volga region and the Urals. Travelling in those days was no simple matter. Part of our journey was by train. There were no dining cars or even snack bars as far as I was aware. But we had a great basket with all sorts of food, plates, cups, as well as a tea pot. At larger stations my father jumped off the train and rushed to the tap for boiling water. And all along the route there were peasants selling food: roasted chickens, sausages, pickles, fruit. All this one often shared with one's fellow passengers. At night, the backs of the seats would be raised and the lower seats extended so that two large double beds were made where we could sleep. Sometimes we put up for the night at the nearest railway hotel or inn.

The journey by ship on the Volga was much more fun than the cramped railway compartment. We visited the towns of Saratov, Samara, Kazan, Zlatoust and Chelyabinsk in the Urals, (these are their old names, most of them changed since then), and visited some of the famous monasteries. I remember next to nothing about the towns, and not much about the river itself, but I have vivid memories of the monasteries,and of the friendly nuns and the elaborate and beautiful embroideries and laces they made. They also made simple silver and enamelled crosses to wear on a chain, rings and small boxes. And their churches, as so many in Tsarist times, were adorned with splendid icons, set as usual in gold and silver frames studded with precious stones. In either Zlatoust or Cheliabinsk we visited an iron-ore works, or rather a factory that produced household and decorative objects from cast iron, and somewhere on the way my father bought me a small pyramid made of local semi-precious stones and quartz, which I cherished for many years. The smell of methylated spirit always brings back memories of this journey. My mother travelled with a small spirit lamp on which she would heat her curler tongs to curl the hair over her forehead.

Another experience which has stayed with me over the years occurred in Kazan, where my father had some business to attend to. We had rented some rooms from a young working-class couple: pleasant and tidy people, the husband a skilled and industrious worker. One night we were awakened by the terrific noise of crockery being smashed, furniture being broken, shouting and crying. I could not understand what was happening, but next morning I learnt that the husband got blind drunk every few weeks, smashed the whole place to pieces and beat up his wife, who then could not go out for several days. When he had sobered up he was crushed with remorse—until his next drinking bout. The memory of it haunted me for a long time.

It is perhaps no wonder, therefore, that for years to come I was always rather chary when passing the noisy drink parlours *(pivnye)* in Moscow, or if I encountered a drunken worker in the street. Even years later in Germany I did not like to pass a pub with a beer-drinking crowd inside, preferring to cross the road. Little did I know that in time I would be a regular visitor to the back room of just such a pub, at many an instructive and inspiring political meeting.

After Margarita Petrovna had left, it was back to school for my sister and myself. Our parents chose the German Peter and Paul School—probably not so much because it was a German school (there had been some talk about sending me to a Russian school which specialised in art) but because of its good reputation among the private, fee-paying schools. Although the school had to conform to the requirements of the Russian education system, and was subject to the regulations and restrictions imposed on all schools by the Ministry of Enlightenment, our school had, it seemed, a freer hand in the appointment of the teaching staff, since it was actually run by the German community.

The German community was made up, firstly, of Germans from the Reich—the German Empire—who, together with their families, had settled more or less permanently in Tsarist Russia, and who occupied the most important and remunerative jobs in industry and commerce. They maintained their ties with Germany and did not particularly assimilate into Russian society—some of the women, after years in Russia, still did not speak the language. One reason for their success was the almost total absence of a Russian middle class. There were the wealthy merchants—the older generation, almost uneducated but shrewd in business, and the younger ones, some of them patrons of the arts. Then there was the Russian intelligentsia—the writers, essayists, teachers and artists—chafing under the censorship and other restrictions, such as the ban on travel abroad, imposed by the Tsarist government throughout the 19th century.

There were also the Russian or Baltic Germans. They owed no allegiance to the Reich. They were, like other nationalities in Russia, subjects of the Tsar (not citizens), spoke Russian, and adapted much more easily to Russian customs. We had the best of both worlds, since my parents retained much of the Baltic way of life, while at the same time falling in with that of the Russians proper. For example we celebrated both birthdays and namesdays, like the Russians. I always had a garden party in the summer on St Margarita's day. We laid stress on Christmas, but also fell in with the lavish Russian celebrations of Easter.

And there were the Volga-Germans, mostly prosperous farmers and landowners, who kept closely together but often sent their children to Russian schools. They were the descendants of German immigrants who settled in Russia in the 18th century encouraged by Catherine the Great, herself a native of Germany. And they were still conscious of their ancestry: some fought on the German side in the Baltic provinces during the war of intervention and civil war after the 1917 Revolution.

Although our school was a German school we had a fair sprinkling of Russian children and a limited number of Jewish children. In Moscow and St Petersburg only 10 per cent of a school's pupil intake could be Jewish. Of these, only those who finished school with distinction (a gold medal) were admitted to universities or higher technical colleges. And, of course, it was only the wealthy Jews, medical doctors or academics, who had the right of residence in Moscow and St Petersburg. The rest of the Jewish population lived predominantly in Byelorussia, the eastern part of Poland then belonging to Russia, and the southern Ukraine, in and around Odessa. Most of them, at any rate in the Western parts of Russia, were small traders or artisans. All were frequently subjected to violent pogroms, sometimes indirectly instigated, and certainly tolerated, by the authorities, when Jews were beaten up and their small shops and dwellings smashed. They could be called up for army service, but could not, as a rule, become officers. Many a young man fled to England or the USA to avoid being drafted into the army.

But if it was not easy for a Jewish child to get a proper education, it was even more difficult, though for different reasons, for a Russian working-class or peasant child. The majority had at best a few years of elementary schooling. Illiteracy was widespread, especially in the villages, because few parents could afford to see a child through school (let alone university) and only the state secondary schools in the towns were free. Yet we find many examples in Russian literature of mothers—more than fathers—working hard and starving themselves to make it possible for their sons to study. And it is equally well-known from the literature how hard some of the Russian students worked at night to make it possible to graduate from a university or Technical High School.

As for women, it was not unusual for middle-class girls to attend at least the Women's Institute for Higher Education. My mother, difficult as it would have been for her to make it possible, was very disappointed when I decided to study music instead of going to university. I have always considered myself lucky to have gone to the Peter and Paul School. Though officially under the auspices of the old Maria Feodorovna, Tsar Nicholas' mother, it was not entirely run by the reactionary Tsarist bureaucrats. The girls' school was a large, three-storey brick building, standing in its own grounds. It had spacious, light classrooms, wide staircases, long corridors and a large hall for special occasions. Every morning we were greeted by the chief janitor, Anton, who at the start of each new school year directed us to our respective classrooms. There was no assembly in the morning, though religious instruction was compulsory and taken by the clergy of the various denominations.

When I was in Moscow in 1961, I retraced my steps and found the school. It was surrounded by a high wooden fence and I saw a woman open a small door and go in. I followed her into a small enclosure where a soldier with a rifle was sitting at a table. 'What do you want?' he barked at me. I explained that this had been a school forty-odd years before. 'Well, it is not a school now,' he explained rudely, upon which I quickly retreated and shut the door lest I found myself in trouble. I remembered that during the First World War our school building had been confiscated by the army. Maybe it was still occupied by them.

The two boys' schools, one a grammar, the other a *realnaya* with the emphasis on maths and science, were a few minutes' walk away. They had a huge gymnasium with the most modern equipment and we were looking forward to being able to use it for our own physical training instruction. Alas, it was not to be—it too was taken over by the army as an army hospital ward.

All pupils in schools in Russia wore and still do wear uniform: the girls usually dark brown dresses and black aprons—white ones for special occasions—and the boys, at that time, a plain grey tunic with a high collar and brass buttons. Most teachers too wore uniform. School hours were from nine in the morning to two in the afternoon, or three in the higher forms when we stayed on for optional lessons such as dancing. The dances were very different from now. Then it was the waltz, the polka, the *krakoviak,* or other figure dances whose names I have forgotten. I was no good at physical training, but I loved dancing, and after every ballet performance I attended I desperately tried to stand on my toes, though without ballet shoes. There were ten-minute breaks between the lessons, and a half-hour break at midday, when we had our sandwiches or, for those who lived near enough, a hot snack brought by somebody from home. At 3pm there was proper dinner at home.

Some time during the afternoon we did our homework, after which we were allowed out. I had a good memory and learnt easily, especially poetry, though unfortunately I forgot it just as quickly. My other interests were history, literature and writing essays. Among the many teachers we had during those eight years were many who, in spite of the regulations imposed by the authorities, were able to give us a knowledge of and longing for a free society. I remember them with warm feelings to this day.

There was our class supervisor, a woman teacher who moved up with us every year: Lyubov Nikolayevna Nägler, middle-aged and unmarried. Her main task was to see to our general behaviour, teach us discipline, keep the register, and help us in one way or another when needed. She was really devoted to us, knew how to handle us and taught us many things we never heard from other teachers. She told us about the wonderful free and open-air schools in Germany, which seemed to us like a dream. She also organised visits to the opera, the ballet, and the Maly Theatre, where the classics were put on at special afternoon performances for schools. It was an exhilarating experience to see the theatres filled with row on row of teenagers, all in their school uniforms, enthusiastically cheering and shouting 'bravo' or '*bis, bis*'—the French expression for 'Again, again'. It was probably my first experience of being not just an individual, but feeling part of a whole.

When we were older, Lyubov Nikolayevna once invited the whole form to her home: an exquisite two-roomed flat furnished entirely in the style of the French Empire, with elegant chairs covered with silk, graceful tables, glass cabinets with delightful china and porcelain figurines, obviously the remains of a once-aristocratic family. She died, after falling from a moving tram, around the time I finished school. We were all very sad.

My favourite teacher, however, was Vladimir Nikolayevich Bunin. Like most of the male teachers he usually wore uniform—black with braid and brass buttons. But he, too, was a liberal, who seemed to chafe under the strict school regime. He often told us of schools abroad and of their different teaching methods. At that age we did not feel the restrictions in the same way as the teachers, but the tenor of what they said made us sensitive to the pervading atmosphere. The teachers obviously found the strict programmes, the system of government inspectors and other rules irksome.

Vladimir Nikolayevich Bunin did have some shortcomings: he could be very sarcastic and had his favourites among his pupils, which I thought was not right even though I was one of them. He also liked to give us nicknames. I acquired mine when one day another teacher reprimanded a pupil for something she had not done. She obviously did not want to expose the real culprit, who did not own up herself. I was incensed. In spite of my shyness, I impulsively raised my voice in protest against the unfounded accusation (without naming the real culprit). The next lesson was taken by Vladimir Nikolayevich, in the course of which he called out: 'Alderman'. Nobody stirred. Then he pointed to me and said: 'Well, aren't you the alderman here, since you speak out for the others?' And that nickname stuck to me till the end of my schooldays. I like to think that I had a kind of inborn sense of fairness and justice.

Vladimir Nikolayevich could grip the entire class with his talks on Russian literature, history, and even grammar. And he could hold even the dullest pupil enthralled when reading a prose passage from the classics (I remember in particular Gogol's beautiful, poetic description of the river Dniepr) or when reciting poetry such as Pushkin's ballad about *Knyaz* (Prince) Kurbski, who left his country and went over to the Poles, because he could no longer bear the arbitrary and ruthless rule of Tsar Ivan the Terrible. You could hear the barely whispered words of Kurbski, as he lay dying, in the farthest corner of the classroom, and nobody stirred when Bunin had finished and Kurbski was dead. Bunin instilled in me a lasting love for Russian history and literature as no other teacher could have done.

A few years later, when I was fifteen, he accused me of 'obviously having boys on my mind' rather than essays or other homework. Nothing was further from my mind, though it was true that—temporarily—I had rather slackened in my work: I was engrossed in reading the classics, such as Tolstoy, Turgenev and Dostoyevsky, or the liberal essayists such as Herzen, Chernyshevsky, Belinsky and others, and was totally absorbed.

Our German teacher in the higher forms was another fascinating, though not exactly likeable person. Previously we had had Herr Krebs, a tall, thin morose man with a big moustache, who sat stiffly at his desk, somewhat aloof but given to fits of fury. One day he failed to appear and we learned that he had committed suicide. It was rather a shock for us. His replacement was another neurotic and somewhat unapproachable teacher, stocky, with penetrating pale blue eyes. He was intense and yet detached, lecturing while staring into the distance above our heads. Yet he was immensely interesting, often digressing into Greek mythology, ancient Persian literature and art and telling us with great intensity of the 'music of the stars'. Not that we actually believed him, but we sat fascinated by his words.

We could choose to study English for two years and these lessons were taught by Miss Ashford, who was Irish. We did not take her class too seriously, and she was quite serene about it, smiling indulgently and benevolently when we fluently informed her: 'I am sorry I could not learn my lesson because I was ill.' Still, we retained something, including the children's song 'Twinkle, twinkle, little star'.

A complete contrast to her, and to most of the teachers, was tiny Madame de Jean, who without any imagination whatsoever made us rattle down French verbs purely automatically, without connecting them to sentences in any way. It was a compulsory subject for several of our years at school, and we did learn something despite her dry and rigid teaching methods.

Once the First World War began some of the older teachers were called up and replaced by very young ones, fresh from their universities, all very shy and somewhat unsure of themselves. There was Rybakov—thin, clean-shaven, a little stiff—who used to entrench himself behind his desk and history books, clinging to the class register for our names, and testing our homework page by page from the book. Since he never moved around the classroom, it was quite easy to read up the pages quickly at the beginning of his lesson, or even prop up the book against the back of the pupil in front and read from it. Young Ivanov valiantly struggled with chemistry experiments in our rather poorly equipped laboratory, under the watchful and mocking eyes of some twenty young girls, who were delighted when an experiment did not come off. On the other hand, the history of art was made interesting and lively by a devoted young teacher who, after the Revolution, became Head of the Icon department of the famous Tretyakov Gallery in Moscow. I met him there, unexpectedly, in 1931. He told me then that the majority of the young teachers were sympathetic to the Bolshevik Revolution. When I asked him why they did not try to influence us, he said they went as far as they could within the school regulations, particularly during our last school year, 1917-18, but few of us seemed to understand or respond to their message.

As a teacher he was such a contrast to our art teacher in the lower forms, Miss Kropotkina. Poor Miss Kropotkina! She was a rather wretched and neglected-looking creature and dressed without any care. She did not have an easy time with us since she had no authority whatever. As soon as she entered the classroom, near-hell broke loose: catcalls, whistling, inky paper balls flying through the air, little explosive bangs from some rubbery material which we used to erase soft pencil marks on our drawings and which we blew up until it burst. How the poor creature stood all this is a mystery to me. She probably did not complain about us, because she feared for her job. But we never realised this.

Our gym classes were equally useless. We did not change, not even our high-laced shoes, and there was very little equipment. Our gym teacher had a simple method: whoever could not jump over a rope, which was gradually moved up higher, or could not do an exercise on the ladders fixed against the walls, had to sit it out until nobody could jump any higher or do the next difficult exercise. Being on the plump side, I sat out most of the time.

Then there was the formidable Fräulein Röntgen, our headmistress, a shortish, but stately person, who carried her generous bosom before her with great dignity, and who walked erect and stiff 'as if she had swallowed a walking stick', as we used to say in Russian. She would solemnly glide up and down the corridors and hall during the breaks and we had to curtsy to her, whereupon she would nod benevolently, and occasionally stop to ask a question. This was particularly vexing if you were in the middle of a good giggle and could not compose yourself quickly enough.

I was very indignant on one occasion when she suggested that a particular girl I was friendly with was not quite suitable company for me. It was a clear case of class distinction. Fanny Schenk, a tall, lanky girl with a slightly apologetic air, came from a rather poor family with numerous children. They were clearly not well off, and she probably attended school on a scholarship. Her dress was old and worn and she did not seem keen on lessons. On the other hand, she knew more about life, love and many other things than any of us. She was reprimanded once in class for not having learned her lesson, whereupon it transpired that her parents could not afford to buy all the necessary school books. I told my mother, who immediately bought the required book, which I gave to Fanny, saying that I had two copies. After that she attached herself to me, and though it was probably compassion more than real friendship, I greatly resented Fräulein Röntgen's interference.

My best friend for several years was Manya Behrens, the daughter of well-to-do German parents. They lived about halfway between the school and our flat, in a large apartment house standing well back from the road. At that time it seemed rather splendid to me. When I saw it again in 1961 it didn't look so grand after all.

I wish I could remember all the things we talked about. She once asked me whether we were rich. I was rather non-plussed by her question, as I had never given the matter any thought. I told her I thought we were, though I must have noticed the difference between our flat and theirs, the fact that they had two maids and we had only one, or that they went to a well-known holiday resort near Moscow while we went to a more modest place. But we never lacked anything at home, as far as we children were aware. Most of our birthday and Christmas wishes were granted and there were visits to the theatre and circus.

Manya's happy childhood was brutally interrupted when the whole family was exiled to Siberia at the beginning of the 1914-18 war, with most other German families. She was only about thirteen or fourteen at the time. I didn't see her again until 1918, when she seemed very mature, reserved, but somewhat bitter about the experience and her interrupted education. Then we lost touch with each other. Her family moved to Germany and there was no postal communication between the Soviet Republic and the West European states for several years.

Then, in 1921, I accidentally met her again in Berlin. I learned then from Manya that her parents had separated, her brother was studying somewhere in Germany and she herself lived with her mother, who was dying of cancer, in a furnished room. She was supplementing their scanty living by doing embroidery. At that time there was a vogue in Berlin for hand-sewn and embroidered lingerie, so she always had work. When I was out of work for a short time I joined her on the small balcony of their room sewing or embroidering camiknickers, having persuaded myself that I could not possibly wear machine-sewn underwear either. This fad of mine did not last long! Their room was always untidy and dismal. Her mother was never out of bed, and Manya herself shuffled around in slippers and a sloppy dressing gown, or an old skirt and blouse. She had one tailor-made navy blue suit and a couple of good silk blouses, and when she went out she looked as elegant and as well-groomed as any lady of leisure.

We became quite close again at that time and she told me a great deal about her love life and adventures. Manya had never been particularly pretty, yet there was something about her that attracted men. She only had to sit in a café for ten minutes before a man would make passes at her from another table. And if she liked the look of him, she would have no hesitation in making an appointment with him and, before long, going to bed with him. I watched her when occasionally we spent an hour or so in a café in Berlin's 'West End'. She seemed to behave immaculately: there was no smiling, no coquetry, but something clicked. I never knew and never asked whether she was doing this for kicks or for money. After her mother's death she married a White-Russian emigre, a former Tsarist officer considerably older than herself, who was running a lingerie and haberdashery shop. I think she was glad of some care and protection and was very loyal to him, helping him in the shop and keeping house for him. But, deep down, something seemed to have been broken in her.

One of the more interesting girls in our class was Lida Zuyeva, one of seven or eight children in a wealthy Moscow merchant family. She wore diamond earrings and occasionally a diamond ring, which we felt was not quite the done thing, although we admired the jewellery. It was rather surprising that our headmistress did not object. Lida Zuyeva's father had amassed great riches in business and they owned a mansion house in the expensive quarter, around the Arbat. On special occasions such as Christmas, they had lavish parties when the large dining and drawing rooms were thrown open; the table, which could seat twenty-four people, sparkled with cut glass and silver, and was laden with the most expensive and delicious food. At Christmas the glittering tree stood in the middle of the drawing room, reaching from the floor to the high ceiling. Yet when I visited Lida informally, the whole family sat around a table in a back room, and the grandmother, an old peasant, ate with her fingers. But they were a hospitable and pleasant family.

There were two other Russian girls in our form. One was Tanya Pshenitsyna. She was rather ugly but had beautiful grey eyes and was very bright and intelligent, near the top of the class. Later, in the winter of 1917-18, when the school was reorganised by the Bolsheviks, she was one of the most active members of our school club and its various debating circles. But I particularly remember her close friend Zhenya Pomeltzova. The two were quite unlike each other, except that Zhenya, too, was very intelligent and one of the top students. She was tall, slim, pale-faced and looked rather aristocratic. She had a very pleasant voice and excelled in reciting poetry.

1912 was the fiftieth anniversary of the liberation of the serfs (not yet quite complete, but nevertheless a milestone in the history of the Russian peasantry). The school was going to have a celebration in the big hall in the presence of all the pupils, teachers and parents. Bunin decided that our form should recite a poem by Nikolai Nekrasov, a 19th century poet whose aim had been to improve social conditions, especially those of the peasants. The poem chosen described a group of bearded, illiterate peasants sitting around a table in a dimly lit hut, listening to a child (about my age) slowly spelling out the Tsar's decree on the abolition of serfdom, with her finger following the lines word by word. The choice of who should recite it was between Zhenya and, surprisingly, me. Bunin may have had a preference, but he left the final choice to the rest of the form, and they voted for me. Maybe the subject of the poem, and the way it was written, had inspired me to overcome my usual shyness, but I suspect that my more robust looks and rosy cheeks also contributed to their decision. I was very excited and my mother was absolutely delighted that her daughter would stand on the rostrum.

The celebration was only three days off when I totally lost my voice! I was upset, but not as much as my mother. I spent most of those three days over a bowl of hot water scented with some herbs, breathing in the steamy air under a blanket. It was obviously 'nerves'. Miraculously I regained my voice on the eve of the day and all went well.

The last two summers before the war, and as it turned out the last we ever spent in the countryside, were particularly enjoyable and memorable. We spent both in the same resort, not far from the outskirts of Moscow. A 25-minute ride on a horse-drawn tram along the forest of Sokolniki took us to the village of Bogorodskoye, then a 15-minute walk through the woods brought us to the resort, with its private and rented villas and houses.

Sokolniki, or at any rate a large part of it, is now an exhibition ground and a recreation park with a small theatre. During the British Trade Fair in 1961 I tried to retrace my steps to the resort of Bogorodskoye, but found everything changed. Instead of the beautiful old trees of the forest—the chestnuts, oaks and elms—there were only young saplings and no undergrowth. Could it be that the forest was cut down for firewood during the war? Speaking Russian without a foreign accent, I did not want to ask too many questions and so draw attention to myself, which would reveal my ignorance of Soviet life. I walked on, but the road became more and more built-up and unfamiliar, so I gave up.

It was of course different in the two hotels I stayed in, where I was in a way under the protection of the British organisers of the trade fair. The hotel staff were friendly and curious about life in England. I did not ask questions about their lives, but I got an inkling when chambermaids asked me to give them nylon stockings, inexpensive slippers, sewing needles or other things one thought nothing of buying in the West.

At the trade fair itself, it was easy to get into conversation by offering English cigarettes. Then the questions started. I particularly remember a group of admiring young people at a stall showing shoes with pointed toes and high stiletto heels, then fashionable in England, and another occasion when a group of students surrounded me in the park and started to ask questions about schools and universities in England. Suddenly a man pushed himself forward and provocatively asked what the British people thought of the very first astronaut, Yuri Gagarin. I had no reason to deny that he was greatly admired. The man then asked me, even more provocatively, what was being done in Great Britain in the field of astronautical research, of which I quite genuinely knew nothing. With his hat and different-style coat he did not look like an ordinary Soviet citizen and I began to feel a little uncomfortable. Then the young people came to my rescue by criticising him and stopping him from continuing his interrogation.

I may have been oversensitive but I could not help being suspicious—and anxious—when one of my interpreter colleagues, an Estonian who had escaped to the West during the war and left a child behind with relatives, suddenly disappeared and I was told she had returned to England. I used to get phone calls in my room in the middle of the night, without anybody on the other end uttering a sound. When I complained, I was told it must be a 'wrong connection'. I shared my room with a young English secretary who was eager to explore Moscow's nightlife, so I asked to move to the room left empty by the Estonian interpreter. The young secretary was never again disturbed by the night-time phone calls: the 'wrong connections' were duly transferred to my new room. Eventually I began to answer in English, and on the last day, shortly before my departure, a 'goodbye' call came, again without anybody saying anything. So I got rather rude (in Russian). Was somebody waiting to see whether I would say 'Oh hallo, is it you, Masha or Ivan, where and when can we meet? I have something for you'?

Those weeks in Moscow were quite a nervous strain—I had no relatives or friends there and did not know a soul—but it was an experience: I was no longer starry-eyed and could observe things more soberly, with interest, but no trace of nostalgia. I had lived in the West, particularly in England, too long for that. I had done what I had always wanted to do: to see Russia and Moscow once more. But on the flight back I nearly burst into tears of nervous relief as we passed over the Soviet-Polish border.

But to return to Bogorodskoye and to our summer *dacha*. These rented houses were usually unfurnished, and the move there and back—with essential furniture, bedding, pots, pans and what-not—was quite an upheaval. The furniture left behind, lamps, pictures and everything else, was covered with dust-sheets. Only my father's room was left intact, though Bogorodskoye was near enough for him to come out every day. In the country it was a lazy life, full of leisure and pleasure, especially for us children, in spite of the vexing task of having to do some school homework lest we forgot what we had learned in the winter. But mostly it was relaxation and summer pleasures.

A welcome caller at the house on hot summer days was the ice-cream man who came with his van and tubs of different kinds of ice cream, which was ladled out into a dishes which we hurriedly brought out to him. Occasionally we helped with the preparations for making jam, pickling mushrooms or gherkins, cabbage and other things for the winter. A boring but not difficult task. The berries and mushrooms were sold in large quantities by the peasant women, who brought them in from the village in large flat baskets made from the bark of birch trees.

This same pliable bark was also used for the villagers' summer footwear: a kind of flat shoe held in place with some binding around the ankle and calf; and, instead of socks or stockings, they wrapped narrow strips of cotton cloth around their feet and calves (like soldiers also did in those days). In rainy weather, or when going to town, the men wore knee-high leather boots with the trousers tucked in. Their cotton shirts, which had to be pulled over their heads, had high collars, and the trimmed or embroidered openings were buttoned up, not in the middle, but on the left-hand side of the chest. These shirts were worn over the trousers and held round the waist with a belt or a cord. Landlords, members of the intelligentsia, students and writers (Tolstoy, for example) also wore these shirts. The peasants and students also wore caps in the summer. The peasant women wore long, loose dresses and embroidered blouses with full sleeves, and often colourful scarves on their heads as protection against the sun.

Jam was made in huge, flat copper pans. The contents had to be frequently stirred and skimmed, and we children usually hung around, not to help but to eat the skimmed foam. Sometimes we were sent to collect milk from one of the peasants in special clay jugs. We could watch the cows being milked and taste the warm, frothy milk after it had been filtered through a thin, cotton cloth. At home it was stored, like all perishable food, in an underground cellar in the back garden. This was lined with wood and in winter packed with ice. To get in, one opened a trapdoor and climbed down a ladder.

Helping with the jam and pickle-making was not an arduous task and occupied little of our lazy existence. We woke up in the morning with the sun streaming into the room and jumped out of bed ready for the day's activities: we played croquet in the garden, rocked in a hammock, and read to our hearts' desire. On the rare rainy days we played Snakes and Ladders or card games. Otherwise we went swimming in a river or the swimming pool, or went for long walks through the dense forest to gather the many kinds of berries and mushrooms which grew there—although somehow I only found just enough to cover the bottom of my basket.

There was so much else to see: the play of light and shade on the leaves and the ground, the song of birds, the red squirrels dashing from branch to branch...perhaps it was just that I was too lazy to search for berries and bend down for mushrooms. Equally pleasant were the walks through green fields with their rich variety of wild flowers, through a cornfield swaying in the breeze, full of red poppies and deep blue cornflowers, insects humming in the heat of the sun. Overcome with drowsiness, we would lie down in the corn or the grass and watch the clouds sailing through the deep blue sky, with snatches of songs from a group of peasant girls drifting through the air. I liked the woods and the forests, but the long stretches of flat land, whether seen on foot or from the window of a moving train, always gave me a feeling of vastness and freedom, a feeling which I have never quite lost.

I liked best the golden days of autumn. No image evoked by these words is as strong as that of our early morning rides to school along the edge of the Sokolniki woods, with the golden, red and brown foliage of the trees. School started in mid-August and if the weather was good we stayed on in the country into September. We had to get up pretty early to get to school on time, but what a delight it was: the brisk walk through the small wood, over rustling autumn leaves and the soft needles of the conifers, before boarding the horse-drawn tram.

In the summer we used the vast green playground, with a football pitch, tennis courts and swings. We all loved the swings, especially one we called the Maypole, with strong ropes fixed to rotating hooks at the top of a pole and slings in which we sat, ran several steps, then pushed ourselves up to 'fly' for a few seconds in the air. If a willing grown-up was around, you could get a special push-up and fly over the heads of the other children.

One such willing assistant was Ivan Zhitkov who was about eighteen, the eldest son in a family of seven children. His mother was a good-looking woman with a broad Russian face. Her husband was considerably older, tall, gaunt and grim. They were an educated family and cared a great deal about their children's education. Tanya, the only girl, was tall, handsome, vivacious and always ready to join in and enjoy anything that was going. She caught her foot on a large rusty nail, never recovered from what we were told was blood poisoning and died within a year. The next in line was Sergei, a serious boy who kept himself very much to himself. The youngest were twins, the same age as our brother, who were cared for by a nanny. They were not much in evidence—unlike their two brothers Kiril and Andrei, who were about eleven and thirteen years old when we first met them. Kiril was the black sheep of the family. They were in the care of a middle-aged spinsterish-looking German governess, a somewhat helpless disciplinarian, whose voice forever sounded in the playground: 'Kiril, Andrei, come here.' More often than not they did not come. Very soon Kiril became my hero for two summers.

What attracted me to him? His non-conformity? His ruffled looks? He had his mother's strong build and broad face, though his hair stood out in all directions and his clothes were always torn and untidy. But his parents, especially his father, eventually had had enough of their son being expelled from one school after another and decided on drastic steps to complete his education. In the late summer of 1914 he was dispatched to Hamburg in Germany, to a well-known tough school, appropriately called, I think, the Grey House *(das Graue Haus)* or the Rough House *(das Rauhe Haus)*. He hated the idea of going there, and I was sorry too. Little did his parents know that within a short time the First World War would break out and Kiril would be cut off.

But the school did not dampen his spirit. When he was fifteen he escaped from school, made his way through enemy territory, across the Baltic Sea to neutral Sweden and, from there, to Finland and finally Russia. It took him months and months. He found our new address (we had moved twice) and came to visit us once. I later heard that he was killed in the Caucasus during the Civil War, but I was never quite sure which side he was on. Sergei made his way into Germany, as did Ivan who appeared quite unexpectedly in Berlin when we too were living there.

A companion of a very different kind during those last two pre-war summers was Lyolya. She was in her last year at our school and stayed with us on some sort of au-pair basis, to keep us company and to keep an eye on us when my mother was busy or in town with my father. Lyolya must have been seventeen. She had the most wonderful hair, brushed straight back to a plait the thickness of a child's arm and so long that she could sit on it. She was strong, happy, and very intelligent. I soon grew to admire and love her and, though she was four years older than me, we became good friends and had many lengthy discussions about everything from trivial happenings on the playground to the meaning of life. I had by that time read many of the Russian classics and could hold my own with her. I can see us now, sitting on an old tree trunk, philosophising about God and the universe, questions that greatly occupied me at that time.

In the summer of 1914 I also became aware of the wider world and its problems and politics. There was excitement and consternation among the grown-ups when my father came home one day with the news that Archduke Franz Ferdinand of the

Austro-Hungarian Empire had been assassinated by a Serbian nationalist. Everybody feared it would mean war. A few weeks later, at the beginning of August, the First World War began. Austro-Hungary attacked Serbia; since Serbia was a Slav country, Russia was bound to come to its aid, and, one by one, practically every country in Europe followed them into the war. Fed on school history and tales of glorious battles and victories, I began to feel very patriotic and imagined the Russian armies marching triumphantly to the battlefields, while the women tended the wounded and sent parcels to the front.

I could only have got such feelings and fantasies from books and newspapers, for there was no display of such sentiments at home. My father was a moderate liberal, who read the ***Russkoye Slovo*** (The Russian Word), a mildly conservative newspaper, and occasionally the ***Russkiye Vedomosti*** (The Russian Gazette), a more liberal paper favoured by the intelligentsia. At any rate, no sooner was he back from town in the late afternoon than Lyolya and I snatched the paper from him and together read the reports on the aftermath of the assassination. Then the axe fell and war was declared.

At first nothing changed and, for most of us, war meant no more than reports in the newspapers. But one day the local policeman knocked on our door and demanded to speak to Lyolya. To Lyolya? Why? It was to inform her that she was immediately to return to her mother and that they would all be deported to Siberia. We were thunderstruck. Were Lyolya and her family enemy aliens who could not be trusted to live in the capital city of Russia? It was preposterous, unbelievable. But the order was there and Lyolya had to leave amidst tears on all sides. Her mother had been married to a German and had thus become, together with the two daughters, a subject of the German Reich. After her husband's death, years earlier, she had not bothered officially to become a Russian subject once more. Neither she nor her eldest daughter spoke a word of German. Only Lyolya had attended the German school. Now they had to leave their home and their living and go to unknown and distant Siberia. When school started again, we learnt that many of our schoolmates and their parents shared the same fate—including my close friend Manya Behrens.

After the war, when they were able to return from Siberia, they told us sad and strange tales about their lives in remote villages and towns, in simple timber houses or peasant huts, with next to nothing to do. Food was cheap, but there was hardly anything else to be had. Nevertheless they had managed to organise some sort of schooling for their children. But three to four years of this primitive life had obviously been a great strain, and left their mark on children and grown-ups alike.

The outbreak of the war and the death of my father soon afterwards marked the end of our carefree childhood. It was also the beginning of the end of the so-called 'good old days' hitherto enjoyed by relatively few. The cataclysm of war and the revolution in Russia changed our lives, the social, economic and political life of Russia and, to a greater or lesser extent, the whole of Europe and the rest of the world.

CHAPTER 2

War and Revolution

WITH the outbreak of war, there were great changes at school. All our general subjects—maths, physics, chemistry, geography—were now taught in Russian instead of German. The girls' school was confiscated by the army authorities and we had to move into the nearby new boys' school, where tuition now took place in shifts: the girls in the morning as usual, from 9am to 2pm, the boys from 3pm and into the evening. So there was Fräulein Röntgen, our ever-vigilant and stately headmistress, standing on the landing of the top floor at 2pm watching over our departure and the arrival of any boys that may have come early, so that—God forbid—we should not meet each other.

We were not unhappy about the move and were looking forward to using the huge, well-equipped gymnasium. Our hopes were soon dashed, as that vast hall was confiscated and turned into a hospital for wounded officers. To my great relief there was now no more needlecraft, or crochet, or knitting lessons. Instead we were put behind sewing machines and assigned the patriotic duty of sewing undershirts and pants for the forces from some unbleached and rather rough cotton material. Unfortunately, I did not do much better than I had done previously at embroidery and always managed to get out two left legs, or two right sleeves. I had to undo almost as many seams as I had sewn. This workroom was in a gallery high above the gymnasium-hospital, now separated by a glass screen. We managed to scrape some of the whitewash off the glass, and no sooner was the teacher's back turned than we dashed to the screen to peep down into the big hall with its rows of beds, the wounded men, and the nurses coming and going between them.

Then, in mid-September, my father died suddenly. My mother came dashing into our room early one morning, but I don't think my father was aware of us any more. My mother was totally devastated and in despair. For fifteen years she had never taken any serious step without my father. Now she was alone with three growing children. All she could speak of on that first day was that she would take her own life and that we should follow her. There was a lot of coming and going: friends, undertakers, florists, the dressmaker. In those days the body remained in the house until the day of the funeral and by that time we were all fitted out with black dresses and crêpe—which we had to wear for many months.

I somehow felt numb, but at the same time aware that something important had happened. Then came the day of the funeral; the slow walk behind the bier to the church and then to the cemetery. My mother was too weak for that and followed in a carriage. And afterwards, there were many, many Sunday afternoons all through the late autumn and into the winter, when my mother would take all three of us to the cemetery to tend the grave. But she rallied in the end and tried to cope as best she could.

The war proceeded and my initial childish enthusiasm and expectation of glorious victories evaporated as the horror and misery of war gradually became more apparent: when we received the touching, half-illiterate letters from soldiers at the front to whom we used to send parcels: or when we watched the wounded in our school gymnasium.

The deteriorating situation in 1915 led to violent anti-German pogroms. My mother was at that time working as a cashier with a large firm selling musical instruments in Kuznetski Most, one of the most fashionable streets in Moscow, the equivalent of London's Bond Street. One day she came home pale, exhausted and frightened. The pogroms had started. Amongst the demolished shops was the one she had worked in. The owner was not German, but he had a German name and the mob made no distinction. Crowds from the street broke in, shouting and smashing everything they could lay their hands on. They dragged the grand pianos on the first floor to the French windows and pushed them out into the street. Other instruments and sheet music followed. Other shops suffered a similar fate. People were injured and some died. All this happened after the Russian army suffered a series of defeats and there were rumours that the pogroms were instigated by government agents and the ultra right-wing *Tchornaya Sotnya* (The Black Hundred) to divert people's attention from such setbacks. Twenty years later the Nazis were to do the same in Germany, unleashing anti-Jewish riots and pogroms to divert the attention of the German workers from internal setbacks, unemployment and shortages.

Shortly after the Moscow pogroms a decree was issued banning all remaining Germans from certain streets in Moscow (and probably other large towns). Since most of them had been deported to Siberia, it affected mainly the old and the children. In some streets there may have been a factory or hospital or some other institution vulnerable to some sort of sabotage 'by the enemy', but in other instances there seemed to have been no rhyme nor reason for this decree. In any case, our street was exempt from this ban and my mother gave shelter to a number of Germans, not necessarily friends or even good acquaintances, accommodating them temporarily on makeshift beds in the corridor or wherever there was room. After a while the whole thing seemed to die down. However, to avoid any misunderstanding and possible unpleasantness, we changed our first names into more Russian-sounding ones: my name was international anyway, but my sister changed her Scandinavian name Helga to the Russian equivalent, Olga (or Olya), which she kept for the rest of her life. My brother Hardy was henceforth called by his second name, Andrei, or Andryusha. Our surname, Watz, was not German, but Latvian or Lithuanian.

When the German army laid siege to the Baltic states Aunt Mia, mother's favourite sister, came to live with us with her three young children. She was terrified of the Zeppelin airships whenever they flew over Moscow. If she happened to be in the street, she screamed hysterically at the well-drilled children: 'Lie down! Lie down!', and they flung themselves on the pavement face down, in a flash. She was also excessively pious, unlike my mother who was simply conventionally religious. As long as Aunt Mia was with us, holidays were holy days and had to be strictly observed and no work was done. In fact, on Good Friday, I remember, I was not even allowed to practise the piano! She most certainly regarded this as a sin. And at parties when we, being older than her children, occasionally played games which imposed a penalty in the shape of a kiss from a boy, she thought it most immoral and vowed that her two daughters would never kiss a man before marriage. (The two girls, when grown-up, had different ideas.)

That summer I spent a few weeks with my Uncle Oskar, who was the garrison doctor at the Kronstadt fortress. It was pleasant enough, though somewhat boring. His young wife was busy with the household and their two-and-a-half-year-old, very independent daughter. So I was left on my own a great deal and got into trouble more than once. The first time I had wandered off on my own into the green and woody parts of the island where the garrison was stationed, not realising that it was out of bounds for civilians. I was stopped and my uncle was informed.

Another incident was rather more embarrassing. I had always been very keen on dancing, and particularly liked the free movements of Isadora Duncan, who discarded ballet shoes and strict classical ballet movements. (She visited Russia after the October Revolution, married the poet Sergei Yesenin, and died tragically in an open motor car, strangled by her own long scarf which wound itself round the wheel. Yesenin, disappointed with the development of the Revolution, committed suicide in 1925.) My uncle's drawing room had two large French windows looking out on to the street, and between them there was a huge mirror, reaching from the floor to the ceiling. We had never had such a mirror in our house. One night he and my aunt were out, the child was asleep and I was on my own. So the fancy took me to dance in front of the mirror—with no clothes on! I was thoroughly enjoying myself, turning, bending and stretching, until there was a noise in the entrance hall and my uncle and aunt entered. I had completely overlooked the fact that the curtains had not been drawn and that anybody passing the house could have looked through the ground-floor window and observe the niece of the respected garrison doctor, with his high military rank, performing in the nude. Uncle Oskar was rather annoyed and Aunt Alice somewhat embarrassed.

I also had a rather harrowing experience that summer. Some time before, I had become friendly with Erika Feldmann, also from our school, whose family were colourful and unconventional. The father worked in some office or other, but at heart he was an artist: he played the violin well and did not observe any hours for eating or sleeping. He had instilled his love for music into Erika. We both had a craze at that time for romantic operas, and over and over again we would play the piano transcript of **La Traviata**, **Rigoletto** and other operas together. Or listen to her father playing in his tiny room behind the kitchen. Together we visited the small local cinema, sitting on uncomfortable benches right through two performances, raving about the Italian actress Francesca Bertini—a tall, dark beauty with a snake-like mouth, who wore long pointed shoes and black dresses which showed off her slinky body. Erika, herself tall and slim, managed to imitate her quite well, right down to the twisting of Francesca's thin lips.

Through Erika I had got to know good-natured Moosya, and her mother, Marya Ilyinishna, who also had a somewhat Bohemian lifestyle. Marya was a real Russian intellectual, a university graduate who worked as a librarian at an art gallery. Her unhappy marriage to a German, a drunkard, had long since broken up, and she had brought up Moosya and a younger handicapped son with difficulty, but with great love and freedom. She loved art, and music, and was also interested in politics; I believe she was a social-revolutionary.

She invited me to stay with them in Petrograd (St Petersburg was renamed in 1914) since I was spending that summer in Kronstadt. It was here that I was introduced to the dismal problem of prostitution. We were staying at a rather luxurious hotel on the Nevski Prospekt, the West End of Petrograd. Having returned very late from some show and a dinner at a restaurant, Moosya, her mother and I were relaxing and chatting, leaning out of the window to the street below and marvelling at the white night. Suddenly I noticed a number of women strolling, seemingly aimlessly, up and down the street. Every now and then a passing man would approach. Some words would be exchanged. Sometimes the man would continue on his way, sometimes a pair would go off together. It took me a while to realise what was going on, and when I tumbled to it, it made me quite sick. I knew about prostitution from literature of course, and perhaps from passing remarks by grown-ups, but I had never yet come across it in real life. I thought it was dreadful. I could not sleep that night, and the memory of what I had witnessed haunted me for a long time.

The war continued its unsuccessful course and the food situation was deteriorating. In mid-1916 bread was rationed to one pound a day, then to half a pound. By the end of the year sugar was rationed too. Bread and potatoes were the staple food of the Russian workers and peasants—now Russia, the granary of Europe, was unable to feed its population adequately as the working men of the villages were sent to fight and die at the front. The women in town took to demonstrating, while armament and other key workers began to strike. Rumours were rife: it was said that the Tsarist Court was pro-German, especially the Tsarina, who had been a German princess. There was talk about a separate peace with Germany.

Then in December 1916 Rasputin was assassinated. He was a crude and uneducated monk who had wormed his way to the Tsarina, who mistakenly believed that this 'holy' man would be able to cure the young Tsarevitch of his haemophilia. Rasputin exerted considerable influence over her and her circle at court, and indirectly over the Tsar. Politicians and members of the aristocracy were dismayed and decided to get rid of him, by poisoning him during a sumptuous supper. But the wily monk was tough and refused to die. So in the end he was thrown, totally drunk, into the Fontanka Canal, where he eventually drowned.

Although we knew what was happenings—defeats at the front, the strikes and demonstrations—we had little inkling of the impending momentous events. I remember demands for reforms and a more liberal constitution, made by the political parties and deputies in the Duma (the Russian parliament established in the wake of the first revolution in 1905), but only vaguely. Some limited concessions had been made to the Duma, and some limited reforms carried out, but by and large it remained an autocratic regime, not ready to grant more rights to the middle class and their representatives in the Duma, nor to heed the needs of the mass of the people.

Thinking back now to that pre-revolutionary period, I realise how little I and my contemporaries knew about the actual living and working conditions of the Russian workers and peasants, in spite of all our liberalism. When we spent the summers in the country, we caught glimpses of the primitive log houses of the peasants, their outdated tools and underfed horses with which they worked the land. We were fascinated and disgusted with some of their customs: when walking through a village towards evening, when the day's work was done and the peasant women sat chatting on benches in front of their houses, you often saw a mother grab one of her offspring and start hunting for lice with a comb, squashing any she detected with a kitchen knife. But of how they really lived, what they ate and so on, we had little idea.

We knew even less of the living and working conditions of the industrial workers, or any other workers in the towns. The caretaker in one of the houses we lived in, for example, was on call day and night. His accommodation was a small room under the stairs. He was responsible for the maintenance of the front entrance of the block of flats. The janitor, who had to clean the back stairs and courtyard, lived with his family in one of the damp and dark basement flats. But his children could play in the courtyard, which we were not allowed to do—except occasionally to make a snowman in winter. So we had no contact with working- class children either. It was not deliberate, conscious, class distinction. It was just a feature of a class-based society.

The poverty in the villages and the abyss between the classes was beautifully expressed by Turgenev in one of his short blank-verse poems: a landlady visits (out of the goodness of her heart) a peasant widow on the day of the funeral of her only son, the best worker in the village. The widow stands erect by the table and mechanically, spoon by spoon, swallows her cabbage soup, her face sunken and her eyes swollen. The landlady is shocked: 'How unfeeling these people are!' And she turns to the peasant woman: 'Tatyana, how can you eat at such a moment?' 'My son has died and I have nothing more to live for,' she replies. 'So it's my end, too. But the cabbage soup has salt in it. Should it be wasted?' The lady shrugged her shoulders and left. The price of salt meant nothing to her.

For me and my friends life continued its normal course. We went to school and were preoccupied with our personal interests: homework, reading, occasional visits to a theatre or concert. But by mid-February 1917 the situation had become critical: massive strikes broke out all over the country, in particular at the Putilov armaments plant in Petrograd, the Dynamo Works in Moscow, the oilfields of Baku. Hundreds of thousands of workers downed tools, sections of the army were in revolt. The women demonstrated and besieged the almost empty shops. There was pressure on the Tsar to abdicate in favour of his son, with his brother as Regent. The middle class was scared of a revolution, and even the Social-Democrats were desperately trying to come to terms with the monarchy. Finally mutiny broke out in some of the units of the Petrograd Guard regiments. While the Tsar was still dithering, the workers and soldiers of Petrograd set up their own *soviet*. Within a month 77 towns had followed their example.

For weeks there were rumours and speculation, but nobody knew anything for certain, and we 16-year-olds understood even less. We continued to go to school until one day—27 or 28 February—we were told that the Tsar had abdicated, that the Revolution had taken place, and we were sent home.

Of course we could not sit at home! Instead we joined the milling crowds in the streets. It was a sunny day and all Moscow was on its feet, lifted on a wave of enthusiasm. Young and old—we were all ecstatic with joy and hope at the overthrow of the autocratic Tsarist regime. Kuznetski Most was thronged with happy people, every one adorned with a red flower: a tumult of talk, laughter, greetings, embraces and kisses, even between strangers. It was an incredible, elated atmosphere.

Then, after a few days, it was back to school. It was the last year for all those who did not want to continue their studies, and in May, as the school year finished, we organised a big farewell party jointly with the boys' school and invited all our teachers. The girls all wore white dresses, and everybody had a red flower in celebration of the February Revolution. It was a wonderful party. We were young and gay and still in a state of euphoria, full of hopes for Russia and ourselves. Our teachers fell in with our mood, full of optimism too.

Yet right from the beginning things had been going wrong. The mass strike movement at the end of February, the massive demonstrations, the mutiny of the soldiers and in particular of the military units in Petrograd, were quite spontaneous. The workers' and soldiers' soviets were set up even before the Tsar was finally forced to abdicate. But there was no leadership to take the soviets and the masses a step further. On the contrary, even the Bolsheviks, whose most prominent leaders were in Siberia or in exile, were trying to hold the workers back from taking up arms. The Bolshevik papers, ***Izvestia*** and ***Pravda***, did not start publication until a few days after the Revolution. Even then, such leaders as Stalin and Kamenev, who arrived from Siberia in mid-March, declared that they would support the Provisional Government, given some meaningless guarantees.

The middle class and their representatives in the Duma had been aware of the crisis, and the inability of the Tsar to deal with it, for months. After the failure of the Russian offensives at the front, even the high-ranking military felt something drastic should be done. The circumstances and the mood were ripe for a palace revolution. But the middle class were not united among themselves. When the workers acted they took fright and turned to the monarchy. The soviets themselves shied away from exercising the power which they already held, preferring to share it with the Provisional Government, which was dominated by the middle class. Alexander Kerensky became Minister of Justice, then Minister of War and eventually President. None of the demands and hopes of the people were met: there was no peace, though the soviets had sent an address 'to the people of the world', declaring themselves for peace without annexations and indemnities. Nor was there any bread.

To everybody around me, the events of that summer were very confusing. We heard that Lenin had arrived from exile in Switzerland at the beginning of April, having travelled through Germany in a sealed train (which soon gave rise to rumours and accusations). The name of Trotsky did not yet mean much to us, so we were hardly aware of his arrival from America a month later, and of his support for Lenin's policy, which was opposed to that of Kamenev and Stalin.

All through the summer there were congresses and conferences of the Bolshevik Party, the Social-Revolutionary Party and the Soviets. A new Russian offensive in Galicia began which unleashed more anti-government demonstrations. I remember marching with one of the demonstrations, presumably organised by the Mensheviks or Social-Revolutionaries. It must have been in the middle of the summer, when the feeling of the masses was high and more and more people were turning towards the Bolsheviks. The crowd I was with was marching along, singing the old traditional revolutionary songs, when it suddenly faced a Bolshevik demonstration shouting: 'Down with the ministers-capitalists! We want peace and bread! All power to the soviets!' There was angry shouting and almost a clash between the two processions. More than once it did come to clashes during those late summer months.

The government counters all this with orders to put the Bolshevik leaders under arrest. In July Lenin goes into hiding. Trotsky is arrested (but later released on bail). The death sentence is restored for those at the front. General Kornilov is appointed Commander-in-Chief of the Russian army—and in the following month leads an unsuccessful coup against the Provisional Government. But the Petrograd and Moscow Soviets support the Bolshevik motions at their conferences, and Lenin writes: 'The Bolsheviks must assume power'.

In October a Military Revolutionary Committee is formed by the Petrograd Soviet and the Bolsheviks declare themselves for an armed insurrection. Other organisations, trade unions, factory committees and railway workers agree. Finally the all-important Peter and Paul Fortress sides with the Petrograd Soviet. On 24 October the Provisional Government issues orders for the arrest of the Military Revolutionary Committee, the suppression of the Bolshevik papers, the replacement of troops who support the Bolsheviks. But it is too late. Lenin comes out of hiding and on 25 October, introduced by Trotsky, appears at a session of the Petrograd Soviet. The October Revolution has begun.

I cannot pretend to have been aware of all these events. We lived on rumours and tried to make out what we could. I used to visit Marya Ilyinishna, Moosya's mother, as she seemed to understand a little more of the political goings-on than most people around me. In any case, I was not vitally interested in politics as such. I spent the summer of 1917 in a relatively leisurely way: reading, meeting friends, coaching two little boys—the sons of my mother's colleagues. One of them was a budding mathematician and could explain multiplication and division to me better than I could explain it to him. I also devoted a great deal of time to practising the piano, a last Christmas present from my father.

After my father's death we had moved to a larger flat so that my mother could take in lodgers and so survive financially. Since then we had moved to a still larger flat, of which two rooms were occupied by a very pleasant Jewish couple, war refugees from Poland, with a teenage son and a daughter in her early twenties. Raheel (how much more musical that sounds than the English Rachel) was an accomplished pianist and was probably suffering from my patient, but sometimes rather ineffective, efforts. One day she came into my room and offered me some advice and suggested regular coaching. I was delighted, especially as I had developed a real teenage crush on her.

As the autumn of 1917 approached I was faced with a problem rather important to a 16-year-old, although rather unimportant measured against impending events. I was starting my last year at school in roughly the equivalent of the English A-Level form. The outward sign of this achievement was a grey uniform, instead of brown. But where to obtain the material? Would my mother find anything on the black market? And would she be able to afford it? In the end a friend of my mother's managed to get some and it was made up in no time. Alas! It was not woollen material and to look fresh and tidy it had to be ironed constantly. But no matter, it was the right colour.

This was the school year I probably enjoyed most. We had fewer subjects, but some interesting new ones—logic, psychology, hygiene—and we learnt well, not because we had to, but because we wanted to. We also practised teaching in the lower forms, or took over the duties of the form supervisors—good training for those who would become teachers after graduating. We were now practically grown up and were treated as such by our teachers. The whole atmosphere in the school had changed since February and the teachers felt more free. Events on the political scene receded into the background, though we were aware of the electioneering activities of the various political parties, which were preparing for the coming National Assembly. All the parties, including the Bolsheviks, were canvassing and distributing leaflets in the streets. But the election never took place. It was overtaken by the Bolshevik Revolution.

How different the two revolutions were. February had been a spontaneous uprising of workers and soldiers, culminating in massive strikes and demonstrations and the setting-up of the soviets. The Bolshevik Party, in the absence of its most important leaders Lenin and Zinoviev, was a restraining rather than an encouraging force. The mass of the population was jubilant at the fall of the monarchy. But their hopes were not met by the Provisional Government that followed—there were concessions but not radical changes. In October the takeover of power in Petrograd was swift and bloodless. In Moscow there was fighting and it took the Bolsheviks eight days to assert their power. We saw no exuberant demonstrations. Most non-political people were bewildered. Nobody had any idea what was happening.

An atmosphere of uncertainty and apprehension set in. At night friends and neighbours sat huddled together listening to every sound of passing cars or motor trucks, fearing arrests, confiscation, enforced requisition of living space or the like. For several days nobody was allowed out into the street without a special permit. We soon learned that it was the Bolsheviks who had started the rising and taken over power, but what their aim was we still did not know. Then we learned that all private houses, including blocks of flats, were to be confiscated. A group of soldiers and civilians came to see our landlord, who lived in the flat just above ours. He was not arrested or harmed in any way, but a House Committee was set up and a meeting called, which my mother had to attend. It was decided to organise watches round the clock as the janitor and caretaker were no longer willing to be on 24-hour call. These two-hour watches were always in pairs and we young ones mostly volunteered for the evenings and nights. But what were we supposed to watch out for? We did not really know. Militia raids? Squads of soldiers passing through the streets at night in armoured cars? Or simply marauders? We were never molested by anybody, and only one person from the whole block of flats was ever taken away.

We actually had a very enjoyable time and often sat out more than one two-hour watch in the entrance hall for company. We got to know the other tenants and made friends with some of them, the young ones. We sat discussing politics or, more often, philosophised about life, art, our studies, or simply played games. I made friends with Kostya, a young student and the son of the now ex-landlord, and eventually became his confidant. He was very much in love with Marussya, a good looking millinery apprentice from one of the flats in the courtyard. She had a beautiful voice and often entertained us with songs, accompanied by Kostya, who could imitate a whole orchestra with his voice.

During the watches in the courtyard we occasionally heard rifle shots in the distance or the rattle of a machine gun. Once my mother was given permission by the House Committee to go shopping. She returned as pale as death, trembling and breathless:

as she had left the shop she had heard a rifle shot and a woman fell down at her feet. Another person was lying in the middle of the street.

We lived in a quiet side street. Even so, detachments of soldiers or civilians, all armed, would pass along it, shouting and occasionally shooting. Sometimes big black cars passed swiftly and silently, and somehow we knew that there were people in them being taken to prison. Or even to be shot? Nobody knew anything for certain, but the house, the street, the city were full of rumours that 'these gangsters and robbers', the Bolsheviks, had overthrown the Provisional Government and were now arresting all the wealthy people, depriving them of everything and even 'nationalising' women. But soon the ban on going out was lifted; offices, factories and shops re-opened; school began again. And we abandoned our amateur efforts to protect ourselves against some unknown danger.

There were marked changes at school. The most important was a decree abolishing tuition fees in all schools, universities and colleges, making them accessible to everybody who wanted to study and was capable of doing so. The main reforms were introduced a year later, when each school was taken under the wing of a particular factory, laboratory or other workplace and specific crafts and skills were introduced on top of the general education programme. In this way, permanent contact was established between workplace and school and children were introduced to the production process. Parents' committees were set up and joint meetings organised with the teachers.

Our tuition became livelier and more relaxed, and our young teachers, replacing the ones called up in the course of the war, took the initiative to form various circles in after-school hours: for drama, literature, history, and the like. No direct efforts were made by the teachers to influence us politically, though some of them were clearly sympathetic to the new regime. And though I attended two or three of those circles, I was always too shy to take an active part in the discussions and the debates.

Within the first few days and weeks of the revolution the new government issued a number of decrees: for the eight-hour working day; banning women and very young people from nightwork; setting a ceiling for the remuneration of commissars and high-ranking employees and others, which was to be no higher than that of a skilled worker; establishing commissions for workers' control over production and distribution. The people were also given the right to recall their deputies to the soviets, including the

Supreme Soviet. Army ranks were abolished, the insignia of rank removed from uniforms, soldiers were henceforth to be addressed with the formal 'you' instead of the 'thou' which stressed their inferior status, and they were no longer required to salute their commanders in the street. The land was given to the peasants—who had been taking it anyway, without waiting for a decree, often burning the houses of the large estate owners. Another decree, a little later, made work for every able-bodied adult compulsory on the principle 'he who does not work, neither does he eat'—those who did not work were simply not issued with food ration cards.

True to their campaign slogan of that summer and autumn demanding 'Peace, Land and Bread', the Bolsheviks issued a decree the day after assuming power, declaring the new government's desire for peace. Lenin called for talks with 'friend and foe', and at the same time declared that the Soviet government would make public all secret treaties concluded by previous Russian governments. Russia's allies feared the propaganda effect on their own war- weary people and rejected any such peace talks. The German High Command, however, agreed to consider an armistice and negotiations began at Brest-Litovsk. Many Russian soldiers had left the front, and the Bolsheviks hoped for a revolution in Germany, which might spread to France and Britain.

But by January 1918, after demands and counter-demands, Trotsky decided to break off the negotiations without signing a treaty, advocating a policy of 'neither war nor peace', which he set out in a most powerful speech, made to the representatives of Germany and her allies but addressed to the German workers. Contrary to his expectations, the German government responded with a new offensive, rapidly advancing on the central front and taking the town of Dvinsk. This unleashed a fierce discussion among the Bolshevik leaders, splitting them half and half into those who were for a resumption of the war and those who, with Lenin, were prepared to accept the now even harsher terms of the German High Command. In the end the decision to sue for peace was carried by one vote—Trotsky now voting with Lenin.

The outcome was tragic for Russia, and for all the fighting men and women drawn into the war of intervention and civil war. Trotsky assumed the post of Commissar for War and rapidly and ruthlessly built up a disciplined Red Army. Fourteen armies closed in on Russia from various sides. When these eventually withdrew, three armies led by White-Russian Generals and anti- Bolshevik followers continued the offensive until the Red Army finally emerged victorious after three more years of war.

But at what a price. The country was ravaged. There was hunger and famine, with epidemics and economic near-collapse. There had been no time for the country to take a breather, for the returning soldiers to work in the neglected fields or build up industry. Instead of leaving the war behind, they were recruited again against the invading armies of the Allies, as well as against their own countrymen. All this required food and transport, and there was no respite for the old men, the women, and their young sons in the villages or wherever work was to be done.

Against this background ordinary people tried to carry on as best they could. In spite of the hardship, there was an enormous upsurge in intellectual and artistic life, and a real effort to improve educational and cultural standards (not always with success). Great efforts, for example, were made to reduce the enormous illiteracy. Courses were organised and individuals encouraged to teach people to read and write. The efforts were not always very successful, but it was an attempt and a beginning, and for the next few years it was a common sight to observe old men and women sitting side by side with young people at such elementary courses.

Some preferred private tuition. Some acquaintances of ours were anxious that their servant girl should be able to read and asked whether I would be willing to teach her. Marfusha herself was not over-anxious to be 'educated'. She was a real peasant girl of the old type. Hard-working, loyal to her masters, and everything but bright as far as learning was concerned. She was trying hard to remember the letters, to grasp the secret of putting them together into words. It was hopeless. Marfusha's brain simply refused to understand why 'D-A-D' should make 'dad', or 'C-A-T' 'cat'. I realised much later that my method was wrong, but at the time only felt sorry for Marfusha, her broad, good-natured face looking quite embarrassed at my desperation. In my own way, I was as stupid as she appeared to be to me. Yet illiterate and uneducated Marfusha knew better than I did, in spite of all my education, what was going on in the country, and what the peasants needed.

We also managed to enjoy ourselves. Apart from attending theatres and concerts, we young people visited each other at home and held parties, playing charades and other games. I remember one fancy-dress party where I appeared as the Queen of the Night, in a long black dress covered with silver stars, and a half-moon stuck in my hair—a most unlikely mysterious queen with my figure and complexion!

In the spring of 1918 I was confirmed, according to the custom of the Protestant Church. My mother had gone to endless trouble to obtain all sorts of food for my party and in a bout of goodwill I offered to help with the preparations in the kitchen, where I rarely made an appearance because of my inefficiency. This time my mother accepted my offer and suggested that I pour the surplus soup into a larger saucepan standing on the hearth. I did it eagerly—only to hear my mother's desperate exclamation: I had poured the clear soup into the dessert, some sort of custard containing milk, sugar, eggs, all precious and almost unobtainable ingredients. We were both very upset, but somehow she saved the day—or rather the supper—by producing something else for the party. But in the conditions prevailing then it was a near-tragedy.

Even so, we were relatively lucky. Soon after the anti-German pogroms in 1915 my mother had been offered a job as manageress of a home for some sixty Germans, old people and young children who had not been deported to Siberia. It was run under the auspices of the Swedish Consulate, which from time to time received food supplies for the home. Occasionally some of the items would be distributed among the employees, so my mother sometimes had a few tins of evaporated milk and a few pounds of sugar to bring home and keep in reserve. I sometimes felt so hungry that I would pinch a tin out of the cupboard, sometimes sharing it with my sister, just drinking the milk out of the tin. Or I would eat a few spoonfuls of sugar.

When the fire was no longer permanently lit in the kitchen, and the pantry got too cold in winter to keep any food there, my mother stored any left-overs for the next meal on a wide window ledge at the end of a long corridor. It was tempting—and many were the times when I could not resist, in passing, snatching up a bit of this or a slice of that. I can't believe that my mother never noticed, but she never mentioned anything, realising that even if we were not starving we were certainly undernourished. Occasionally we visited her in the home where she worked. They had a very good cook there who was also very kind. She always treated us to delicious crisp potato chips (fat was already scarce at that time), or some special kind of potato pancakes.

It was at the home that my mother met Willy Schünemann. He had come to Russia in 1904 to work as an accountant for a German company, had married and had a little son. But his wife died, Willy was interned in Siberia and young Willy was looked after by a relative. He was six years old when his father returned from Siberia. The father had found life in Russia before the war very agreeable, and did not know much about the conditions of life after the revolution, so unlike many of the other Germans released from Siberia during the peace negotiations he did not leave for Germany itself but accepted a job as an accountant with the new German Consulate. His work involved checking the ledgers of the Home for the Elderly and Children. He and my mother met, got on well with each other and decided to get married—though not before my mother had consulted us, especially me as the eldest. She had clearly been lonely all those years and had had to work hard to keep us going, and she was still young enough to have a life of her own (she was only 38). And he seemed quite a pleasant person. So they got married and Willy and his son moved in with us. Whether it was a real attachment or more a matter of convenience, I cannot tell at this distance of time and then I was too young and inexperienced to know. Perhaps it was a little of both. He, too, had had a hard time.

I was busy, too, that summer, practising assiduously at my piano, with Raheel's help. I had decided not to go to university, but to sit the exam for the Philharmonia School of Music. My mother was disappointed, but she did not protest. At the same time I got a temporary job in the office of the Swedish Consulate, which represented German interests during the war. It occupied a spacious house in the midst of a lovely garden. But I felt utterly miserable. Dull office work was the last thing I had ever thought of doing. Yet the people there were very pleasant and considerate, since I did not know the first thing about the work. The hours were not bad, and the consulate was quite near our flat. The first day or two I could hardly stop myself from crying. I simply could not resign myself to this kind of life when all my thoughts and desires were directed towards studying, learning, doing some interesting and useful work. But I realised that I had to help my mother at least a little. Food and clothing were becoming scarce and very expensive on the black market. It was there in that office that I taught myself to type, on a typewriter which today would seem quite ante-diluvian, with two separate keyboards, one for capital letters and the other for lower case.

Late that summer I sat my exam for the School of Music. I remember it as if it were yesterday. It was a glorious sunny day. I went through my scales and finger exercises; I played something by Bach and something by Mozart. The school stood in its own grounds surrounded by a garden. The windows were open, the sun was streaming in, I could hear the birds in the garden, and I was trying to make the sounds of Mozart as pearly and crystal clear as possible; I finished up with a piece by Schumann. When they told me I was accepted, I was overjoyed.

In the autumn the serious work started. For the first time I had a teacher who knew how to explain things: the touch on the keyboard, the phrasing, the different approaches to each piece of music. Valeria Vladimirovna appreciated my efforts and greatly helped me. She used to say that I came into the class 'like a pink cloud on the pale blue sky'. I was indeed pink and plump, but she expressed it rather poetically. I still see her quite clearly: she was all round and soft, with her brown hair loosely and softly combed up into a bun, but ruffled and fluffed towards the end of the day; with plump, flexible fingers, extracting such a variety of sounds from the piano. I immersed myself in this new world with great zeal and delight.

I became very friendly with two of her students. One was a young woman in her mid-twenties, from Siberia. Tall, slim, with a sallow face, black hair, and rather spidery fingers, she had slaved and starved in order to come to Moscow to continue her musical studies. The abolition of tuition fees had at last made this possible, though there were of course still the living expenses. We often delighted in listening to her playing Tchaikovsky and Grieg concertos, or pieces by Chopin, Liszt, Scriabin, much of which was still too difficult for me. My other friend was Lyolya, who became very close. She lived near us and we spent long hours together, practising and talking about music, going to concerts together, discussing what we had heard, and disagreeing on Scriabin, who at that time was rather too modern for my taste. Lyolya's mother and sister ran a small dress-making business. As money began to lose its value, some of their clients were able to pay in kind—with food or other goods, which was a great advantage.

Lyolya and I enjoyed each other's company and tried to ignore the material difficulties of life. We made it a rule never to discuss them. We both knew there was no bread, no meat, no tea, no fuel: we could do nothing about that, so what was the good of chewing it over again and again? And we kept to our vow for a year and a half, until we were forced to part. We were both desperate when my family finally decided to leave Russia, and promised to write to each other. But for some years there was no postal communication between Russia and the West. Nevertheless I faithfully kept a kind of diary in the form of letters, firmly hoping that one day I would return and we would exchange what we had written. When I did visit Moscow, years later, I did not try to find her again. I was no longer quite the same person. Nor would she have been.

In the meantime, food and fuel were the main topics of conversation, especially among women, on whom the burden of feeding their families lay. 'Today such and such a shop is selling pickled herring. The corner greengrocer has received a barrel of pickled cabbage. Yesterday somebody managed to get horse-meat.' When my mother first served horse-meat, she did it surreptitiously, without telling us what it was. Eventually we noticed it, and in the end she was quite proud at having managed to buy some. In time, horses that were collapsing in the street from weakness were surrounded by a crowd, killed and cut up there and then. We were terribly distressed when the last of our potatoes became frozen in the winter—but we had to eat them all the same. Oh, the vile taste of those sickly, sweetish potatoes! And what a treat when the scanty ration of heavy black bread, three or four thin slices a day, was supplemented by our inventive mother with pancakes made from carrots or potato peelings.

All through 1918 the situation deteriorated. It became still worse in the winter of 1919. For months we never saw any butter (margarine was unknown in Russia at that time). Fat was equally scarce and so was cooking oil. We finished up by using castor oil for frying, until the chemists, on government orders, stopped selling it without a doctor's prescription. Luckily onions were plentiful, so we smeared the frying pan with onions to give the potatoes some flavour and stop them from burning. The worst thing was when, for weeks on end, there was no salt in the shops. A pound of salt could be bartered for a whole *pood* (an old Russian measure of 36lbs) of flour in the villages.

And there was no tea, so we drank a substitute made from dried peel or rose leaves, dried blackberries, even birch bark, anything that was at hand and could be sweetened with saccharin, as sugar too was scarce. There was, however, usually a regular ration of dried, salted flounder. This fish had to be repeatedly soaked and tenderised with a wooden mallet to make it at all eatable. Even so, undernourished as we all were, the members of our family more often than not refused to eat their salted fish ration. I was either more hungry, or less discriminating than everybody else and benefited from their squeamishness.

Clothing and footwear had become a problem for most people. Olya reminded me recently how very pleased she was when our mother obtained a coupon for boots for her. Olya had to queue up half the night, and in the end it was a pair made of some coarse cloth on wooden soles! Nevertheless she was delighted and they kept her feet warm all through the winter.

Demobbed soldiers continued to wear their old uniforms and greatcoats. It was difficult, but there was no alternative. People, houses, streets—everything looked drab, especially in winter.

Then another major problem arose: heating, especially if you had central heating as we had. It simply stopped—no joke in winter when the temperature in Moscow could drop to minus 25 degrees Centigrade. This intense cold, unbearable for any length of time, resulted in burst pipes, cracks in the walls, water freezing up overnight. But people with the old type of ovens were hardly better off, since neither wood nor coal was easily available, and those ovens consumed a fair amount of fuel. They usually stood in a corner of the room, reaching almost to the ceiling, shaped like a large box covered with tiles and with a small door near the floor where the fire was lit. The tiles gradually released the heat.

People resorted to all sorts of alternatives, installing oil stoves, small iron stoves, or anything they could get hold of. In my mother's room, which also served as a dining and living room, we had a small hearth built from bricks. All of these still needed an outlet for the fumes; so a pipe from the stove had to be erected across the room, to give off as much heat as possible, with an outlet into the chimney of the original oven. For us, with our central heating, the only outlet was through the one small window pane which was not sealed off for the winter and which was the only means of airing the room. Of course the pipe had to be sealed off, making it impossible to air the room.

There was still the problem of obtaining fuel. Sometimes friends or neighbours tipped each other off that in a particular street a timber house was being pulled down. Then we would sneak up at night and steal a few planks of wood or logs from under the militia man's nose. Sometimes he would be kind enough to look away. (The militia had replaced the police after the revolution, and instead of a uniform they only had armbands). Or people would burn any old pieces of furniture that could be spared. The last thing to go into my mother's stove was a beautiful antique sideboard, with winding columns and polished a reddish golden colour. Inherited from my grandmother, it somehow had survived all our moves. It finally ended its existence by comforting us when we so badly needed it.

These small stoves were by no means always easy to light, and often enough the wind would blow the smoke back into the room, making us choke. Nevertheless they kept us going, and even served to heat up some simple food, when we could no longer keep up a fire in the kitchen hearth. It was then so cold that when the kitchen table was wiped with a damp cloth it immediately became covered with a thin crust of ice. The only advantage was that the cockroaches, common in Russian kitchens, disappeared.

There was no heating in my room, and how I practised the piano there, I do not know. Perhaps my zeal helped me, or perhaps we did not feel the cold so much during the day. At night, however, it was pretty awful, but also rather comic. I often came home late after a concert, a lecture, or a theatre performance, after a day of near fasting, when the family was already asleep. There was always some food left for me in a pot, kept hot wrapped up in newspapers and blankets. I always found it tasty, even when it wasn't. Having eaten, still with my winter coat and hat on, I rapidly undressed, washed and went to bed, covered with several blankets and a thick, heavy sort of eiderdown. (In Russia they were usually put on top of the mattress rather than over you, and so were filled with feathers, rather than down, which made them rather heavy.) With my head wrapped up in a shawl, and with gloves on my hands I would settle down in bed and immerse myself in a book for an hour or two and then go happily to sleep full of impressions of the evenings outing and stuffed with philosophical problems or images and descriptions of works of art, or a classical novel. Fortunately, although the electricity was cut off for several hours every night, an exemption was made for streets with public buildings and important institutions. We were lucky to be living near a hospital.

The acute shortage of fuel for heating also hit the theatres and concert halls. But even that could not dampen people's spirits. The audience simply sat with their coats on, and the performers shed theirs just before coming on to the stage. I remember concerts where the pianist took off his gloves at the last moment, while an attendant was warming the keyboard with an iron filled with glowing charcoal. Even when public transport stopped for a time, and cabs were no longer available or too expensive, audiences were not deterred, though it meant a walk home in bitterly cold weather with the glistening snow crunching under your feet. Nor did it stop the actors, musicians and writers, few of whom had as yet left the country.

It was a remarkable feature of those early post-revolutionary years, this upsurge of artistic and intellectual activity on the part of performers and other artists such as painters and sculptors, and interest on the part of the people, in spite of all the hardship. It seemed like the blossoming of all that had lain dormant, those years of *proletcult*—the culture of the proletariat.

Keeping clean was also a problem. As fat became extremely scarce, the manufacture of soap all but stopped. But people still found an ingenious solution: they began to get hold of any and every scrap of fat by legal and illegal means and make soap themselves, for their own use and for sale at enormously inflated prices or barter on the black market. Soap-making was soon declared illegal and a punishable offence, which by no means stopped people, only they tried to do it more secretly. That, however, was difficult, as the boiling of the inferior fat and other substances gave off a penetrating, vile smell, which gave the show away. Our Aunt Tori was engaged in this enterprise, but luckily was not caught—at any rate not while we were still in Moscow.

The 'black' market should have been called the 'free' market, since it functioned openly and was obviously tolerated by the authorities. I remember the black market that my mother used, on Sukharevski Square. Peasants from the countryside brought in their produce to exchange it for all kinds of things: household utensils, clothing, jewellery, even home-made soap. If money was accepted at all it was at astronomically inflated prices.

In these circumstances the physical resistance of the townspeople was extremely low: the smallest cut would fester and take days to heal; epidemics were rampant and hospitals were overcrowded, with patients lying on mattresses on the floor in the corridors. In the winter of 1918-19 it was Spanish 'flu, in 1919-20 typhus. Thousands upon thousands of people died during those two winters.

All these difficulties and hardships were not of the making of the Bolshevik Revolution as such. The renewed German offensive in the winter of 1918, against a country that had already experienced four years of war; the harsh conditions of the peace treaty eventually concluded with the German High command in March 1918; the Allied wars of intervention and the civil war which engulfed large parts of southern and western Russia—these devastated the young Russian Socialist Federal Soviet Republic (RSFSR) (with other Soviet Republics this later became the USSR—the Union of Soviet Socialists Republics). All the country's reserves had to be directed towards the army which Trotsky, as Commissar for War and Commander-in-Chief, created out of men who had voted for peace in 1917 by leaving the trenches and battlefields and tramping home. But the further years of war added to the decimation of the industrial workforce. Though basically a peasant country, Russia before the First World War had a modern, developed industry with three million workers. By

1920 their number had shrunk to one and a half million.

But it was not only the renewed war that the young Soviet government had to deal with. Right from the beginning it faced insurmountable difficulties. The flight of the aristocracy and of hostile politicians was probably no great loss. (Some of the aristocracy finished as taxi drivers and waiters in Paris and other capitals of Europe; some of the women as chambermaids with the post-war *nouveaux riches*—the yuppies of those days, if we are to believe a witty comedy staged in Berlin in the 1920s.) Far more serious was the exodus of many intellectuals and experts in various branches of industry and commerce, civil servants, bank clerks, accountants and others. This was more than a calamity. There were also acts of sabotage by former government officials and those who ran the railways, the post and telegraphs, who refused to hand over documents, plans, ledgers and files to the largely unskilled Soviet representatives, leaving them high and dry. This made communication and the supply of goods to the towns at times impossible.

Faced with all these difficulties the government had to resort to arrests, imprisonment, even executions, in order to survive. Yet such drastic measures, it must be emphasised, are not part of a socialist revolutionary programme. They are the reaction to violent and obstructive actions on the part of a hostile minority opposed to any radical social change.

Lenin was fully aware that in backward, impoverished, peasant Russia, they could not embark on the road to socialism on their own (as no country in the world could have done then or could do today). Nevertheless the Bolsheviks struggled on, still hoping for a revolution in Germany. Eventually the Kaiser was toppled in November 1918 and revolutionary councils of soldiers and workers were set up in German towns. Soviets even took over some German consulates abroad, which had been re-opened after the peace treaty of March 1918. In Moscow the consulate became the German Welfare Commission for Prisoners of War, Internees and Repatriates, attached to the Central Revolutionary German Soldiers' and Workers' Soviet. I had to visit the Welfare Commission in connection with my mother's work at the Home for the Elderly and Children. The offices struck me as very similar to those of Russian soviet institutions, where you went for ration cards, and vouchers for clothing or shoes. There were red flags and posters, slogans on the walls, instructions on a noticeboard, a rough and ready atmosphere full of activity and confidence, some muddle, and soldiers and civilians coming and going.

Meanwhile in Germany the Social Democrats were as scared of a full-blown workers' revolution as their counterparts had been in Russia in February 1917. With their connivance the revolutionaries Rosa Luxemburg and Karl Liebknecht were murdered in January 1919 by the Frei Korps, which had been formed by the most reactionary army officers at the end of the First World War.

By and large I do not think that many people in Russia really understood the implications for Russia (or Germany itself for that matter) of the success or failure of the German Revolution, nor did we get much news of it. We were too busy trying to survive.

In 1918 I accepted a permanent job as a typist with the Commissariat of Finance, though as a student I was not liable to labour conscription. The salary was pitifully low measured against black-market prices: one loaf of bread for a month's salary! (My stepfather, who eventually had to leave his job with the Welfare Commission, could afford two loaves a month on his new salary.) The perks attached to the Commissariat job induced me to accept it: the Commissariat was running a children's home outside Moscow in an old converted monastery, for the children or young relatives of their employees. So my sister and brother, and in time little Willy, were able to go there. It was an enormous help: the children were well housed and well fed; they were taught by a number of teachers, and supervised by other staff, who organised games, competitions and outings to neighbouring children's homes. They were happy there. I even managed to spend a fortnight's holiday there myself in the summer of 1919.

The Commissariat of Finance occupied an enormous building in the style of London's Kings Cross Station, right next to the gateway to Red Square. In the corner between the building and the gateway there was a tiny chapel with a famous icon of the Virgin of Iberia, where candles still burned. But over the chapel there was a large banner: 'Religion is the Opium of the People', and another referring to education and enlightenment. The chapel was eventually removed and the huge building became the Museum of the Revolution. It had three or four floors, with long wide corridors and very large rooms. The offices of the Commissariat, like any other offices or institutions, were supposed to work from 10am to 4pm (after the Revolution working hours were reduced to seven hours a day for factory workers and six hours for office and other workers, including lunchtime). But in winter it was quite impossible to heat those rooms and corridors, and however thick the walls of those old, solid buildings, however wrapped up you were in your padded or fur-lined coat and boots, it was practically impossible to work efficiently, or even work at all for any length of time.

Our department manager was a mild man who used to walk through the vast unheated rooms with his army greatcoat hung over his shoulders, now without its epaulets, sadly and understandingly shaking his head when told that so-and-so had not come in yet or, at three o'clock, so-and-so had already left having felt half- frozen. We tried to warm ourselves with hot tea or a few brisk exercises in between. At 1pm we were ready for lunch and as the Commissariat had no canteen, we had to go out to one of the public restaurants, or rather 'food centres'.

The opening of such eating places was certainly one of the progressive measures introduced by the Government and it was the fault of neither the central nor the local administrators that they were far from satisfactory. I am sure that the staff of these centres, the Commissariat of Food Supply, and the Co-operatives, did their utmost, but it was just not within the realms of possibility to get and cook decent food, decently served. This was the usual procedure: you queued up for between half an hour and an hour; when your turn finally came, you were given an enamel or tin plate, a tin spoon, fork and knife. (Later you had to bring your own plates and cutlery because, in spite of their poor quality, people were pinching them—hardly surprising when the towns were invaded by crowds of soldiers from the front who owned nothing, people from the provinces and peasants who now discovered that you ate food other than with wooden spoons out of a common bowl). Into these plates the usual Russian cabbage soup was dished up, then you had to look for a seat on a bench at one of the tables with soup or tea spilt all over the place.

After having thus strengthened (or exhausted) yourself, you went back to the office, and within an hour or so were again frozen and stiff. So by about 3.30pm it was time to stroll home. In January 1920 a new decree was published making absenteeism, lateness and a similarly lax attitude to work a punishable offence. Though recognising that this decree was fully justified, I for one would have found it rather hard to comply, though the lax situation at work was imposed by conditions rather than unwillingness to work.

The Commissariat was right in the heart of Moscow, near the Bolshoi Theatre, the College of Music and the Trade Union House (formerly the House for the Assembly of the Nobility) which was also used for concerts. So in between working hours, foregoing the cabbage soup in the tin plates, I often spent some time in one of those establishments. My visits to the Bolshoi Theatre came about quite accidentally. Passing the stage door one day, I ventured to open it out of curiosity and went in. There was nobody around, so I explored the theatre, including the stage and the dressing rooms: the holiest of the holy for me. Nobody asked me who I was or what I wanted. There must have been so many new people going in and out in those days. In one dressing room I rummaged through a trunk containing all sorts of props and discovered a pair of worn ballet shoes that fitted me! I was so delighted that, I must confess to my shame, I could not resist 'expropriating' them to practise in at home—the dream of my childhood.

It was so simple to get into the theatre that, whenever time permitted, I started to go to rehearsals and even performances. Thus I got to know the workings on the other side of the curtain, the behaviour of the actors, and so on. Once I stood barely two yards from the great Shaliapin as he waited for his cue in the wings. He was already Tsar Boris Godunov, working himself into the part, with his eyes rolling, his heavy breath responding to the words spoken on the stage by his Boyars. Another time I watched ***Das Rheingold***, in the days when I still used to go to Wagner performances. It has a beautiful scene, when you are sitting on the right side of the curtain, as three lovely mermaids swim in the Rhine, guarding the Nibelungen gold. The illusion of water and waves was produced by a green gauze curtain and lighting effects, behind which the mermaids were singing and swimming playfully. However, I was on the wrong side overlooking the entire stage and its machinery. My illusions were shattered: the mermaids, one of them pretty plump, were perching in cradles, which were moved up, down and sideways on pulleys operated by hefty men behind the stage backdrop; the waving of their arms and the movements of their tails looking pretty silly seen from that angle. Another eye-opener was a performance by the famous ballerina Geltzer. As the audience applauded she was all charming smiles; but behind the curtain she abruptly changed into a rather old hag, giving her young partner a vicious dressing-down, using the crudest Russian expressions, for having trodden on her toe; a minute later, more radiant smiles for the public.

I discovered a couple of chairs in two tiny boxes right behind the curtain. They were probably for members of the company—but I often made myself comfortable there. On one occasion I put my fur hat on top of some wooden balls in an opening in the wall by my side. The opera ended with a thunderstorm, skilfully imitated by the orchestra. Suddenly there was a terrific rumble and crash by my side; I thought the whole wall was coming down. Then I realised it was the balls, somehow set in motion to imitate the clap of thunder. But my hat! Where had it vanished to? I could not possibly afford to lose it. I descended into the lowest regions of the theatre and luckily found it in the basement, among the stage machinery and rubble.

There was one other unique incident. At the end of a performance, after a few curtain calls and what seemed the end of the applause, I took a short cut across the stage to the nearest exit. Suddenly there was a new burst of clapping. The curtain went up and there was I, right in the middle of the stage! Luckily, the actors all flocked in again, some of them already with their coats on, like me. They lined up once more and we all sang the *Internationale*. And nobody noticed a foreign body among the singers.

But soon I embarked on a very different, rather unusual but instructive activity. The black market had gradually dried up and food had to be sought, especially in winter, from much farther afield. In spite of the absence of the children, it was difficult to exist on our scanty rations. So with our young maid Katya I joined the stream of pilgrims to the villages. The peasants had, by that time, become rather choosy: some wanted, and received, pianos, gramophones, pictures and pieces of furniture. Our offerings were more modest: household goods, linen, clothing, trinkets—anything we could spare and could carry which had any barter value.

One fine autumn day Katya and I set out to explore the villages in the vicinity of Moscow. She returned with a sack of potatoes on her back and I had a sack of flour. The flour was easier to carry, as it did not cut into your back like the potatoes but, even so, it was quite a job for me to walk the several miles to the station and the short walk from the Moscow station home. At the start I fervently hoped not to meet any of my former schoolmates or teachers; later there came a time when I was looking out for somebody to show my success in coming home with the precious booty. It was not easy, this kind of barter, but having got over the initial embarrassment at so strange an activity on my part, I found it interesting and at times even romantic. And I really got to know the life and lot of the Russian peasantry at first hand.

Some of the peasants resented us 'beggars from the town' and did not hide their feeling of superiority. But most received us with kindness and even invited us to share their meal or to stay overnight. So there we sat with bearded men, worn-out women and a crowd of children with flaxen hair, all around a large table in the middle of which stood a big wooden bowl with cabbage or potato soup, and sometimes pieces of meat in it. In front of every one of us there was a chunk of bread and a wooden spoon. Katya, coming from a peasant family, felt quite at home of course. For me it was a new experience. After the father or grandfather had given the signal, everybody was allowed to fish out a piece of meat. Katya and I were always encouraged to eat as much as possible as they knew we would not get such food in town. Then there were endless glasses of tea from the *samovar*, which supplied the hot water to dilute the tea extract in the small teapot.

Occasionally I would talk to the younger people, some of whom had been prisoners of war in Germany. They spoke of the superior style of work and life of the German peasants or farmers and were determined to introduce their modern methods of farming as soon as it became possible. I do not remember any political talk about events in the country or the policy of the Bolsheviks. The peasants' attitude seemed to me to be 'wait and see'. Of course, the more politically conscious peasants were glad at the overthrow of the Tsarist regime and the distribution of land to the peasants (the setting up of collective farms came much later), but for now they were taking advantage of the plight of the town population to improve their own standard of living. I once had a special request from the young daughter of a farmer to bring her some face powder, for which she would give me—unknown to her father—an extra half a *pood* of flour or buckwheat. I managed to get some powder but in my ignorance of cosmetics did not bring her French powder. She was very disappointed, but gave me the extra flour all the same.

The rough log houses, draught-proofed with hemp, were extremely primitive. You entered the house through some sort of shed, which on one side led into a cowshed; I am not sure, but perhaps the horse was kept in there as well; certainly the pigs; the hens were everywhere. Straight on, a door led to a shed for all kinds of equipment. The door on the other side led into the dwelling part of the house. All this was under one roof. The living quarters consisted of just one large room with a massive oven along one wall; part of this served as a bed for the old folks and perhaps one of the younger children. It was the warmest place in the house. From there the old ones could overlook the entire room and climbed down only for their meals. At one end of the high oven was a hearth for cooking the meals. This part could be screened off by a curtain. In the middle was a deep recess for baking bread or heating milk until it had a thick brown crust. This part opened up right into the room. Under it was a fair-sized open space, where chickens slept and clucked in winter; and sometimes even piglets, very young lambs or kids.

Along two walls of the room there were simple benches, a table and a few chairs. There was also a bed for the parents or the young married couple. Somewhere there was also a chest of drawers. The rest of the family slept on the benches, on sheep-skins, which also served as blankets. If we stayed overnight, we joined them on the floor. Needless to say, the air in the room at night was pretty stuffy. In one corner of the room there hung, as in most Russian homes, an icon, with a small oil lamp in front, the flame of which was kept alight from one Easter mass to the next to keep away evil spirits. For washing there was a cylindrical container filled with water, and with a rod protruding from the bottom. As you pushed the rod upwards, into the container, the water would be released and you had to be quick to catch it and give your face, and with luck your ears and neck, a quick lick. In the summer everybody washed at the pump in the yard.

The most strenuous part of these expeditions were the journeys. Unless you have gone through a similar experience you cannot remotely imagine what it was like to travel in those days. First there was the queuing up for tickets, not for hours, but sometimes days. Everybody would get a number in the evening, entitling you to join the queue again the following morning without losing your place. Then you would try to find out when and from which platform the train would leave—although any train would do. No suburban train would deposit you more than ten or fifteen miles away and you would always find a village there. But time was the big problem. You sometimes sat in a train for hours in a tightly packed open carriage. A few times Katya and I even spent the night in the train, at the station in Moscow, a 15-minute walk from home and our comfortable beds. But we could not risk losing our space, or missing the train altogether.

Somehow or other the time would pass and eventually the train would leave. It often took two, three or four hours to cover the distance. In the middle of some woods the train would stop, puffing and panting. The doors of the carriage would be opened and Red Army or militia men would invite everybody, in a business-like or joking manner, to step out into the deep snow, the women to clear the track, the men to chop wood to feed the engine. As everybody was anxious to continue on the journey as quickly as possible, we all complied. And after all, wasn't it only fair, since the engine and the engine driver were doing us a favour by carrying us to our destinations?

Eventually we did arrive. Then there might be a six or seven-mile walk to the village through knee-deep snow. This was even more difficult on the return journey when we might have to get up at 4.30 in the morning to catch the train, all the while carrying our heavy sacks on our shoulders. I was sometimes so tired that I literally fell asleep standing up in the train, supported from all sides by the people crowded around me. Sometimes we travelled throughout the night in a cattle truck with just a few benches, without backs, down the middle—one was lucky to get a seat at all. Often the trains stopped to let army trains through, taking soldiers to the civil war fronts or bringing back the wounded. These trains obviously had priority.

I vividly remember one of our trips. The train had stopped, the people were streaming out and setting off in a hurry for the lengthy walk ahead. It was a dark day, or dusk was already setting in. Suddenly I stumbled over something: a small bundle. Inspecting it, I found that it contained salt! About a pound of it, at a time when salt was more precious than gold! What was I to do? My first impulse was to find the person who had lost it, but how to go about it? Perhaps forty or fifty people were already ahead of us struggling through the snow. Had I called out whether anybody had lost something, half of them might have been upon us. And would our voices have reached them anyway? So in the end, with heavy hearts Katya and I decided to keep it and exchange the salt ourselves. I still have my doubts whether I did right. In the end it was a question of principle versus practicability.

On one journey, lucky to get a seat, I found myself next to a Red Army soldier with a big, filthy sheepskin hat on his head. He was obviously dead tired, and kept nodding off then jerking awake again, until sleep finally overtook him and his head dropped on to my shoulder. There was no room for me to move away, and in any case I would have been scared of offending him. At the same time I was just as scared of his hat, a sure breeding ground for the widespread typhus lice, the source of the epidemic spreading through Moscow. But I sat there all the same, stiff inside and out.

It was surprising that in spite of all those journeys, the walks in the bitter cold, the filth and the dirt, and insufficient food, neither Katya nor I ever caught any serious disease. On the contrary, I was as healthy as ever before and looked it, so that on a sunny summer day two young men in the street, apparently from the provinces, pointed at me, remarking much to my indignation: 'Look how they starve in Moscow'.

In time it became more and more difficult to find things to barter. The peasants, or at any rate the wealthier ones who had the food the towns so badly needed, had accumulated everything possible. And we had less and less to offer. The last things I exchanged were my mother's and father's wedding rings.

All this bartering and trading went on illegally. There was often a Red Army control at the exits of the railway station and it was possible that after all the agony of getting a ticket, the journey, the walk through the snow, the haggling with the peasants, the sleeping in stuffy, unhygienic huts, the sack of flour or whatever you had brought back would be confiscated before you left the station. No crying or begging ever helped. It was done on the government's instructions in an attempt to stop the illegal trade, though admittedly this was directed primarily against the speculators, who sold the products in town at enormously inflated prices. That this order was not carried out with 100 per cent strictness may have been sheer physical inability on the part of the Red Army guards; on the other hand, they may have been discriminating between the speculators and people like Katya and me, who, fortunately, never had to suffer such a loss.

Whatever the difficulties associated with these trips, I still had sufficient interest and strength left—much to Katya's amazement—to rejoice at the landscape and nature around us: the beautiful autumn colouring of the fields and woods, or even the two-hour walks through the deep, soft snow through wide fields or thick, dark pine woods, their branches laden with glistening snow, with heavy, grey clouds in the sky. I used to call it a symphony in black and white. I do not know whether this meant anything to Katya, but she always listened attentively. Sometimes we sang folk songs together. Only when Katya began to sing Bolshevik songs did I walk on in silence. If somebody had asked me why I was apparently against the Bolsheviks, or what they stood for, I would not have really known. I had no opinion of my own on this matter. I seem to have disliked what I thought was pure politics, and simply accepted the opinion of the people around me. Yet our family or friends had never suffered any personal harassment from the Bolshevik government. And if you had asked Katya about the Bolsheviks, she would hardly have known much more than I did.

Katya was a good-natured, simple-minded, but by no means stupid young peasant woman. She had a brother, a Red Army Soldier and a Bolshevik, who occasionally came to visit her. She was unable to argue with him and therefore accepted everything he told her. She had been brought up in a patriarchal peasant family, where the father could dispose of the children as he pleased. Katya had been married for only six months when her husband was called up at the beginning of the war and shortly afterwards was reported missing. In Moscow she had no friends at all and I don't remember her ever going out in the evening, except on one occasion when her brother took her out to a fairground together with some of his army friends. Months later Katya suddenly decided one evening to do some thorough cleaning: she scrubbed all the floors in the corridor, the kitchen and bathroom, dusted and wiped here and there, much to our surprise. The next morning Katya had disappeared and did not show up the whole day. We were at a loss, until we learned from the former caretaker's wife that she was in hospital and that she had given birth to a little girl—the result of Katya's one and only outing. We were dumbfounded. There was my mother, who had given birth to three children, and our lodgers, one of whom had two children, and nobody ever noticed a thing; though my mother had remarked once that Katya was getting fatter on the little food we had. Was it lack of interest in her on our part? I hope not.

When she came back from the hospital with the little baby, my mother naturally told her that the baby would be welcome, but Katya would not hear of it. She was so scared of her father in the faraway village and what he might do to her that she would rather give up the child. She could never have gone back home if it had become known that she had this child. Yet the Soviet government had abolished all legal distinction between legitimate and illegitimate children; young mothers received higher rations and there was every chance that, once the country had pulled through, there would be nurseries for babies, education facilities for children, and sufficient work for mothers. She was a nice little baby, and when she cried I used to take her into my room. She lay on my bed while I practised the piano, which usually stopped her crying. We talked and talked to Katya, but no, she could not overcome the age-old fear of her father.

One evening she took that little bundle—as unnoticed by us as when she went to the hospital—and came quietly back without the baby. She had left it lying on the steps of a pleasant-looking house, which, as she told us afterwards, she had carefully chosen for this purpose.

It seems to me now that it must have been a sign of the toughness of life and the hardship most people suffered that we did not protest more vigorously and force Katya to keep her child.

She never expressed her feelings about it and never really confided in us. Were we all too occupied with ourselves? Katya stayed with us, willingly sharing all *our* troubles until we left for Germany. We would have dearly loved to take her with us, but she did not want to leave her country.

My stepfather had gradually become disillusioned with life in the new Russia, and was finding it rather inhospitable. He kept talking about Germany as the country of order and sufficiency, as he had known it before he came to Russia. But leaving was not easy. In the first place the repatriation transports to Germany had stopped towards the end of 1919, and to leave illegally, as emigrés, was out of the question as far as we were concerned. We saw no reason for it, in spite of the harshness of life at that time, as we had all grown up in Russia, and even to my mother, born in Riga, Germany was a foreign country. We were non-political and had not suffered any more than anyone else under the Bolshevik government. So none of us, except my stepfather, was inclined to go.

Nevertheless, the question of leaving or staying had gradually become a permanent cause for discussion at home. I was particularly fierce against leaving. However difficult and complicated life had become, it was still running in the familiar groove, whereas a new life in Germany frightened me. Millions of other people had stuck to Russia and lived through it all, why not us as well? We were only three adults, surely we could manage to get through. The children were well looked after in the children's home. Every time they came home on a short visit we were surprised how good an influence the home had had on them, especially on my barely twelve-year-old brother, who had become helpful, polite and considerate as never before. Olya, being rather quiet and shy, always got on well with everybody, and little Willy could hardly have missed parental care, of which the death of his mother and the internment of his father had deprived him earlier. So there the matter rested, until one day late in December 1919 or early January 1920.

Then my mother suddenly became ill and our family doctor diagnosed typhus. It is a terrible disease, which leaves the patient prostrate and delirious. It is also highly infectious. It was a notifiable disease and by law you were not allowed to keep a patient at home if there were people other than family living there. We were at a loss. To take my mother to hospital would have almost certainly meant death. The hospitals were overcrowded, patients were lying in the corridors on straw mattresses and dying like flies. There was not enough medicine or food to go round, and the doctors and nurses worked to the last ounce of their strength through day and night. Our doctor decided not to notify the authorities and we tried to keep it a secret from our lodgers. But they could not help guessing, and were all so decent that they never mentioned it and never insisted on my mother being taken to hospital despite the danger they themselves were in.

Our doctor, who had treated us for years, came round twice a day. He had grown terribly old and thin over the past year or two. He was one of the old people who were unable to reconcile themselves with the new regime, but he stayed on, treating patients as efficiently as ever in spite of the lack of medicines and the most elementary things, such as bandages. He was extremely kind to us in those days and helped us a lot, and we felt bad that we could not adequately express our gratitude to him, but money had lost its value and we had hardly anything left to offer him. In the end we gave him two Chinese vases, which he may have appreciated, being a cultured man, or found useful for barter.

My mother's illness was a great trial for me. Her health had never been good, but she had never been really ill either, and I had no experience in nursing. Now I had everything on my hands: my mother, the household (small as it was), and providing meals, which was quite a job. The disease is transmitted by body lice, especially among large crowds. My mother may have been infected when visiting the markets in search of food. Or I might have given refuge to some lice that may have dropped on my shoulder from that Red Army soldier's sheepskin hat.

Wherever the infection had come from, the results were devastating. After a few days of high temperature my mother became delirious, talking wildly for days and nights. It was agony to witness how her fantasies tormented her. She raved on incessantly, continually threatening to throw herself out of the window. She accused herself of having caused the outbreak of the war because she had taken some sheets out of the trunk of one of the lodgers to barter them for food. She had set the world ablaze and would now have to pay for all the destruction, the lost lives of the dead soldiers and sailors. (I never knew whether her story was true. It wasn't as if she had young children to feed, and we had never actually starved. Besides, nobody would have left a trunk unlocked with so many people in the flat. I cannot imagine my mother ever having even thought of such a deed whilst of sound mind.) So while she was ill my stepfather and I took turns to sit by her during the night. The same room also served as a sitting and dining room, and we prepared our simple meals on the small brick stove. Even Katya preferred to sit with us and my sick mother, rather than in the freezing cold kitchen or her own small room, which had no window. Those were terrible days. Then the crisis came and she survived. But she was terribly weak, unable to walk properly for several weeks, and really needed plenty of milk and other quite unobtainable foods to build up her strength.

This was the state of things when my stepfather came home one night and announced that there would be one last train to Germany. Whatever we decided to do, he would be leaving with his little son. And we had to decide at once—the train would leave in three days. My mother was still so weak that she could hardly grasp the situation. The children were in the home. So the decision lay with me. My resistance was broken through my mother's illness. I could not take the responsibility for her recovery and things in general all on my own. I was ready to go. But to leave everything and everybody within three days! That was the awful thing. I had so many friends to say goodbye to. I had, with the help of my stepfather, to wind up our household, such as it was, and pack.

I started that very night, clearing out my books, my notebooks, letters, numerous little tokens from friends, sheet music, photographs. How difficult it was to part from all that I had collected over years. But we were allowed to take with us only what we could carry, and were forbidden from taking out of the country any letters, photographs or other written or printed matter. I don't remember whether that referred to books as well, but I took with me two library books that I had not finished reading, as a kind of parting gift—though I knew this was wrong. One was a book on astronomy, which I still have, now of course quite out of date, the other a biography of Tchaikovsky which I lost somewhere on my subsequent travels. I cried all night as I cleared out my things.

The following day I went to see Lyolya and my piano teacher Valeria Vladimirovna. Lyolya was as desperate as I was. Valeria was very sad but tried to console me by telling me about the excellent academies of music in Berlin. But somehow I felt that this was the end of my music studies, that in Germany everything would be different. Then I saw Aunt Tori, who had stayed with us for so many years and was now married to a fellow Latvian. She was terribly upset and came round immediately to help. I gave her my most cherished letters and photographs to look after.

In the meantime my stepfather was chasing around trying to

obtain some Polish currency, later to be changed into Deutschmarks. It was extremely difficult to buy foreign currency on the black market and one had to pay a pretty high price for it. In order to get some cash in the first place, we had to sell our furniture, and whatever else we could find buyers for. The selling was a tricky business. After the revolution confiscation was the order of the day—meaning the expropriation of big business, the nationalisation of banks, the railway network, big estates, trusts and factories. But this order was carried so far as to declare every chair in a household, every bed, as national property, on loan to people for their own use. Normally there was no interference on the part of government officials; you continued to live in your rented flat, sit on your chairs, sleep in your beds as before—unless of course you belonged to the propertied classes, in which case your house was likely to be confiscated with everything in it. But the snag for people like us was that you *were* forbidden by law to sell anything, and as soon as you carried a piece of furniture, a carpet or anything across the street the authorities were liable to pounce and ask for *bumagi*—papers testifying that you were entitled to shift this object. Fortunately practically everything in our rooms was taken over by the various people who lived in the flat with us. My piano, my father's last present to me, I could have sold for quite a lot of money, but sentimental reasons stopped me. So I left it with my friend Lyolya, convinced that I would return to Moscow within a short time. (I presume I must have given her a duly signed paper to enable her to move it into her home.)

The last thing was to fetch my sister and brother. This was Katya's job and it turned out to be quite an odyssey. Early in the morning, on the last day before our departure, I went with Katya to the railway station, where we queued up for the ticket. Finally she got it and left for the platform. I turned towards the exit to hurry home to continue packing our essential clothing into one of those old-fashioned basket-trunks, which two of us could carry...but the exit was closed. The crowd of people milled around, talking and dashing to and fro. I went to another exit. The same thing: closed and guarded by a militia man. The same at yet another exit. Nobody knew anything, only one thing was clear: nobody was allowed to leave the station.

I was in a panic. I simply had to get home, where my sick mother was expecting me and where I still had so many things to do. I ran from one militia man to another. I went to the commandant of the station. All efforts to get out were in vain. They had orders not to let anybody leave and there was absolutely no exemption from this order, whatever the reasons. I was in despair and fluttering around the station like a wild bird in a huge cage, when a young girl, an employee at the station, took pity on me and offered to show me a way out somewhere beyond the platforms, past some sidings with endless trains shunted on to them. At last I was free and ran home, still stunned by fear that I might have to stay there for I knew not how long.

But the excitement was not at an end yet. The day passed and no Katya and no children turned up. Of course there could always have been a delay, but it got later and later and still no children. I was getting more and more anxious. The train for Germany was supposed to leave in the morning! What could have happened? Finally, shortly before midnight, they arrived, upset, exhausted, hungry and sad. It was very hard for them to leave the happy children's Home in that big old monastery and all the friends they had lived with for a year. But they were also a little curious about the future, at least the two boys were.

Now Katya told us her adventures. She had got on the train, which left fairly punctually, but after a while she noticed that it had taken a different route. She discovered that every man or woman who was at the station that morning, whether as a traveller or not, was being taken some miles out of town—the women to clear the tracks, the men to fell trees and chop wood. They would be safely back in Moscow in the evening. Katya realised that she would be unable to fetch the children. So she jumped off the slowly moving train, somehow managed to get another, then a peasant cart, then she had about an hour's walk through fields and woods to the children's home. It was early February, but the weather was pleasant and sunny and Katya knew she had a job to do.

The road from the station to the monastery was usually quite deserted, but on that day first one cartload with singing and chatting children came along, then another. She hardly glanced at them and continued on her way, until she heard the second cart stop and her name called out. It was the children from the home, on a visit to a neighbouring children's home. My sister and brothers had recognised Katya and stopped the cart. Now they heard that in less than 24 hours they would be on their way to Germany! So the whole excursion sadly turned back to help them pack, exchange token gifts and take leave of friends and teachers.

The following morning—it must have been 7 or 8 February 1920—we bade a final farewell to our friends and acquaintances and sat waiting for the transport to the station. When it was delayed, I decided to make a bonfire in my room of all my remaining papers. I made a neat pile on the parquet floor and set it alight, thinking the pile would burn to ashes in no time. But it went on and on burning, with the thick smoke filling the room and escaping into the street through the small open window. Luckily nobody in the street took any notice. When the flames and smoke finally subsided, I was aghast: I had burned a big black circle into the floor, leaving the House Committee and my successor in the room to deal with this rather disastrous damage.

Our train, like all the previous ones for those who wanted to return to Germany, had been provided by the Soviet authorities (presumably with the cooperation of the German authorities) and was equipped with an ambulance carriage with medical staff, and a kitchen. We deposited the little luggage we had in our compartment and, with Aunt Tori, waited for the train to leave. It was a long wait and a weary one, especially for my mother, and we were getting hungry. The kitchen did not start working until the train was on its way. Not till the afternoon did the whistle finally blow. A hasty embrace from Aunt Tori, a last desperate glance at Moscow, and we began our long journey into an uncertain future.

There must have been between five and six hundred people on that train, the vast majority former prisoners of war. Most of the others were the remains of German families who had tried, like my stepfather, to resume their pre-war life in Russia. But there was also a sprinkling of people like us, whose accidental link with Germany enabled them to leave Russia.

We settled down as comfortably as possible. There were two or three carriages, all of the third-class type with hard seats, for families. The majority of the ex-prisoners of war travelled in former goods trucks, fitted out with benches and a small stove for warmth. The compartments in our carriage did not quite reach to the ceiling and there were no doors to the corridor. Each compartment had two top and two bottom bunks, which could be extended to form a very big double bed at night. You could not fall off, but if you wanted to get down, you had to slip out at the foot end. We were given one or two blankets each, and also covered ourselves with our coats. I don't remember it being cold in the carriage. At night, which fell early since it was mid-winter, a candle lantern dimly lit the corridor and the compartments. The train swayed gently, chugging along, slowly, painfully, with endless stops. It took us days to reach Borisov, the last town before the war zone between Russia and Poland, where at that time there was something of a truce.

The journey was a trying time for everybody, especially those with children, though the staff on the train did their best. Twice a day doctors and nurses would go the length of the train, examining the sick and the weak, distributing medicines, or whatever was required and available. Of course we kept it secret that my mother was only just recovering from typhus, and luckily nobody fell ill because of her during the journey. The food we received was simple but relatively good. Many of us had not had such substantial meals for weeks or months: at midday we had a thick soup, sometimes with bits of meat in it. Those who could afford it, supplemented this with food offered by the peasants all along the route. And at the stations there was always a rush to the cistern to get boiling water for tea.

Our greatest difficulty during the journey to Borisov was to keep clean. Often we just rubbed our faces, ears and necks with snow. At longer stops we managed to get some warm water which trickled down from an engine pipe. Every now and then we had a 'spring-clean' in our carriage: mattresses were carried out and brushed, blankets shaken out, the benches washed down with carbolic disinfectant supplied by the ambulance staff. It was surprising that with all this we did not get into hysterics or fall out with each other. On the contrary, everybody was friendly and tried to make life in the carriage as bearable as possible.

Of our fellow passengers I remember clearly only one, a Madame Belkina, an intelligent woman in her mid- thirties. In Moscow she had worked with a theatre and concert ticket agency, and knew all about artists, singers, dancers, musicians, about operas, ballets and music. I liked to talk, or rather listen to her. Or I immersed myself in the two books I had taken with me.

Finally we reached Borisov, a town in Byelorussia, which had been part of Lithuania, Poland and Russia and became one of the sixteen republics of the USSR in 1922. There we stopped, and it suddenly became doubtful whether the Polish authorities would let the train pass at all. The big spring offensive—when the reactionary Marshal Pilsudski marched his troops into the Ukraine and was turned back by General Tukhachevsky, a former Tsarist officer who had joined the Bolshevik Revolution in 1917—had not yet begun. But skirmishes between the two opposing armies had been going on for some time and we were caught up in them. There were daily negotiations about whether to let the train through to the Polish-German frontier. Early in the morning the train would move up quite close to the war zone, where we could hear rifle shooting and machine guns. In the evening we would be taken back again—only for the same thing to happen the next and every day for about a fortnight. It was a nerve-racking time. However reluctant we were to leave Moscow for Germany, now that we had packed our bags there was nowhere else for us to go. So the whole train hoped and waited.

In the meantime we made the best of a bad thing and used to go exploring the nearby villages to get some extra food and find proper washing facilities. They were wretched and poor Lithuanian villages, which had suffered badly during the war. The population was predominantly Jewish, the men wearing long black kaftans, skull caps and long locks *(peisaks)* dangling from their temples. The women used to bake a special kind of flan from coarse flour on flat baking tins in the old ovens, which we bought to supplement our monotonous train diet. At times the weather was gorgeous, the snow sparkling in the sun. It was February, the worst cold and frost was over, and we greatly enjoyed these excursions, stretching our limbs and breathing the fresh air.

And at last, one bright morning, we were told that we could proceed. We had to walk for six or seven miles though the snow to board a Polish train. Fortunately some sleighs were available for the old, the sick and the small children, and my stepfather had also managed to buy a child's sleigh for our basket-trunk. We could never have carried it across. We entered an enclosure where our documents were checked by the Soviet and Polish military. Then we passed through a wooden gate.

Russia was behind us now and there was no way of getting back. I stopped and looked over the undulating snow-covered countryside, with a row of dark trees on the horizon. I will never forget the sight of that long line of people, winding their way across the bare white landscape. Most of them were returning 'home'. Yet they all—at least to me—looked infinitely sad, forlorn, joyless. They were not refugees, yet seeing photographs of the many refugees through the years since then, people who have been, for one reason or another, driven from their homes and countries, has always reminded me of that melancholy picture at the Russian-Polish border. It seemed like a forerunner of the many and tragic migrations to come.

Having crossed the no-man's land, we boarded the Polish train which took us to Warsaw. There we spent the night in a reception centre, where we were deloused, disinfected, and sent to the bath house for a good scrub. Our clothes were disinfected and returned to us smelling of cheap petrol. The following day we were free to walk around. We strolled along the Krakovska, the

Bond Street of Warsaw, with our stepfather, marvelling at the window displays in the shops, eating the Polish national dish—*flaky* (tripe)—in a restaurant, and indulging ourselves eating chocolate cake and drinking coffee in a café.

After one more night we were finally put on another train which took us to a quarantine camp at Heilstadt, near Koenigsberg (today this is Kaliningrad, and part of the USSR). It was there, at the beginning of March 1920, that we started our new life in a land unknown to us, which turned out to be very different from the 'land of milk and honey' that my stepfather had visualised.

Part Two:
Germany

CHAPTER 3

Berlin

WE WERE to spend a fortnight in quarantine, but the fortnight became three weeks, and three weeks a month, a terrible, never-ending month. I was in black despair most of the time, and lay on my bed crying and sobbing for hours. My poor mother must have suffered badly, seeing me like that. I don't remember her ever complaining. Yet she must have suffered at least as much as I did, having been so rudely torn away from all her previous life, and still weak from her recent illness. I did not realise it at that time and, selfishly, felt only the acute sadness of having had to leave behind almost all that I had loved and cherished for a whole nineteen years. And I saw only the bleakness of the present and uncertainty of the future. Never once did I experience the thrill of setting out on a new life. I was so engulfed in my own grief that I was hardly aware of the rest of the family. Even my stepfather with his little son could not have felt very happy at this start to a new life and this welcome to the country of his birth.

We lived in large barracks, thirty or forty people in each, all jumbled together. We were relatively lucky, as our beds were right at one end so that we had a corner to ourselves. The beds stood in two long rows with a wide passage between. In the middle of this passage was an iron stove where we dried our washing and occasionally cooked. Meals were provided, but sometimes we wanted something else. There were no partitions, except round the washroom with its row of wash basins. There we lived, with nothing to do, within the confines of the barbed wire which surrounded the camp.

In time we did manage to slip out and go to the nearby village. I could not believe my eyes when I saw how those German peasants and small farmers lived. Their houses had two, three or more rooms, with proper bedsteads with metal frames and shiny brass knobs. For a meal the table was laid with a separate plate for each person, with a spoon, knife and fork for everybody. It was amazing compared to the Russian villages. Sometimes we went for short walks over the meadows. My mother even managed to get some Easter eggs for us and hide them in the grass so that, according to our old custom, we could look for them. These were the few lighter moments. But everybody's nerves were on edge and there were arguments within the families and quarrels among the different groups of inmates.

To top it all, there was the news of the right-wing Kapp *putsch* on 13 March 1920, when heavily armed troops marched on Berlin and declared the Social Democrat government overthrown. The Social Democrats themselves simply fled. But the militant workers started to arm themselves, the trade unions declared a general strike, and Kapp and his supporters were ousted. Only then did the Social Democrats return, to re-impose 'law and order' with rigorous methods. The news did not mean much to me or my mother but it must have been disquieting for many of the ex-prisoners of war and repatriates, including my stepfather. I do not remember him ever discussing politics, but I do not think he was particularly right-wing.

Eventually, at the beginning of April, we were on the move again, to Berlin. My first impression, from the train which runs right through the centre of the town from east to west, was of huge, solid, grey buildings. I had exactly the same impression when I returned from my first visit to Paris in January 1935: massive greyness and heaviness.

We arrived at another repatriation centre, in a confiscated school building in the western part of Berlin, near a railway station. Here men and women were accommodated on separate floors in the large classrooms. The children remained with their mothers, unless they were teenage boys. On the ground floor was the dining room, where we were fed peculiar dishes, such as barley gruel with prunes—pretty revolting. We were issued with vouchers for articles of clothing from a special store, as we could not very well walk around in our Russian winter coats in April. I got a dark green, loosely woven, cheap-looking spring coat with which I wore a black and white beret which I had made myself in a style rather the vogue in Moscow at that time.

I do not remember how long we stayed at that refugee centre, but as soon as my stepfather had found his feet and my mother had regained some strength, the hunt for a flat began. We were on the list of people needing accommodation, but flats were scarce in Berlin. And we could not afford to rent anything expensive. In her desperation my mother began to ask strangers in the street if they knew of a flat or furnished rooms to let. Eventually she met a working-class woman who used to spend the summer months with her retired husband in a shack on a small allotment outside Berlin. She was willing to let us have their flat for a few months. It was in the well-known working-class district of *Roter Wedding* in the northern part of Berlin. (The name *Roter*, meaning Red, came from the predominance of Communist voters, but *Wedding* is just a name and has nothing to do with English marriages.) The flat was tiny, in a drab block: you entered through a very small kitchen, then there was a living room, and off that a small windowless room, more like a large cupboard, which served as a bedroom. No entrance hall, no bathroom, just a tap in the kitchen and a sink. But it meant escape from that dreadful refugee centre—anything was better than that.

Contrary to his expectations, my stepfather could not get work with his pre-war employer. Nor could his relatives help him. He had a bachelor brother, a very respectable teacher at a boys' grammar school, and two portly spinster sisters, all approaching middle age, all three living together, seemingly comfortable, respectable and middle-class. They were quite friendly towards us, but without any warmth. Even with their long-lost brother their relations seemed rather cool. All this must have been very disappointing for him. Quite by accident my stepfather met an old school friend in the street, who managed to get him a job in the town hall or some government department, not the job he had hoped for and not well paid either, but a beginning. That same friend also recommended me to an acquaintance of his at a bank. Much to my surprise, they took me on.

My sister was still determined to become a hospital nurse, but she could not start training until she was eighteen. So my mother found her a job at a chocolate factory near where we lived and for several months she sat there, with young working-class girls, wrapping up chocolates and placing them one by one into pretty boxes with pretty pictures on them. They were searched every day as they left the factory, but were occasionally allowed to buy chocolate cheaply. Yet my poor sister did not have even the minimum preparation for a working life that I had had! My brother and stepbrother had to be found places at a school, but my brother found it difficult to adjust to the school curriculum, different from that at his school in Moscow or the children's home. He never really settled down.

Eventually the housing authority offered us a flat in the heart of the West End of Berlin, in a street off the Kurfurstendamm, famous for its expensive cafés, restaurants and theatres, and the elegance of its inhabitants. The new flat was at the other extreme from the flat in *Wedding*, and we knew we would feel quite out of place. But we had already turned down a couple of others, and if we had refused this time we might be taken off the register altogether. So we accepted it. As it turned out it was not in the front part of the house, but at the back, across the courtyard. Most houses in Berlin, as in Russia, were built around a courtyard, sometimes even with a second courtyard beyond that, and the quality of the flats—and the rent—diminished according to the distance from the street. In our new house only the front part had a staircase laid out with lush red carpet runners and decorative plants in pots in the lobby. There was only one caretaker for both parts of the house, a snobbish woman who, having seen us move in, considered us somewhat inferior to the people in the flats at the front.

The flat itself was beautiful: four rooms, bathroom, kitchen, all very spacious, and a large closed-in balcony overlooking a back garden with tall trees. We had plenty of space, of air and sun—only next to no furniture! We had beds, a dining table and a few straight chairs, some saucepans and crockery, given to us by our stepfather's sisters.

I had a large room to myself and I managed to hire a piano, still hoping to be able to continue with my studies. It proved impossible. I was working full-time and did not know how to find an evening music school, if there was one. I also had little time to practise, especially as my stepfather objected to it in the evening. Now he was no longer a newcomer into our home. Now it was his house. I felt I could not impose my own will any more, even though I more or less earned my own keep. Above all, I felt that serious study had to be everything or it was nothing. I did not like the idea of just dabbling so I gave it up. For ever. It was a wrench, and for a year or so afterwards I avoided listening to music and could hardly keep back my tears when I accidentally heard the sound of a piano from somebody's open window.

At the bank I was introduced to such simple tasks as filing and checking the entries of stocks and shares by a thin, friendly girl and a fat, good-natured boss. I was soon transferred to another department, sharing a desk behind long counters with a girl slightly older than myself. Gerda was my introduction to Germany's middle class. In time we became good friends and continued to see each other long after I had left the bank and she had got married. Sitting opposite each other, adding up endless columns of marks and pfennigs, all of which had to tally with parallel entries by the end of the day, we evolved a method of adding up and talking to each other at the same time. We discussed philosophy and she introduced me to contemporary German writers—Strindberg, Thomas Mann, Hermann Hesse—and others hitherto unknown to me, such as the Norwegian dramatist Henrik Ibsen.

I was lucky to have met Gerda, because her friendship made life in Berlin a little more bearable. Her mother was a very shrewd widow who had managed to preserve the money her husband had left her by dabbling in stocks and shares and property. She had a sharp face and a sharp mind for business, but she received me at her house in a very friendly way. She had a middle-aged brother who was a homosexual—the first I was aware of meeting. He was a very pleasant person and rather intrigued me.

Gerda was a girl of strong principles: she had been in love with a cousin but decided not to marry him because of the possible harmful effect on the children of such a close marriage. The cousin announced that he would console himself in a monastery where he could indulge himself in his two other passions: books and wine, while Gerda accepted the proposal of a very pleasant, quiet young man just out of university, who was very much in love with her and frequently came to meet her after work. She was pleased every time it rained because then they could walk with arms linked under one umbrella, which would otherwise have been considered improper as they were not yet officially engaged. I found it somewhat ridiculous that she was already putting by things for her future married life: linen, cutlery, anything that she might be given as a present or that she had bought herself from her monthly salary. She had a special trunk for this 'bottom drawer'. If such a custom had ever existed in Russia, it had faded years ago.

On the other hand, I was also introduced to less prudish behaviour between the sexes, and to jokes or remarks which I either did not understand or found objectionable. There was a young woman in the office who often looked rather tired and pale on Monday mornings, and her male colleagues took this as an opportunity to make suggestive remarks, which she accepted with amazing equanimity. Then there was a pleasant, good-looking and rather shy bank clerk who used to pass my desk rather more often than necessary. Eventually we became acquainted and he invited me to go sailing with him and his friend on Sundays. The friend had a girl friend, a jolly, plumpish widow in her early twenties. That was very enjoyable. But one evening he put the text of a new hit-song on my desk, which went something like

'Why must it be great love straight away? Why can't one be happy just for one night?' I was indignant. Relationships between the young of both sexes in Russia were free and easy, as far as I was aware; there was no flippancy, nor was there an excessive obsession with sex. I don't remember now what happened to that young man, but before he faded out of my life I had an enjoyable evening with him at the opera, listening to Wagner's ***Die Meistersinger***, and in the dress circle too!

I had eventually overcome my grief about the end of my music studies, and when I earned a little more I regularly queued up on Sunday mornings for opera tickets—gallery, of course! You had to arrive long before the performance to get a good standing place, but I preferred to sit on the steps in the dim light with other young music-lovers and follow the score, borrowed from the library. I also began to visit museums and picture galleries, concerts and theatres, in which Berlin excelled. There was the Reinhard Theatre, and the left-wing Piscator, and guest performances by Soviet companies: Tairov, Meierhold, Vakhtangov and the Hebrew theatre Habima. Yet I never lost the feeling that all this was only temporary and that sooner or later I would return to Russia.

At the same time I was trying to take up some sort of training or studies. University was out of the question, primarily because I had no Latin, so I enrolled with the Berlin Handelshochschule, a school of economics or commerce. It offered a variety of lectures in the late afternoon and evening. But it was not primarily economics or commerce that interested me—more often than not I attended lectures on civil rights, philosophy, politics, and even chemistry. During the second year I dropped out altogether, having decided that commerce was not for me: it would only lead back to an office, albeit in a somewhat more elevated position than that of a shorthand typist.

We didn't make any contact with the emigré organisations in Berlin. My mother was probably too preoccupied with everyday care for the family, or too exhausted. Olya had started her nursing training at last and lived in the hospital, and I was probably too shy. Possibly, being of mixed origin and with a German stepfather, we did not quite fit in either of the two groups, German or Russian. Moreover, the majority of the Russian emigrés at that time were people who had fled the country in 1917 and 1918, and by devious routes, via Finland, Turkey, Siberia and even China. The great majority found their way to Paris, where they settled. Those who came to Berlin were mostly intellectuals and former well-known members of the various political parties. As newcomers, we had no contact with them.

In 1921 I did, however, join the Russian Famine Committee, set up to help alleviate the terrible suffering in Russia. Among its Russian organisers were some well-known politicians, including Milyukov and Gessen. There I met the young Nabokov, who later became a famous writer, author of the novel **Lolita**. He always seemed to me slightly conceited in his attitude to people who were not his friends.

But I did make friends with a Russian-Jewish girl, Lida, and her two friends, both Russian students. In the summer of 1921 we all went on a hiking tour through the Riesengebirge, a mountainous area in the south east of Germany, near the Czech border. It was a rather ridiculous walking tour, but we enjoyed it. None of us had ever done this before or carried a rucksack on our backs, and we had no idea where to begin. We bought a map of the area, took a train to some station or other, got off, and began to climb right up to the mountain crest, staying with farmers on the way. We carried our food with us, occasionally buying something from the farmers. Instead of being up at the crack of dawn, we used to get up at nine or ten in the morning, dawdle around, walk through the midday and afternoon heat and by four or five in the afternoon start to look for somewhere to spend the night. And we just marched on, never descending into the beautiful valleys or small villages on the slopes.

After about eight days of this we reached the foot of the highest mountain, the Schneekoppe. We stayed at one of the two inns and managed to get up at six in the morning to tackle the peak, over five thousand feet above sea level. But when we sat around the breakfast table on that grey windy morning and watched the hikers in the distance struggling up the mountain against the wind and rain, with no prospect of a view from the top, we wondered, was it worth the effort? And decided it was not. So after a good meal and a further rest, we turned our backs on the inhospitable Schneekoppe and made for the railway station in the valley below and the train back to Berlin. The zig-zag run down took three hours. I found it rather ridiculous and disappointing to climb for eight days and then get down in three hours. But we had had a good time.

Regrettably, our friendship did not last long. Lida was anxious to study engineering, and the only place she could find was at the technical college at Bingen, on the Rhine, a long way from Berlin. The two boys also started on some studies and we gradually lost touch with each other.

So I did get to know people here and there. Olya was among people at the hospital: patients, doctors and nurses, and became friends with a few of them. It was not easy for her. The work was hard, the people and customs strange, but she was training for something she had always wanted to do. And she used to come home on all her days off. Andryusha was worse off. He left school as early as possible and became an apprentice gardener somewhere out of Berlin, though he did not last there very long.

I think the most lonely person of us all was my mother. She must have been very homesick, without friends, no money, sitting in a half-empty flat, feeling the contemptuous looks of the caretaker upon her every time she came home with her meagre shopping. Far from the 'land of milk and honey' visualised by our stepfather, we had arrived just as the German inflation was gathering speed, to reach astronomical heights by 1923. Even in 1921 we ate mostly hash made from ox lungs, margarine, cheap liver sausage and artificial honey, with my mother eating the tiniest share, enough just to survive. I remember her sitting forlorn on a straight chair against a wall, in a long brown cardigan, sipping hot tea from a glass in a holder. I really think she gave the family all the food there was, living primarily on tea. No wonder she never picked up properly, either physically or psychologically. Although we did not realise it, she took out all her frustration and disappointment on little, defenceless and puzzled Willy—who just could not do anything right. I really felt sorry for him.

But my mother was not well. In the summer of 1923 the doctor diagnosed tuberculosis of the lungs and suggested a few weeks' rest at a sanatorium. But she would not hear of it, though she could probably have gone under the national health insurance scheme. It was bad luck for my stepfather, too, having already lost his first wife. It was not surprising that there was a certain tension between them, though at that time I did not notice it. I did not contribute to her peace of mind either—to my eternal regret—still moaning about Moscow and my music studies. In addition, I began to develop rather progressive ideas about free love, the status of illegitimate children and so on, and began to expound these ideas to my mother. Though I was not living up to these ideas, I must have worried her at times.

I also began to question the alleged wickedness of the Bolsheviks. Though still not particularly interested in politics, I could not help hearing about financial crises, economic instability, changes of governments, and the strife among political parties in this or that country. Yet the Bolsheviks had managed to hold power for four or five years now. The civil war was over, and conditions seemed to be improving, especially after the introduction of the New Economic Policy (NEP) in 1921, which had allowed the limited re-introduction of private enterprise, while the government retained control over the important branches of industry. There was a trend among some of the Russian emigrés to become more conciliatory towards the Bolsheviks and a group started to publish a journal, ***Smena Vekh*** ('The changing of the Milestones'), which no longer viewed the October Revolution through the eyes of deprived owners of confiscated property. I do not remember who the initiators of the journal were, or how well founded and objective was their analysis of Bolshevik theory and practice—whether it merely reflected the New Economic Policy. The journal interested me greatly and for a while I began to wonder about the past and to argue in defence of the Soviet regime.

By contrast, the economic situation in Germany had been deteriorating for some time. Inflation had reached astronomical heights, then came to an abrupt end. It had reached its peak in the late summer of 1923, with the value of the Deutschmark falling continuously and prices in the shops doubling practically every few hours. (As a guide, when we arrived in Germany in March 1920 the rate of exchange was already 240 DM to £1. By the summer of 1923 it was 265,000 DM to £1, and by December it reached 15 billion DM to £1.) Yet I never saw anybody carrying their wages in suitcases, as is sometimes said now. There was no need to. The bank notes were simply printed over, so that a 10 DM note became overnight a 100 DM note and then 100,000 DM or more. The bank I worked for paid our salaries every morning, enabling us to go shopping over the lunch hour—by evening the prices might easily have doubled. If shops did not take their money from the tills to the banks in time, they no longer had enough to replenish their stocks for the following morning. Food became scarce, because the peasants and farmers no longer wanted to sell their produce for German money. A few dollars, however, represented a fortune.

The end of inflation, which came abruptly at the end of 1923, was catastrophic. For anyone with money in the bank, businesses and wealthy people, it lost its value overnight. Working people suffered less in this respect since people who were paid hourly, weekly or monthly did not have bank accounts and lived from one week or month to the next. Olya and I kept our money in envelopes marked for rent, for food, or a relatively large purchase such as shoes or a coat. Many firms were unable to survive.

Early in January 1924 my mother fell seriously ill. My stepfather was doing a lot of overtime—it was the time of the year when ledgers had to be closed and balance sheets drawn up. One day he was not back home by midnight and my mother went to meet him as he walked home through the Tiergarten, a huge park near our home which divided Berlin in two. In her frail state, probably not dressed warmly enough, she caught a chill on that frosty night, took to her bed, and never got up again. Even today, more than sixty years later, I cannot think calmly or without pain of her illness and death, and the loneliness of it.

I was then working with a small merchant bank quite near our flat, which enabled me to go home at lunch time to give her something to eat. But for the rest of the day, till the evening, she was on her own. Even in the evening she did not have much company or attention from any of us. Then my sister took leave of absence from the hospital to look after her for the last few weeks. Even so, we three grown-up people never sat with her at night to offer her a glass of water, or say a few comforting words. Then one Sunday afternoon she began to slip off into a coma, alternately lamenting her children, especially me—as the eldest I would have to take on some responsibility for the family. She made my stepfather promise to look after us and he assured her, 'Your children are my children'. Then she lost consciousness, but lingered on through the week till the following Saturday morning. It was 24 January, the same day that Lenin died.

I don't remember that winter very clearly. My sister returned to the hospital. My brother, I believe, was still an apprentice and my stepfather was out a lot. I do not even remember mourning my mother very much. I think I felt that in some ways it was a blessing for her to be out of it all and not have to worry any more about whatever may befall us.

After the inflation, my small bank lingered on till the end of April 1924, then folded up—and I found myself without a job. Luckily I found another within a few weeks, dealing with correspondence and bookkeeping (of which I knew precious little) for a firm that sold wallpapers and furnishing materials.

One Sunday afternoon I went for a stroll, feeling rather melancholy as I watched other people walking in pairs or small groups. I stopped to look at one of the windows of a large department store, and when I turned round to go home, I bumped straight into a man behind me. We both apologised, and realised that we were both Russian. There was thus a bond between us, and he asked for my permission to see me home. He was a Georgian from Tiflis. When we parted in front of my house we kissed and made another appointment. This was the first of three totally accidental encounters, which, each in its own way, changed the course of my life.

We met again and it seemed only natural that I wanted to invite him home. To my surprise, my stepfather banned him from 'his' house and wanted nothing to do with 'this exotic Georgian'. He warned me that Rapho had no intention of marrying me and would only get me 'into trouble'. The thought had not even entered my head! I knew that my stepfather wanted me to marry a weedy young student, a member of his own ex-students' club who once took me to the horse races (the only time I ever went, and I promptly lost twenty marks).

After the October Revolution Georgia had enjoyed a short period of independence when the right to self-determination was conceded to some nationalities. Rapho had been elected a deputy to the Georgian parliament, under the new president Chkheidze. When, in 1921, Georgia became one of the Soviet Socialist Republics and was again incorporated into the USSR, Rapho had emigrated, together with other politicians. In Berlin they lived on subsidies from the government-in-exile. Rapho also had some connections with the Georgian Orthodox Church, and had an estranged wife in Tiflis and two small sons. He told me something about a civil divorce, but that was not recognised by the Church.

The only result of my stepfather's warnings was to estrange me even further from him, and send me head over heels in love with Rapho. I was too busy to concentrate on my rather exacting work. Rapho's frequent visits to my office, in a small house behind the shop, did not help. And when I finally bridged the gap between the theory and practice of free love, and everything in my personal life became simpler and clearer, it was too late to save my job. My predecessor had left me detailed instructions for the payments due to various authorities, but, probably dreaming of her impending marriage, she had omitted to draw my attention to the next tax payment due shortly after she left. I was not yet experienced enough to detect it. So the inland revenue people were upon us. They were reasonable and realised that there was no ill intention behind the non-payment, but my bosses got cold feet and, much to their regret, had to replace me with a more experienced person. I think that was the only time in my life that I was simply sacked.

At home things had been going from bad to worse, and eventually came to a head. My stepfather gave me an ultimatum:

give up the exotic Georgian or leave 'his' house—which meant he would also wash his hands of my brother and my sister, who was about to sit her final exams. I reflected very carefully and came to the conclusion that if I did let him dictate my life, we had no guarantee that one day he would not find some other excuse to get rid of us. The very fact that he linked his 'care' for our brother to my behaviour made me suspicious. So I took a furnished room near where I worked. My stepfather did not even let me take my mother's sewing machine, which he did not need, or a tea and dinner set which I had bought as a present for my mother. Nothing but my personal things.

My moving out was a godsend to him. Soon after his arrival in Berlin he had met an old childhood friend, a war widow with a son of about twelve. She had come to our house once, when my mother was still alive, a plump, robust and jolly person. I later had the feeling that my stepfather's overtime hours were spent with her rather than in his office. And sure enough, we heard a little later that Willy Schünemann had married for the third time. None of us ever saw him again—or little Willy, which we regretted. At the time I felt that had I met him in the street, I would not have stopped to shake hands. But with the distance of time, I thought that perhaps he, and above all little Willy, had found a pleasanter and quieter life with his third wife. He had behaved in a mean way towards us and towards our mother, but, after many hard years, perhaps he was entitled to an easier life.

The day I moved out was the day I was given the sack. Not suspecting that might happen, I had rented a comfortable furnished room near my work, with breakfast and supper provided. It was much too expensive now that I faced unemployment in four weeks, so I paid my rent in advance and gave notice. In the meantime I enjoyed the comfort and Rapho's unrestricted visits.

The labour situation was difficult at that time, but I hoped for the best and began to look for another job and another room. My sister had finished her training and opted to live out of hospital so that I could live with her. We took a cheap room in a good middle-class area of Berlin, but at the rear of the building. Our room was long and narrow. Behind the door was a washstand (the water had to be fetched from the kitchen) and a wardrobe, opposite a largish bed. Beyond the bed was a table with two chairs; the window faced the door, and opposite the table was a rather dilapidated red plush sofa. We also had limited use of the semi-dark kitchen, which we shared with the landlady. Her husband was hardly ever visible, and I think they only had one other room. But they were quite pleasant people and tolerated Rapho.

Rapho used to visit fairly frequently, and when my sister was on night duty the whole set-up became rather comical. She had to sleep beforehand so we would shield her from the light of the lamp by opening a big black umbrella behind her head and one door of the wardrobe, to cut her off from the rest of the room. Today I cannot understand how she ever managed to get the required rest, but she never complained.

Rapho and I would sit reading or talking very quietly; sometimes he would read poetry to me, or charm me with Georgian songs (he had a pleasant voice), or with skilful drumming of the most intricate rhythms with his fingers and hands on the edge of the table. He taught me one or two songs in Georgian, one of which I still remember. He also taught me how to cook real Caucasian *pilav* (or *plov*)—rice with braised lamb, chestnuts, scrambled eggs and whatever else you fancy, all placed in little heaps under the rice. I taught him German and discussed how he could find work. It was pretty hopeless but—although I was in love with him—I could not understand how a grown man could go on living on subsidies, instead of trying to earn his living, be it only selling matches or flowers on a street corner. This was of course an absurd idea and Rapho would have found it quite beneath his dignity. I strongly objected. If I had learned anything from the Bolsheviks it was that no honest work was dishonourable (though selling matches on street corners was not exactly work of social importance). And there were so many examples, as I pointed out, of members of the Russian aristocracy now having to earn their living as taxi drivers or waiters.

After a while there was talk that the funds of the Georgian government in exile were running short and the subsidies might be cut altogether. But Rapho had also been a member of some Church Council; he therefore approached the Papal *nuncio* in Germany for assistance. He was eventually offered lodgings and an allowance in a Catholic institution in Vienna. He obviously did not want to leave me and Berlin, but it seemed the only way out for him. I was pretty desperate, and we both hoped the separation would be temporary (especially as I did not share his religious leanings). In the meantime, however, we were—with my sister's assistance—very happy on my unemployment pay.

One day a neighbour let me know that a local engineering works, the Berlin-Anhalt Maschinen AG, or BAMAG, was urgently looking for a typist. I applied and got the job, a most boring one: typing out endless tenders, detailing machine parts, tools and equipment in the minutest detail. But it was a job. During those three months of unemployment (the only time I had ever been unemployed) I had started to teach myself shorthand and mastered the rudiments fairly quickly (the German system used at that time was very much simpler than the English one). It was just as well. Soon afterwards I was asked by the personnel department if I would be interested in a transfer to the department that dealt with foreign correspondence. Of course I was. And with the help of a manual I converted the German shorthand into French. So with some application on my part and no doubt some indulgence on the part of the actual correspondents, I tackled the job.

In the midst of all this came Rapho's departure. I must have been distressed, but I remember little of that time, except that we frequently wrote to each other and hoped that we would be united again before long.

There followed a period of which I am not particularly proud, except that I knew when to extricate myself. I was occasionally 'loaned' by my department to the director-general and once or twice to the head of the finance section, a Herr Stadler, whose secretary was ostensibly rather busy. This was, as I later realised, a mere pretext; he had simply got his eye on me. I was perhaps a little flattered, and I felt lonely without Rapho, so I accepted an invitation to a dinner dance in a garden restaurant one summer evening. And I continued to accept his invitations to elegant restaurants, having wine and lavish meals served with a confusing array of cutlery. Thinking back, I must have been very naive. I don't know what attracted me to Stadler. He was not particularly good-looking, quite a snob and rather conceited. But he was a good conversationalist and particularly knowledgeable in economics, which he tried to explain to me. He came from a wealthy, old-established bourgeois family from the Ruhr. A childhood friend of his, a man called Hofmann, worked for the same firm in Berlin. He had charmed and seduced a very sweet and innocent girl, and sometimes we four spent a pleasant evening out or a Sunday in the country. Hofmann had a fiancée waiting for him in Düsseldorf, whose trust he could not possibly betray. It did not matter about Hella, who was deeply in love with him and kept hoping he would forget that other loyal girl. The hypocrisy of his behaviour, especially as he was a Catholic—so was Stadler—did not strike either of them as objectionable.

But it was, of course, also a question of class: Hella was the only child of a grocer who had made good during the war. Her parents had given her a very good education and she was also good-looking, with delicate features and large grey eyes. So though she was good enough to be the sweetheart and plaything of a young, bourgeois gentleman, she was not fit to be his wife. I found this attitude shocking. Hofmann confessed to me that he himself loved Hella but he could not go against tradition and the expectations of his parents and bride-to-be. Eventually Hella had a nervous breakdown and a broken heart, and was shipped off by her parents for a long stay with relatives in Sweden.

For my part, I felt that my relationship with Stadler was plainly unsatisfactory. When he started to tell me about the elegant and entertaining young women from the 'rag' trade, with whom I neither could nor wanted to compete, and as his phone calls became less frequent, I made short shrift. Olya and I had moved into two very pleasant rooms near the Tiergarten. On the ground floor there was a café, and night after night there came the sounds of the latest hit-song 'Yes, we have no bananas'. Olya was, as always, very patient and understanding with me, and accepted whatever I did. But our brother was more troublesome. He had left his gardening job and managed to find work with an insurance company based in Hamburg. He upset a colleague and got into trouble with his firm, so that I had to go up to Hamburg to help sort things out. Perhaps I should have helped him more in one way or another, being the eldest. As it was he rather drifted, unable to settle.

As our mother had died of tuberculosis, all three of us were under medical supervision. Now I began to have some trouble with my lungs. The doctors were very careful and put me on the sick list for two months, to be followed by three months in a sanatorium. Fortunately BAMAG allowed me full pay for all of those five months. As it was spring, Olya and I decided to rent a room out of town, but near enough for her to commute. The room we found was small but adequate and it had a pleasant garden. The only snag was the mosquitoes—a veritable plague, as they bred on a nearby pond. We could never sit out in the evening, and before going to bed we had to splash a bottle of ammonia all over the room so as not to be eaten alive.

The sanatorium was also near enough for Olya to visit me on her days off. I had a really enjoyable and restful time there, and spent much of it reading, as we had to rest on deckchairs in the garden for most of the day. The majority of the other patients were not severely ill and some, myself included, were allowed out for short walks in the surrounding countryside. I even started to learn Spanish there. At weekends we organised our own entertainment, and, as we were all girls, there was a relaxed and uninhibited atmosphere.

Rapho finally faded from my life. I remember him briefly visiting me at the sanatorium and bringing me a Russian book, an anthology of prose and poetry, which I still have. He had had an offer of work in the Papal library at the Vatican, in Rome. Any getting together again was now hopeless.

When I returned to BAMAG I found I had been transferred to some other work and now shared a room with an extremely pleasant ex-naval officer. When work was slack he would tell me of his feelings as he stood on the deck of his cruiser, or whatever ship it was, observing the sea and the sky and the stillness of it all when there was no fighting, which gave him a somewhat detached and philosophical outlook on life. We got on well together when I occasionally had to work for him, but he confessed that he would not like to have me as his private secretary, as I tended to be too independent. I, for my part, was more than ever determined to break out from routine office work and the subordinate role of a woman at work.

But before turning my back on BAMAG there is one other memory, of Isya, a young engineer temporarily posted to the head office in Berlin. I don't know how we met, but our point of contact was again that we were both from Russia, or rather in his case the Russian area of Poland. He was very proud of being a descendent of Sephardic Jews from Spain (the East European Jews were Ashkenazi). Isya sang old Jewish and Yiddish songs, of which I espeically remember one, a song about 'The Old Question', to which there are many answers yet no answer. In the actual song both question and answer are merely hummed without words, yet perfectly conveying both. Isya gave Olya and me our first wireless: a small wooden square with some wire spirals, a crystal, and a needle which had to be manipulated until you hit upon a sound. I might have forgotten Isya had it not been for his old Yiddish songs and his wise advice not to mourn things past, but to try 'to catch the melody of each new minute'.

Except that there was not much melody in my life right then. I seriously began to rack my brain to see how I could earn my living and at the same time acquire new skills. I began to scan the newspapers. At that time eurhythmics were very fashionable in Germany—a style of movement—sometimes to music, sometimes just to a beat—developed from Isadora Duncan's ideas. There was a proliferation of classes and schools, run by well-known dancers who rejected classical ballet. I had been keen on dancing since my childhood so I looked into the possibility of joining such a school. Unfortunately, practically all required full-time attendance in order to get a teaching diploma, which would mean finding evening work. There seemed to be nothing except work in cafés and bars, serving or performing with other girls. I did not care, and innocently went for interviews, to be told by one or two potential employers that my figure was not quite suitable or my legs too fat. One very kind and grandfatherly manager asked me why I actually wanted a job in a bar, seeing that I was not quite the type. And he very gently told me so.

Then I saw an advertisement for a fairly well-known dancing school which was looking for young girls to join a team for performances at a very large dance-café, twice nightly, at 5pm and 12 midnight—and no contacts with the customers. I applied, was given an audition, and was accepted! I simply could not believe it. The engagement was for a trial period of a fortnight, but this would be extended if the management and customers approved of us.

Then the rehearsals started. On one occasion we were practising a jump and turn which I could not manage. The trainer got rather impatient and asked me where I had been trained that I was unable to do this. I timidly admitted that I had never been to any dance school and had never done anything except social dancing. She was astonished, showed me how to do it, and kept me on. Then another surprise: the leading dancer in the short piece from the ballet ***Si j'étais Roi*** had to give up for some reason and her part was given to me. But that, I think, was more because of my innocent looks and long blonde hair, when most girls had already had theirs fashionably cut. The other dance was the 'Blue Danube' waltz, which I really liked, and for which we wore flowing gauze dresses. Unfortunately, our *Madame*, as we called her, had tried to save on our costumes, and they were simply not lavish enough for that café. After the trial fortnight the contract was not extended. So there I was again: still at the BAMAG and nothing else in sight.

I seemed to be drifting in an unsettled search for an aim in life. Olya and I still lived together, but we had moved so often that we had adopted an attitude that if we did not like a place we could always move out again after a month's notice. I was still looking for the chance to train at a school for eurhythmics, and for a suitable job to go with it.

Then, in the spring of 1928, I found both. The job was as secretary (and office girl, being the only employee) with Herr

Herring, a tall, stern and very German man— so he seemed to me— who had recently returned from years of working in South America and had taken over the German sales of some medical equipment manufactured in France. This involved a great deal of correspondence in French, and occasionally English. I also had to boil his two eggs daily for lunch and make him coffee or cocoa— and the grumbling there was if the eggs were not done precisely as he liked them! He was a great grumbler. I often thought later that it was from him that I learned to grumble, having up to then been quite an easy-going person. But he was satisfied with my work and also took a certain personal interest, unwanted and unasked for, in me and Olya, knowing that we lived on our own and had no older friends or 'protectors'. We were even invited to his home several times, a large house out of town, with a garden. He had two charming little daughters and a somewhat subdued, self-effacing wife, who was very pleasant and hospitable to us. He must have been quite a despotic husband as he was rather a despotic boss.

But he paid me well and had full confidence in me. I had the keys to the office and the showroom, as he usually came late, was often out during the day, and left early. Actually, I rather objected to any private contact with him, as in many ways he had quite a wrong image of us, or at any rate of me. I was not at all the 'well-brought-up' young girl with a lady-like outlook on the world that he imagined me to be, and I objected to his Germanic ways and Aryan views. Once, when I lost my temper, he gave me a little lecture on the Scythians or Tartars, who invaded and dominated old Russia for a long time. According to him, this had made the Russians so unpredictable and had caused all that violence after the Revolution! He also made disparaging remarks about the Jews, which made me secretly wish that his two blonde little daughters would one day defy him and marry Jews or some other non-Aryans. But I kept quiet, appreciating the well-paid work, the relatively short hours, and above all my relative freedom at work.

Years after I had stopped working for him and soon after Hitler had come to power, he contacted me again and asked me to dinner. His wife had died and he had become friendly with a member of the old Russian aristocracy, a princess, and he wondered whether I happened to know her. I didn't. But more interesting was his confession that he had for some time been a follower of Hitler. However, he had become disillusioned with Hitler's policies: the execution of the Röhm group ordered by Hitler, the persecution of the Jews, and the obvious drive towards a war. So after all my ex-boss did apparently have a broader view of things. He was now at a loss what to do and where to turn.

During the winter of 1928 I had also made the acquaintance of the Pruzhans and Semyonovs, two Russian couples, refugees, though definitely not aristocratic! I answered an advertisement from a Russian woman, who had 'just come back from Paris and was now accepting trainees'. It was not quite what I wanted, but I thought it might lead to something.

The Pruzhans, Margarita Dmitrievna and her husband David Venyaminovich, had left Russia after the October Revolution. She had been a medium landowner, while he had been a journalist. In their youth they had both been interested in politics and belonged to the Social Democrats—and David told us once how he had taken part in a bank raid in aid of the party. Margarita had a young daughter from an earlier marriage and a son, Igor, who had attended one of the well-known 'free' schools in Germany. She was an ardent farmer and gardener and disliked city life. In Berlin she kept an allotment, which she tended most eagerly. I never quite knew what David did for a living, probably a bit of writing for the Russian emigré papers and a bit of small-scale business, as so many of the Russian refugees did. At any rate they survived, in two furnished rooms.

After a visit to Paris, Margarita had the idea of opening a beauty salon in Berlin, combining it with eurhythmic exercises, stimulating baths and light treatment. Her ideas were interesting, but it came to nothing and before very long they left for France again. Before that, however, she had taught me face massage, manicure and in spite of the big age gap we became good friends, and remained so right up to her death some time in the 1960s.

I lost contact during the war but caught up with them again in 1947. They were as warm and hospitable as ever. Yet I was somehow disappointed in Margarita Dmitrievna. She had always been so composed and serene and I somehow needed the support of an elderly person with a more detached view of life. Perhaps it was naive of me, but I was all mixed up. The war had been a terrible experience. Not just the bombing raids and the constant anxiety you felt for yourself and people close to you, on both sides of the divide, but also for all those being maimed and killed at the front. I also had mixed feelings about the war itself, and what attitude to take. I recognised by then that the war was a consequence of the economic and political system, and as such had to be opposed (as indeed a small group of Trotskyists did before and for a while even after the war had started, by propagating a

Socialist Anti-War Front, with its own publication). But there was also the strong pull, especially from the anti-fascist German refugees, including those on the political left, to support the war against Hitler. And when it was over, and we felt such compassion for the starving Germans, I also felt resentful that the millions of Social-Democratic and Communist workers had ever let it come to Hitler assuming power and unleashing the war. Also there was the disappointment and disillusionment that our hopes for radical changes after the war were not fulfilled.

So I somehow expected—perhaps unfairly and unreasonably—that Margarita, being considerably older than me, would have a more detached attitude. She might help me regain a more balanced view of things. But that was not the case. She was still burning with resentment, not to say hate, against the Germans who had invaded and looted the enemy countries, and also against the French, who had put up such a poor show in so many ways.

I only later realised what a tough time they had all had in France. She, David, Igor and his young wife, who, amidst a fierce bombing raid, gave birth to their first child in one of the farm outhouses—without electric light, hot water or medical assistance—had set out on foot with thousands of other people for the unoccupied Vichy region of France, fleeing from the invading German army. Motorcars, horsecarts, bicycles, people on foot, with children, bundles, pots and pans, all mixed up, all pushing each other, without regard for the old, the sick, the weak. And the French peasants along the road, sensing business, not giving a glass of water to anyone without a payment. Eventually the Pruzhans found it impossible to carry on and had turned wearily back, surviving the rest of the war lying low on their smallholding. It was unjust of me to expect a serene attitude from them.

Through the Pruzhans I also got to know Tatyana and Yuri Semyonov, both much nearer my own age and also Russian refugees. The two couples had met in the Caucasus, on their way out of Russia, where they drifted into a commune run by a Russian-Caucasian theosophist—to my mind half philosopher, half charlatan. There Tanya had learned his interesting theories about movements, which demanded great concentration and muscle control. I became her pupil for a short time. Her husband Yuri was a writer and journalist and seemed rather serious and important to me. They too had quite a hard time making ends meet. Tanya was supplementing Yuri's earnings by hand-painting silk scarves for a shop. They had a child, a little boy, the image of Tanya. She was not an exuberant mother, but when I watched them looking at each other, I felt they were somehow communicating, deeply and silently, and one could feel the common bond between them. Sadly, the boy died from diphteria before he was four years old. Later, when I had already left Germany, they had another son, a blond and blue-eyed Russian boy like his father. But I think Tanya never managed to forget her first-born.

Olya kept in touch with them after I had left and until she left Berlin herself. Through mutual friends I traced them again after the war. They had had a very bad time in a German internment camp and after the war they starved, as practically all Germans did. By the time I managed to send them a food parcel they had left for Sweden. I received a letter from their former landlady informing me of this, and adding that in view of the situation, she hoped that I would understand that she and her family had kept the parcel themselves.

But in Berlin in the winter of 1928 I was lucky. I discovered a school that ran courses in the early evening, five days a week. There was my chance. I had a job where I could, as a rule, leave on the dot of 4pm; I could reach the school easily by 5pm. After two years I would get a diploma and the right to run classes and courses myself. Those two years were very hard work: three to four hours daily, plus theory, essays, later the devising or improvising of lessons. No theatres, no concerts, no cinemas any more, except occasionally at weekends. Yet those two years were a most enjoyable and carefree time. I was mentally absorbed and physically acquired a feeling of lightness, almost of weightlessness. The owner of the school, Ruth Allerhand, was very pleasant and an imaginative teacher. She had a young woman assistant called Johnny, slim, with short hair, rather boyish looking and a very good dancer. Johnny and Ruth lived together and we all assumed that they were lesbians.

The pupils, with one or two exceptions, were working girls: secretaries, clerks, and the like. Some seemed quite unsuited to eurhythmics, but all were enthusiastic and did their best. At weekends the entire school or perhaps just a small group of us would go on an excursion out of town, and in the fields or swimming pools we would again improvise all sorts of movements and dances—on those occasions mostly comic ones, at which I was not all that good as I was still rather self-conscious and reluctant to expose myself.

In time I made two lifelong friends at that school. There was Berta, eight years younger than me, curly-haired, small, plumpish, with tiny feet and hands, charming in her movements, full of fun and imagination. She came from a wealthy Jewish family. Her mother was a widow and semi-paralysed, spending her days in a wheelchair. Her sister was a medical student and later worked as a doctor at the Jewish hospital in Berlin.

Berta was very independent. After she had finished the eurhythmic training, she made off for Paris on her own and without any financial assistance. There she found herself a job at a laundry, sorting out dirty linen. I always admired her for her spirit of adventure, coming from that bourgeois home. Eventually she returned home. We maintained only very loose contact until I met her again in Prague in 1936, where she befriended me for a couple of weeks after my escape from Hitler's Germany. Her sister remained in Berlin, not wanting to leave their disabled mother. When the persecution and gassing of the Jews really got under way at the beginning of the war, Berta's sister administered poison to her mother and herself. It was one of the many tragic stories of Hitler's Germany. Berta and I met again in London and still see each other.

My other friend was Lore. She was the complete opposite of Berta. A year older than me, she was not so much stiff as totally unable to relax, either physically or mentally, and totally unsuited to gymnastics or dancing. I never understood what made her take up eurhythmics. But she was good at theory. Perhaps her talents were for teaching, yet it is impossible to be a good teacher without being able to inspire, to improvise, and, up to a point, to perform whatever one teaches. Yet she stuck doggedly to the work and did get her diploma.

Lore and I got on well together, having discovered a common interest in literature, art and even philosophy. She lived in a studio flat together with her artist friend Gertrud, a painter and a teacher. I loved to visit their studio. It was a totally different world. They introduced me to a lesbian café, which was strange to me—I did not particularly take to it. And once a year the stiff and somewhat withdrawn Lore let her hair down at the fancy-dress ball of the Berlin Academy of Arts. It was the art event of the year with the rooms splendidly and artistically decorated and everyone in imaginative costumes. Lore thoroughly enjoyed herself. It never attracted me, though. I was once invited to such a ball, but could not enter the spirit of it—whirling around with whoever happened to pass by and catch you.

Having finished at the eurhythmic school and still thinking of branching out on my own, I took a six-month course in physiotherapy and massage at one of the teaching hospitals.

Massage was taught by one of the staff nurses, and as a model she used an old paralysed patient who knew every move by heart, a chap full of humour and jokes in spite of his disability.

Throughout those two years I kept in touch with the Pruzhans and Tanya. Yuri, her husband, must have had contacts with the Soviet cultural organisations in Berlin because occasionally he would get tickets for a private film show or a lecture. One day he was busy and Tanya asked me to go with her. The film was **Turksib**, about the building of the Turkistan-Siberian railway at the beginning of the first Five-Year Plan, linking Alma-Ata with Siberia. The film shows the tremendous difficulties of the construction, carried out by enthusiastic teams of young workers, watched in amazement by the local population riding along the tracks on their camels, trying to race against the first engine, jubilantly decorated and manned by some of the workers. (The film was shown in London in 1971 at the National Film Theatre; and more recently in a shortened version on television). It was a splendid film, yet I hardly knew what I was looking at. This sounds paradoxical, but will become clear.

During the interval, when the lights went on, something made me turn round and my eyes caught for a moment the greenish-grey eyes of a man standing at the back, leaning against the wall with a few other people. Nothing more. Then the lights went out and the film continued. After a while the person next to me left and his seat was taken by the man from the back! Our elbows accidentally touched. I felt as if I had touched a live wire. I could no longer concentrate on the film. It must have been cold that day because I had my hands in a muff. Before long I felt a hand reaching for my muff and pressing a little note into my hand.

The man left hurriedly as soon as the film ended and I went out with Tanya, still clutching the note. It asked, in Russian, for an appointment the following day, suggesting a place. I could have ignored it, but that was beyond me. So I went, and we strolled the length of the Tiergarten. He apologised for the note at the cinema and then we got into conversation, both delighted to have met a compatriot with whom to speak Russian. That was one point of attraction, but there were others, physical and intellectual. Thus began the most romantic and inspiring months of my life—with far-reaching consequences.

Vladimir was a Soviet Russian, sent to Berlin by the Soviet government for an unspecified period of time. I never got to know anything about him, nothing beyond his first name, that he was born and brought up in Byelorussia and was of Jewish parentage;

and that he lived somewhere in the centre of Berlin. I did not know his surname, his address, his telephone number, whether he had a wife and family in Moscow. Nothing. I accepted all this without a murmur. He must have had a strong personality and I suppose I felt it was this or nothing, though he later often said he would like to take me back to Moscow with him. Even then, I never asked any questions. Vladimir was far too interesting and fascinating a man, and far too attractive to me to give him up because of non-compliance with conventional customs and habits.

But he was also a very busy man and we met mostly in snatches and at the most unexpected times. Not being master of his own time, we rarely made appointments in advance, but he would ring me, sometimes as late as ten in the evening, or at odd moments during the weekend, and we would go to a small café near where Olya and I lived, or for long walks through the Tiergarten. Very occasionally he would visit me at home for a short time.

When I eventually learned about the life and work of Soviet workers abroad, I realised he must have felt trapped in a private apartment. He seemed to feel most at ease on walks, in a café, or occasionally in a hotel room. Even then, he would go off quite suddenly, saying he expected a phone call from Moscow (mostly late at night, whilst I usually stayed on). It was all very unusual. In the middle of a walk, a discussion, an interesting conversation, a carefree, high-spirited mood, he would look at his watch and we would part abruptly. And if it was not too late, and not too far, I would accompany him to the corner of the street where he lived, in order to delay the parting for another half hour or so, and then we would say goodbye and turn in opposite directions. Sometimes I wondered whether I should follow him surreptitiously to find out which house he would enter. But apart from the fact that he would probably have easily detected my intentions, it somehow seemed undignified to me, something, which in the circumstances I just could not do. That was the rule of his game, and I accepted it.

Vladimir was an intellectual, well read, well versed in literature, music, art, all the things that interested me too. He had joined the Bolshevik Party during the 1917 Revolution whilst still a student. I once wondered why he did not try to proselytise and convert me to communism, not noticing that without the sledgehammer technique of some party members I met later (especially activists and officials) his way of opening my eyes to social conditions in the world around me influenced me far more than any propagandist or agitator could have done. He gave me a German edition of Larissa Reissner's book **Oktober**, which I still possess. It contains brilliant reports by this young and talented revolutionary journalist from the battlefield of the civil war, vivid studies of coal-miners, reports from Afghanistan, from Germany and so on. I was fascinated. She died in 1926, not on a battlefield but of typhus; she was greatly mourned, according to Vladimir, who attended the State funeral, by a grief-stricken Karl Radek, her companion after the death of her husband Raskolnikov.

It was Larissa Reissner's stories, and Vladimir's own attitude to his work that made me wonder: what is it that makes these people renounce their personal lives and ties, and live first and foremost for their work? What force is there behind the communist idea and the Communist Party that can extract such sacrifices? I began to ask questions, but, most of all, I decided to find out for myself. But I had to do it my own way, without any assistance from Vladimir. On the contrary, I did not even want him to know. In this rather childish way, I thought, I could also get something of my own back. I depended so entirely on Vladimir. I could never make a move of my own in regard to him. We never went together to a theatre or concert. When I took a fortnight's summer holiday at the seaside, Vladimir said he might join me for a couple of days, but of course he never came. So now I felt that I must act independently.

I had heard of the Internationale Arbeiter-Hilfe (IAH), the International Workers' Relief—a mass organisation, officially independent, but actually run by the German Communist Party (KPD). I am not sure how I heard about it, whether Vladimir mentioned it, or in connection with the strike of the Berlin transport workers, which was taking place at that time—the IAH had organised soup kitchens for the strikers and their families. I went to see the Berlin district organiser, Erich Lange, and—ridiculously and naively—offered to organise keep-fit classes for working girls and women (I had finished my training and had my teaching diploma). Erich Lange, though still young, was even then an old hand as a party official and organiser of the Berlin district. Diplomatically he thought my suggestion a very good idea but suggested I should first get a little acquainted with the activity of my local group—and he told me where and when the branch met.

So one fine evening when walking around with Vladimir, it was my turn to be secretive. I stopped at a corner in front of a pub and told him I had some business there and had to leave him now. He did not ask questions either, and did not stop me. But to anybody versed in the work of party organisations in Germany it must have been quite obvious what I was up to.

So I joined the IAH and from then onwards attended the branch meetings quite regularly. I do not now remember whether I eventually told Vladimir about it or not. But when I began to show an outspoken interest in communist ideas, Vladimir told me of the years of the revolution and the civil war, when he was already an active member of the Bolshevik Party. He told me about Mikhail Borodin, who was sent to China by the party to conclude an alliance, which in fact handed over the Chinese communists to Chiang Kai-Shek—a policy which Borodin did not agree with privately, but nevertheless carried out. Vladimir also told me other stories, which later made me think that with all his devotion to Soviet Russia, he was probably not a one hundred per cent follower of Joseph Stalin.

Then one day, in October or November 1930, Vladimir vanished from my life as suddenly and unexpectedly as he had entered it. He rang one evening—how lucky that I was in!—to tell me that he had been transferred to Paris and that he was leaving in a couple of hours. There was no time to meet or say goodbye. It was not in his hands; he simply had to obey instructions. And in any case, what difference would it make? What could we say to each other that we hadn't said before many times?

I was stunned. Would I ever hear from him again? How would I ever get to know when he would have to go back to Moscow? Or if anything happened to him? I would hear about it, he said. How, he did not say. And I never heard anything. Two years later, when some Soviet delegates came to an IAH conference I accompanied one of the Russians to the Soviet Trade Delegation to see somebody there on business. I suddenly had a hunch, and asked the man whom the delegate had come to see, a head of department or some other high official, whether he knew Vladimir and whether he could tell me anything about him. He said he did not know him, but from the momentary consternation on his face and the lowering of his head, I could see that my intuition had been right. But it no longer seemed to matter that I did not get a satisfactory reply. By that time I was involved myself and personal concerns had moved to second place.

Even the parting itself did not make me despair, as would have seemed natural—there had been so many partings since leaving Moscow. I had a new outlook on life, new ideas and a new activity, and Vladimir had also managed to instil in me a certain self-discipline and strength of mind. My first impulse after that last phone call was to go to the street where he had lived to see whether I could still catch him coming out of one of the houses. But then I saw the senselessness of this and accepted the truth of his last observation: what could we tell each other in a hurry that we had not already told each other about ourselves and our feelings for each other?

Yet I could not remain at home. I dressed and went out, retracing our many walks through the Tiergarten, and then I returned home. That was the end. I was immensely sad, but not in despair. On the contrary. I felt I was now free to become more active. After a few days I went to the district office and enrolled as a member of the German Communist Party. I felt that in this way I was closer to Vladimir and, as I had already been active in the IAH for some time, it seemed the logical step to take.

CHAPTER 4

Communist Party

IT WAS the end of 1930. My boss Herr Herring had decided to close down the office; he had not been as successful with the sale of medical equipment as he had hoped. He regretted he had no contacts to recommend me for another job, unless I wanted to go to South America. Unemployment in Germany was rising and he thought it would not be easy for me to get another job. He also thought Germany was going to the dogs. If I wanted to make use of his South American connections, he would gladly help me, and recommend one or two families who might take me in.

He meant well, but it was out of the question. I had my teaching diploma in eurhythmics and my diploma in physiotherapy. By rights I should be starting to work on my own in that field. Instead, I accepted an offer from Erich Lange to work full-time at the Berlin district office of the International Workers' Relief. The pay was small, the hours of work unlimited, the work—whatever came along. But it was the first time in my life that my interests and my work for a living coincided, and for the next two or more years I became completely involved in the organisation's activity.

In addition to my daytime work I regularly attended the local branch meetings of both the Communist Party and the International Workers' Relief. The membership was predominantly working-class. I had long since realised that my original offer to organise gym classes was totally out of place, so I sat back, absorbed the milieu, and began to study party literature, as well as basic books on Marxism, including ***Das Kapital***—though I must confess, I never got beyond the first volume.

I became rather humble, greatly impressed by the members' ability to get up at meetings and put involved questions to the speaker or make involved contributions to the discussions. I felt I would never be able to get up myself, knowing so little about the theoretical and practical aspects of the items on the agenda. I did not realise at that time how much waffle there was in all those discussions and how much muddle-headedness and inability to argue clearly and succinctly. True, I never properly mastered this art myself, but neither did I feel compelled to make a contribution just for the sake of saying something.

However I had to admit to myself that those German workers and their wives knew far more about current affairs and the problems of working life than I had ever imagined. I had to catch up on an enormous amount. It was probably only then that I began to read newspapers regularly, mostly the Communist press, which was very one-sided and rather crude. But for me it was probably the right thing to do. Regrettably, everybody else in the movement seemed to do the same, thus ignoring subtle shades of policy in the camp of 'the class enemy'.

The head office of International Workers Relief was in the Friedrichstrasse, one of the busiest thoroughfares of Berlin, dividing the town from north to south and close to the working-class district of Neukölln. The Berlin district office was nearby. The founder and head of the organisation was Willy Münzenberg, a dynamic and exceptionally able person, Somebody once remarked that in different circumstances he could have become an equally successful business tycoon. As it was, he had joined the Communist Party in his youth and became founder and secretary of the Young Communist International. However, after a congress in Moscow he was demoted for some deviationist views. That was in 1921, the year the New Economic Policy was introduced and the USSR was engulfed in a famine which affected 25 million people, caused by both the devastation of the civil war and droughts in important grain-producing areas.

Münzenberg was known to be a brilliant organiser, so Lenin suggested he should raise help in Germany for the starving people in Russia. Münzenberg therefore set up the International Workers' Relief. It was a great success. In later years he concentrated predominantly on Germany, helping striking workers, recruiting members and sympathisers both for the organisation itself and for the Communist Party, many from among intellectuals and artists. He used every means available. He published newspapers and an illustrated journal, organised mass rallies, films, festivals and entertainments with well-known left-wing artists.

When Hitler came to power Münzenberg escaped to France, where he continued his political activities, but was denounced by the German Communist Party as a renegade, since he had become critical of their policies. After the outbreak of war, the political refugees in France, Münzenberg among them, were rounded up by the police and escorted to camps in the region of France not yet occupied. But progress was slow and when it became clear that they might easily be overtaken by the German army a handful of refugees, including Münzenberg, broke away to make their own way south at a quicker pace. There all traces of Münzenberg vanished. Some time later a corpse was found in the woods with a wire around the neck. It was identified as that of Willy Münzenberg. There had been, among that small group, a person whom nobody knew or had seen before in the camp. Suspicion fell on the Communist Party, as in other similar cases of the violent death of so-called renegades and known Trotskyists.

I met both Willy Münzenberg and his wife, Babette Gross, at the head office, when I had to go there on business. Münzenberg was easy to get on with. Babette struck me as somewhat distant and aloof. She was a kind of business manager rather than directly involved in political work, as far as I knew.

I worked in the district office, not far away. It was usually teeming with people coming and going. The atmosphere was friendly and comradely, and hectic. But I was conscious that we were dealing with people and their needs, not with goods and profits, and for the first time I never objected to having to do the donkey work for senior colleagues. There were letters to be typed and sent out to the branches to direct their activities, speakers to be found for their meetings—often from among well-known intellectuals, among whom there were many sympathisers just as there were in England in the 1930s. Sometimes special campaigns and big rallies had to be organised throughout the district to recruit new members and collect money for various purposes. Or there were instructions to be typed for Lucie Peters, a comely middle-aged woman who was responsible for the social-welfare side, with special emphasis on women.

Erich Lange, the district organiser, was, like his boss Willy Münzenberg, a fount of ideas for new ways of organising rallies, finding speakers, attracting an audience and raising money. He was actively assisted by a variety of people who worked on a sort of freelance or part-time basis, if they had other jobs to make a living. There was a man called Katz who knew everyone and who always managed to find a hall to rent, a band to engage or some special performers. At big rallies and meetings we often had the composers Kurt Weill and Hanns Eisler, with well-known singers to perform their famous agit-prop songs. One of these was particularly popular—it likened the Social Democrats to radishes: red on the outside and white inside.

One of Erich Lange's fruitful ideas was to issue stencilled

educational courses, in Marxism and dialectical materialism, for the branches both in Berlin and the provincial district. Julius Hollos, a Hungarian journalist, was entrusted with the task of working out a syllabus and I was assigned as his assistant. And not just for such menial work as typing the stencils but for the actual work of drafting the separate courses. I, a Communist and Marxist of a year's standing! However, we did it and the branches used our outlines and recommended reading lists. It was of course interesting and enlightening work for me, which I did mostly in my spare time at home.

Conveniently, Olya and I had recently taken over the flat of a friend of ours, whose newly-wed husband had been transferred to Frankfurt for six months. It was marvellous to be on our own and not in digs. There was just one drawback: the furniture was so new, conventionally middle-class and highly polished that we hardly dared sit on the chairs, use the dining table or sleep in those comfortable beds. But it was convenient for Hollos and me to spread our books and papers on the table, and for meals and informal occasions there was always the kitchen.

The move necessitated my transfer to a different branch of the International Workers Relief and I made friends with the branch chairman, Paul, who occasionally used to come round for a chat. He was unemployed at the time, like so many other members. I think he had been in the printing trade, though to me he looked more like a baker: flaccid and dimply, white and rather fat. But I remember him as a very unyielding chairman, a proper Communist Party member with rigid views. At that time I only sensed this in a vague way, perhaps because his physical softness and roundness did not seem to go with his unbending attitude. Yet his influence, or rather the influence of the movement in general, had become rather strong on me. I had absorbed, to the best of my ability, not only the political ideas of Marx, Engels and Lenin, but also the entire Communist ideology of that period. I began to preach it to my brother, but with such intensity that I nearly drove him into the opposite camp.

Andryusha had given up his job in Hamburg and had turned up in Berlin with a girlfriend. For a while we shared the flat with them. While he was looking around for work, she lazed around all day, never doing a thing, though Olya and I were working. My brother and I used to have endless discussions about politics, and most of the time he opposed everything I said—remnants perhaps of our childhood fights, though by then we used to get on well together. Then Paul intervened, and in a man-to-man discussion they thrashed things out. In the end my brother, too, joined the movement and became a member of the Communist Party.

Only Olya kept out of it. She was probably just not the type and she also found great satisfaction in her work as a hospital nurse. She had pleasant colleagues—and then Arnold, a German-Russian from the Volga region, also an emigré, appeared on the horizon and started to woo her assiduously. So she had no inclination to be active in any other field. She knew all my friends, she was always prepared to have them come to our house for meetings or just discussions, but never took part in them herself, except for absorbing, to a limited extent, some of my ideas. She was always very supportive and never opposed or objected to anything I did.

Some time during the winter of 1930-31 the International Workers Relief organised a two-week residential course somewhere out in the country to which I was sent with twenty-three other activists. A local member had placed a small house at our disposal, right in the wilderness, about three miles from a small town where the organisation had a branch. There was a small kitchen, two small bedrooms and a large living room, an outside lavatory and no washroom, only a loft to be reached from the outside by a step ladder. To this loft I used to repair every morning with a bucket of water for my ablutions, to the great amusement of all the others, who simply had a lick under the kitchen tap. There was only one other girl there, with whom I shared a pair of bunk beds, the other two being occupied by three or four men. The rest of the comrades, including the two lecturers, slept either in the second bedroom or on mattresses on the floor of the large room, which served as dining room and lecture room. But the more the merrier. It was warm inside, whilst outside the snow was piling up—enjoyable all the same on our daily walks and occasional trips to the town for shopping. Most of our food we had brought with us from Berlin, and a comrade from the local branch used to do the cooking.

One of our lecturers was Fritz Globig, a small live-wire who had had one arm amputated, and who tried hard to keep up with the young comrades, jumping over the chairs or tables. He was a rabid Communist, with whom I got into such a fierce argument that I nearly left the course and the movement, had it not been for the intervention of Peter Maslowski, the other lecturer. He was probably an equally Stalinist Communist, since he remained in East Germany after the war, and was still active there in the early 1960s. But he was also a person of great charm, cultured, obviously of middle-class origin and education, and a brilliant and convincing lecturer on dialectical materialism.

This subject appealed to me more than political economy, of which I was pretty ignorant. We had some seminars, and also had to write essays, at which I was quite good. I remember Peter saying that I might go some way in the movement and he would like to know how I would shape up in the years to come. But when it came to speaking—I just could not do it. I failed completely, and to my great chagrin the same Peter said that I would not be of much use to the movement if I could not speak.

Walter Friedrich, who was Erich Lange's brother-in-law, was also on the course. He and his wife Liesel became two of my closest friends. Then still only in their early twenties, they were very active members of my branch and we often saw each other. Walter's father had died in the war. His mother had brought up her two boys by taking in washing and working as a charwoman. His brother eventually became a policeman. Walter survived the hungry war years, including the winter of 1917-18 when the only thing to eat was swede, by going to bed as soon as he came home from school—no playing with other children in the courtyard or in the street; he simply did not have the physical strength. Yet he grew up a tall and good-looking man. He used to do some clerical work, but was already unemployed when I met him.

Liesel and Erich's parents (their father was some sort of highly qualified worker) had been Communists almost since the foundation of the German Communist Party. Their other daughter, Friedel, became the wife of the well-known writer on dialectical materialism Kurt Sauerland and both later escaped to the USSR, where Kurt eventually perished in a camp or prison. Friedel returned to East Germany after the war, still as staunch a Stalinist as ever. So were Erich and his wife. Only Liesel and Walter became Trotskyists, soon after the collapse of all organised mass resistance to Hitler and his coming to power. After the war Liesel used to send food parcels to her parents in East Berlin, to help them survive. They accepted the parcels, at the same time accusing Liesel of being 'an American agent'.

The residential course deepened my understanding of the class struggle, and strengthened my acceptance of Marxism as an analysis of the capitalist system—an analysis which is still valid today—and an outlook for a socialist future. For the first time I no longer felt my stay in Germany was only temporary. I had found an aim in life, and it was no longer all that important where I lived and worked. And I fervently hoped that I would remain true to my ideas and ideals. But I still could not speak in public! Despite this, I was occasionally delegated to speak at small branch meetings. When I complained to Erich Lange that I did not know what to say on the burning questions of the day, he simply replied: 'Well, read today's ***Rote Fahne*** (Red Flag) and you'll find there everything you will need to know and to say.' I found that rather unsatisfactory, as the branch members had no doubt already read the day's issue themselves. I felt instinctively that rather more was required to be a speaker. But I tried my best from time to time.

In the late summer of 1931 the International Workers Relief organised an international conference to which delegates from other countries were invited. It was a really big affair with many well-known speakers, organised jointly by Willy Münzenberg and Erich Lange with their usual aplomb. They even invited Clara Zetkin. She was then 74 years old and very frail, but she did come, although she had to be supported by two women when she stood up to speak. Yet her short speech was inspiring. And I wished then, without in the least aspiring to be anywhere like Clara Zetkin in the movement, that I would be able to retain such vigour and idealism into my old age.

For the first time since the mid-1920s Soviet delgates came too, six in all, including two women. The conference was a great occasion and very successful. The Soviet delegates spoke no German and I was appointed their interpreter and guide. All six were highly placed officials in various trade unions. I became good friends with two of them: Katya was chairman or secretary of the Social Security and Health Service Workers' Trade Union, and a member of the Supreme Soviet (the approximate equivalent of a Western parliament); Stepan was chairman of the Oil Workers' Union. During the occasional private conversation he confessed that he was very interested in Trotsky's writings and that he had managed to get one or two books in Berlin. He was reading them as fast as he could there and then. He also told me that such books were sometimes smuggled into the USSR in suitcases with false bottoms. It was an amazing confession, but it hardly registered with me then. I knew Trotsky's name, but that was about all. We did not know much about his role in the party or his exile.

Katya invited me to Moscow. If I could pay my fare as far as the Soviet frontier, from then on everything would be free, she would see to that. She had been about the same age as me when the October Revolution broke out, working as a messenger girl in a factory. Shortly before the election for the National Assembly in October 1917, somebody pressed a stack of leaflets for distribution into her hand in the street. It was an appeal to vote for 'List No 5'—the Bolsheviks. She read the leaflet, became interested in their slogan—'Bread and Peace'—and became a Bolshevik herself. She joined the party, fought in the civil war, became the chairman of a revolutionary tribunal at the front and condemned more than one White-Russian prisoner to death. She confessed to me it was awful, but at that time there seemed no other way out than to be ruthless. After the war she trained to be an engineer. Later she switched to social security and health insurance and gradually worked her way up to the position she was in when she visited Berlin. She was a very efficient, matter-of-fact person, business-like, yet pleasant and kind. In 1931 she was still an enthusiastic and convinced Communist, but in a soft moment she spoke of the 'difficult road to socialism', of the hard work to be done, of her occasional longing for the life of an ordinary citizen, of an ordinary woman.

Of the remaining delegates one was a rather old man, who had been active in the revolutionary movement long before the revolution; one was an up-and-coming young girl, and the other two I do not remember. They were proud of the achievements of the USSR, which was then in the third year of the first of Stalin's Five-Year Plans, and hoped it would catch up with, even overtake, the economic successes of the United States of America.

The conference elected a fraternal delegation of about twenty people to visit the Soviet Union for the celebrations of the October Revolution. Most of the delegation were unemployed workers. By arrangement with Erich Lange, however, I accepted Katya's invitation. As an employee of International Workers Relief, it would not have done for me to be one of the delegates, but two weeks' holiday were due to me, and I could afford the fare to the frontier.

We set off in due course by train, with great expectations and enthusiasm, especially when we crossed the frontier and drove through the huge arch which welcomed visitors to the Union of Socialist Soviet Republics. In Moscow the delegates were accommodated in a hotel in the centre of the town, while I stayed with Katya at her flat in the Dom Pravitelstva (The Government House), a huge block of flats just across the river Moskva, newly built for members of the Supreme Soviet and high-ranking officials. It had a special shop and a cinema, which in later years opened to the public. All entrances to the building were guarded by special janitors who questioned everybody about their business, and would not let any unauthorised person pass. Were they possibly members of the GPU, the dreaded state political administration?

For the rest of each day, meals, sightseeing and the like, I was attached to the official delegation. We visited factories, crèches, workers' flats in new houses, and of course the Kremlin, the Tretyakov Art Gallery, the Lenin Mausoleum and above all the Red Square Parade on 7 November to celebrate the anniversary of the revolution (in 1917 there had still been a 13-day discrepancy between the Russian and European calendars). I remember how, as delegates from abroad, we jumped the enormous queue at the Lenin Mausoleum and were shown straight in by the military guard. And there was no murmur from the patient crowd in the queue. It was rather peculiar to see the body of Lenin lying there under a glass cover, looking like a wax figure, with a pinkish, slightly subdued light streaming from above. There was a hushed silence and a slow but steady movement of the crowd under the watchful eye and gentle prodding of the guard. I don't remember having been deeply impressed or moved, but perhaps one did have a general feeling of awe and respect for Lenin as he once was.

We attended meetings, conveyed fraternal greetings to the Russian workers, we were fêted—the lot. And we never noticed the shortcomings, the difficulties and protests, behind the facade. I particularly remember the delight of one young German worker, Fritz Renner, an unemployed member of my own branch. He was like a child, full of delight for all he saw, and walked around Moscow with a perpetual expression of wonder on his face—wearing a red tie, which he must have bought in Berlin specially for the trip, the only man in Moscow to wear one as far as I could see.

Since we were quite a crowd when walking around, it was sometimes difficult to hear the explanations of the official interpreter, so I acted as an unofficial one to the small number of delegates I knew personally. Sometimes I also had to act as an intermediary between the delegates and the hotel administration to arrange a tour somewhere or tickets for something.

At meetings, too, I was sometimes asked to interpet for our group. On one occasion I was asked to address a large crowd of women workers and to convey to them greetings from German women workers, ostensibly as their representative. For greater effect, it was suggested that I spoke in German and my words were then translated into Russian, to the warm applause of the audience. I never quite saw the phoneyness of this at the time.

The delegation left Moscow after a week for some other town and I was given the option of going with them, or accompanying a Professor Goldschmidt to Kiev, Baku and Tiflis. I chose the latter and was not disappointed. Professor Goldschmidt, a well-known writer and publicist, was one of Germany's 'red' intellectuals, a strong sympathiser with the Soviet Union. It was no doubt to the authorities' advantage to arrange this special visit for him and his wife and to present the activities of the trade unions and other aspects of Soviet organisation in as favourable a light as possible. He was in his sixties then and quite a shrewd person, humorous and entertaining. His wife, rather younger, was less so; she was very middle-class, ostentatiously displaying their prosperity in her dress and make-up, and not particularly intelligent or interested. In one factory I was pulled aside by a few women who discreetly asked me whether Frau Goldschmidt was really also a communist, as make-up was then rather scorned among women in the USSR, and such dresses either did not exist or were not available to ordinary citizens.

Our young interpreter, named Vsevolod, who was no doubt an employee of the GPU, was pleasant and efficient in smoothing out any hitch on the journey. He taught me a couple of songs from popular Soviet films and from the Komsomol (the Communist Youth Organisation). And he cleverly tried to give plausible explanations for some of the obvious discrepancies between the theory and practice of Soviet life, which I for one lapped up only too readily.

We travelled in luxury in two compartments of an International Wagons-Lits carriage. Just as well, since the journey took two days and three nights. I shared a compartment with Frau Goldschmidt, while the other was occupied by the two men. Our first stop was Kiev, where we were supposed to visit a famous new tractor factory, but were unable to do so for some unexplained reason. Later I heard some talk about labour trouble at the plant. Instead we were taken to another factory where young Komsomol workers told us about their work. This involved a fair amount of overtime and weekend work, which they did only too willingly in order to fulfil the plan set for their factory. Much of this enthusiasm must have been quite genuine.

In Tiflis and Baku Professor Goldschmidt was primarily interested in interviewing trade union and local Soviet officials. It was very interesting for me and gave me a far better understanding of the functioning of the system—at least of how it functioned in theory—than all the sightseeing and being fêted in Moscow.

While in Moscow I had tried to contact Stepan, the other delegate I had made friends with in Berlin. I was told he was in Baku. That was even better from my point of view. I must have been given the address of his hotel and I sent him a telegram. He contacted me at our hotel and, although quite pleased to see me, was visibly disconcerted, whether by being openly contacted by a foreign communist or for some other reason, I did not know at the time. Nevertheless we met once or twice during my short stay in Baku and he explained to me—unofficially—that he had been sent to Baku by his trade union because of a fierce fire in the oilfields. Officially we were not told about it at all.

As well as the talks arranged for Professor Goldschmidt, we were taken sight-seeing to the new workers' flats, but had to go through one of the old, narrow streets where the old dwellings still existed. One worker's family seemed to be living in a storeroom or small warehouse. As we passed, we could see through the high wide open double door, which gave some light to the seemingly windowless interior. There were some dilapidated pieces of furniture and a couple of children playing near the entrance. When I remarked on it to our guide, he explained that new houses had not been erected fast enough to keep up with requirements. Even then, enthusiastic as I was, it seemed to me a somewhat lame excuse. We were also taken to the graves of the twenty-six commissars, who had been shot by the White-Russians in a mass execution during the civil war.

Baku was rather picturesque, with camels resting in the streets, but there were oil rigs on the horizon and a smell of oil in the air; an old town, hot and dusty. Tiflis was quite different. You could still feel the old elegance and lightness. The buildings in the main street were well maintained, with plenty of trees contrasting with the white houses, clean air and sun. A train took us up a mountain, from which we had a splendid view over the town. For me all this had an additional interest because of Rapho and what he had told me about his home town and country.

Professor Goldschmidt had the usual informative talks with officials. We were taken to a theatre to see a Georgian play and saw Stalin's mother in one of the boxes—a little old woman, all in black. We were shown a beautiful ancient church and talked there to a Georgian priest or monk. And we were taken to Mzkhety, some distance from Tiflis, right in the mountains, where a hydro-electric installation was being built on the river bank. On the opposite bank was a tiny, ancient chapel, greatly revered by the orthodox Georgians, and nearby an enormous statue of Lenin, several times life-size, stretching his arm across the river and commanding that electricity be generated. 'Socialism is Soviets plus electricity,' he had said.

As well as collecting material for a serious study on certain aspects of the Soviet economy, Professor Goldschmidt observed the everyday life of the people, and later published a book with sketches of his impressions: some were plain descriptions of our experiences, some amusing, or satirical in a good-natured way. One such story was about 'Flushers and non-Flushers'. This referred to the filthy state of the lavatories in our otherwise modern and clean hotels. Some of the visitors there from the Asian republics of the USSR had never confronted a flush toilet before. They did not know what the chain and the water cistern were for; they climbed upon the seat and used it in the way the French did (or do) in those old café toilets with just an opening in the floor.

In Moscow I went to visit our old Aunt Tori. She and her husband, a highly skilled engineer, now had an eleven-year-old son. They still lived in the same two-room flat, without a bathroom, in a wide street with pleasant two-storey timber houses, each built around a courtyard. Access to the first-floor flats of the inside wings were from galleries that ran all around the houses. The atmosphere was somewhat rural, but spacious and clean, and the tenants mostly skilled workers or craftsmen. But in 1931 Aunt Tori and her husband Ivan had to share their flat with another engineer and his wife, which meant each family had only one room and had to share the kitchen. They received me hospitably, dishing up tea and precious home-made jam, according to the Russian custom. The jam was incredibly sweet, but how could I refuse it? They also quite sincerely suggested that Olya, Andryusha and I should return to Moscow and bed down with them until we had found work and somewhere to live. This was, and probably still is, the spirit of the people, certainly between family and friends.

Ivan was a hard worker, and earned rather more than the average skilled worker because of his special qualifications and possibly for overtime and piecework. He was also a party member and quite content with life under Stalin. Not so his colleague and flat mate, another skilled engineer but rather older than Ivan. He was full of bitter complaints against the regime, and its shortages and shortcomings. This greatly surprised me, all the more as his five children all had university or technical college training, an opportunity he and they would hardly have had if they had grown up in Tsarist Russia. So I dismissed his complaints as the discontent of a disgruntled individual. But it is interesting that in 1931 a person was not afraid to be so outspokenly hostile in the presence of a workmate and a stranger, a foreigner at that, and I had not disguised the fact that I was a German communist.

In 1961 I tried to find out whether my aunt and her family were still alive. I found the street, but as to the house—my mind went blank. For thirty years I had remembered the number of the house and the flat, and now I did not know which was which or whether the numbers had changed. Some houses had been replaced by larger, stone-built ones, but one side of the street was the same. I went into several courtyards, looking up at the galleries. Nothing seemed to fit. In one there was an elderly man sawing logs. He looked up and asked rudely: 'What do you want?', to which I meekly replied that I was looking for a family with such and such a name, who had lived here thirty years ago. To which he equally brusquely replied: 'Never heard of them'. And I made off quickly, unsure of what might follow. I have often wondered whether this lapse of memory was purely psychological, my wanting and yet being relucant to find out what happened.

We returned to Moscow from the Caucasus in time for the grand parade, the climax of the delegation's visit. From very early in the morning the centre of the town was cordoned off and all traffic had stopped. There were militia and army men everywhere. Only officials from factories, other large enterprises, government departments and individuals with special passes were admitted to Red Square. The International Workers Relief delegates had all been given passes and we planned to go to the square together. I had to make my way to their hotel from Katya's flat across the river. I advanced with difficulty through the throng of people and the various checkpoints, where I invariably had to show my delegate's pass. I was also invariably asked for additional explanations, which were not always readily accepted. Eventually I got wise to the game and simply waved my card, saying in broken Russian *'Delegatsiya'*, until I finally joined my comrades in the hotel. From there we were marched off to a front row in Red Square, just below the Kremlin Wall and quite near the Mausoleum, where we now had to stand and wait.

The whole square was empty, except for the invited guests lined up behind ropes, and militia and Red Army guards. The walls of the vast GUM multi-storey shopping centre were decorated with huge portraits of Marx, Lenin, Stalin and other Soviet leaders, with banners, inscriptions, exhortations, and the like; a very colourful, if somewhat crude, picture. Gradually our side of the Square began to fill with other foreign and Soviet delegations, all with their flags or banners. It was pretty cold, though the snow was not very deep, nor the frost too severe.

At last, when the clock on one of the towers of the Kremlin Wall was chiming ten, the huge gates opened and Stalin and his entourage drove out in big black cars. They got out and lined up on the wall above the Mausoleum, behind the balustrade: Stalin in the middle, flanked by the entire Politburo on one side and military dignatories on the other. The national anthem was played (I think it was at that time still the *Internationale*), then the parade started: first the armed forces—infantry, cavalry, tanks and heavy weapons; followed by contingents from factories and other large workplaces; other organisations followed, including the Komsomol, the young Pioneers and the sportsmen, all shouting salutes to those taking the parade; then came the foreign Communist delegations and those from other parts of the USSR. All with flags and banners flying, salutes and heads turned towards Stalin on the Mausoleum wall. There was solemn music, and the singing of old and new revolutionary songs. For four or five hours we shouted back and sang and applauded, and it was difficult to say which was greater, our enthusiasm or our exhaustion.

Then it was all over and everybody drifted back to their homes or hotels for refreshments and the evening celebrations, which included magnificent fireworks on the banks of the river Moskva. The Mosfilm Studio had shot a film of our delegation in the square, and I fervently wished for Vladimir to see it and recognise me. Then it was all over and we were getting ready to return to Berlin.

On the last day I went to the cinema at the Government House, where Katya lived, and saw a film about the life and work of young Komsomol members. I felt very sad and shed a few tears, realising that I had to go back to Germany, with its rising unemployment and tense political situation. I regretted that I had not responded to a further invitation from Katya to go on a short visit to Leningrad, but I felt I could not exceed my leave.

Back in Berlin, I could not refuse after this trip to speak here and there at branch meetings about life and work in the USSR. As I returned one night from out of town together with my co-speaker, a tall, handsome, impressive man known as the Red Pastor, he told me how surprised he was to see me at such a meeting in Germany! He had also been in Moscow, he told me, and seen me come into the hotel lobby one evening in a dark-grey, tightly belted coat, a black beret, and boots, with cheeks flushed and eyes sparkling from the cold outside. 'Typical new Russian Woman', he had thought, obviously as starry-eyed as the rest of us. He was quite a rare phenomenon in the German communist movement: a practising Lutheran pastor and at the same time an active—and popular— member and speaker for the Communist Party and the International Workers Relief.

Another amusing incident—though it did not seem all that amusing at the time—happened at a public meeting, attended by about 200 people. I had prepared my report very carefully and tried to keep strictly to my notes. Suddenly the lights fused and we were plunged into complete darkness. Luckily, before I could gather my wits and start to improvise (which might even have been better), the fuse was mended and I could continue. I don't remember what sort of applause I got, but to my surprise and great satisfaction twenty people handed in membership applications after the meeting.

It was possibly on this occasion that there was no train back to Berlin after the meeting and I had to spend the night. I was kindly invited to stay at the house of the branch chairman, an unemployed comrade, and his wife. They were very hospitable and gave me supper. But I had to share their double bed with them! And the sheets on the bed looking as if they could well do with a change. Whatever the sleeping arrangements, there was no other way out and I could not have hurt their feelings.

It did not do me any harm to experience how some people had to live. I sometimes said to Erich Lange that I would really like to work in a factory for a while, to see what it was like. He did not think it a good idea, since the membership of both the International Workers Relief and of the party was predominantly working-class, while they had relatively few intellectuals or people with better than elementary school education.

In the spring of 1932 I left my job and went to work with DEROP AG, a Soviet oil company working under the mantle of a German company with a German director as figure-head. Known as the DEROP, its official name was the German company for the Distribution of Soviet Oil Products. In those days there were many companies, Soviet in all but name, to promote trade between the USSR and other countries.

For the first six months at the DEROP I worked in the personnel department, as assistant to the senior assistant to the Russian head of the department. In actual fact it was the senior assistant who ran the department. She was a German Communist, daughter of a dustman, very efficient in her job, very intelligent in general, and pleasant to work with. She also understood the work and personal problems of the German staff, and was upset if she had to give somebody notice. Our Russian boss was a somewhat bewildered man, unfamiliar with German labour laws, tax laws and so on, so he left everything to her.

We three got on well together and when times were slack had quite a few discussions on various subjects, including, I remember, children's education. In those days before Hitler, and before the Moscow Trials, the atmosphere was not so tense and there was not quite so much suspicion on the part of the Russians as there was later. They both had young children and the two families occasionally spent Sunday together out in the country, using the Russian's car and picnicking in the woods or by a lake. But they had very different views on children's education. My German colleague greatly disapproved of the Russian's 'modern' ideas of giving even a small child complete freedom. The Russian's little daughter, for example, was allowed to eat whatever and whenever she wanted. If she ate too much that was her look-out and would teach her not to over-eat on chocolate or whatever. The children were also allowed to butt into the grown-ups' conversation and tug at their parents' sleeves until they got attention. My German colleague did not approve of that and brought up her two little boys in a stricter, more conventional, way.

The DEROP employed about half Russians and half Germans. The Russians were in all the leading positions and all what one might call confidential positions—book-keeping and drawing up balance sheets for example. There was a special department, equipped with the new Hollerith machines, which exclusively employed young Russian girls, specially trained to punch the holes into the cards which replaced the old ledgers. Obviously the system required great accuracy. No one except the girls and their elderly Russian boss was allowed into the department, except of course their Russian superiors. It was this that led to the trouble.

Sometimes there were slack periods and the Hollerith girls had little work—which would not do at all! What would the bosses say, if one of them strayed in and saw the girls idly sitting around? So the machine had to be kept going all the time. But what with? Well, there were always noughts that could be punched, and that, on the surface of it, could do no harm. But they could and they did! When the time came to draw up the annual balance sheets and prove the fulfilment of that year's plan, the girls could not remember how many fictitious noughts had been punched, or where. All the book-keeping had gone hay-wire! And the bosses in Moscow were pressing for the figures! So a year's work had to be done all over again.

With the best will in the world this was impossible. The old chief accountant was in despair, the chairman was frantic. Somehow or other he managed to get additional funds for temporary labour to draw up the accounts in the old-fashioned way, for which the DEROP tried to get fifty German book-keepers, practically overnight. The labour exchange was quite unable to provide so many, in spite of the high unemployment, and instead sent all sorts of unlikely people, including engineers and ballet dancers. The personnel department was certainly kept busy. Somehow a more or less suitable temporary staff was selected, the accounts disentangled and sent off to Moscow. Whether they proved satisfactory or not, none of us ever knew. But I seem to remember that the old chief accountant was recalled to Moscow and nobody ever mentioned him again.

Eventually the Russians decided that it was a waste of time my working in the personnel department, especially as I knew some Russian shorthand. This really counted for something. They had plenty of typists, but hardly any shorthand-typists, as the Russian shorthand system was difficult and took a long time to master. Letters were usually scribbled out by hand and then passed on for typing out. There was only one stenographer, Zinochka, a slender, overworked girl, working for the company chairman, primarily for confidential work, and that was all. So I was transferred to the secretariat, a purely Russian administrative department consisting of the chairman of DEROP, his personal assistant and secretary, Zinochka the stenographer, and me—mainly working as secretary to the boss's personal assistant.

The chairman was relatively young, in his mid-thirties probably, lean, quick in movements and in grasping things, a live-wire who could assert himself when necessary. Because of his position and his manner almost everybody was in awe of him, though I think he was not a bad chap. He had a sharp, somewhat boyish face with a touch of humour to it, and he always wore a bow-tie and dressed in a slightly dandyish way. His personal assistant was older and extremely cautious, almost unsure, and sometimes irritatingly slow in taking a decision for himself. But he was quite unyielding when it came to carrying out the chairman's orders. I got on quite well with him and he was very helpful when I was uncertain about something.

In fact I got on well with all the Russians I came in contact with. Working at the centre of the enterprise, I often had to go to see the Russian heads of other departments. There were two in particular who were very interested in what was happening in Germany and in the progress of the German Communist Party.

Whenever I had to see one of them and he was alone, I would be questioned about the party, the mood of the German workers, the Social Democrats, and so on. But as soon as another Russian entered the room, the conversation would abruptly switch over to business matters. I never questioned why.

One day Zinochka could not cope with her workload and the chairman asked me to type something for him. It was marked 'confidential', some purely business matter which did not mean anything to me. Yet the boss had, strictly speaking, no right to let me see it. But there are rules, and rules to be broken if need be. The fact was that the DEROP, like every Soviet institution or enterprise, had a confidential department, which no unauthorised person, either foreign or Russian, was allowed to enter. These departments handled classified material, which probably existed in many companies. The personnel had to be cleared and specially admitted to work of a confidential nature by higher authorities, including no doubt the GPU or, as it became, KGB. No doubt these departments kept an eye on the Soviet employees as well. I was now occasionally entrusted with these confidential reports or minutes of meetings. I was surprised, but tactful enough not to show it.

Later that year, 1932, when the presidential election campaign was taking place in the USA, the Russians were rather tense. The contest was between Roosevelt, for the Democrats, and Hoover, for the Republicans. The day the election results were announced, the chairman happened to be ill at home, but he rang early to give me some instructions. Then he asked eagerly: 'What is the result of the elections?' When I said 'Roosevelt' he was greatly relieved. He explained to me later how much more advantageous for Russia they expected Roosevelt's presidency to be. He had good reason.

Earlier that year Olya and I had had to move again as our friend was returning to Berlin. Tired of lodgings, we decided to rent our own flat and found a very nice one somewhere between the predominantly working-class Wedding district and the more mixed district of Gesundbrunnen. It was a spacious and sunny flat on the fourth floor of a new block. There were two largish rooms and a very small one, a kitchen and bathroom, a covered balcony overlooking a large garden with green trees, and the use of space in the block's loft and cellar, each of which could be locked.

We had no furniture and hardly any money to buy any. However, we managed to get a few things second-hand from one of our previous landladies, and with a couple of small occasional tables, a bookshelf in each room, and a few boxes covered with colourful materials, we each had a comfortable, pleasant room. The stoves in the spacious kitchen, where we had our meals, and in the two large rooms had to be heated with coal, which we stored in the cellar. It was marvellous to be in charge and not have to take special care with somebody else's precious furniture. We were happy with what we had and did not want to acquire too many possessions. A young comrade, a working-class housewife, used to come in and clean for us once a week, as we were both working all day long. We felt free and independent.

In November 1932 there was the election for deputies to the Reichstag—the lower chamber of the German federal parliament, the upper chamber being the Bundesrat. To celebrate this independence from landladies, I decided to display a huge red banner with a communist slogan for the November Reichstag election. It stretched almost across the width of our two front rooms, proclaiming to the whole street (and the nearby police headquarters) the way I would vote. Olya did not protest (she never did) though it marked her too, of course, at a time when the political atmosphere was already tense.

At the DEROP I had made friends with a newcomer from Russia, a young woman about my age called Masha. She was burning with enthusiasm for the Soviet Union and communism in general, and was full of zest for life. She bubbled over with youth and health and interest for a lot of things apart from politics. One day she accepted my invitation to come home with me. It was quite a distance by underground and on the way she read out to me a letter she had received from her mother, and we talked very animatedly about this and that, in Russian of course. A man sitting opposite suddenly turned on us and rudely said we should stop jabbering in a foreign tongue, which nobody could understand, and were we discussing German politics? I exploded and told him to mind his own business, there was no law against speaking Russian. He piped down, but when we got out at our station he followed us, stopped us and showed his police badge. He took us to the stationmaster's office. This was a blow, more so for Masha, as she was a Soviet citizen and could get into trouble. As for me, I had a small suitcase with me, full of International Workers Relief literature, and a party membership card in my handbag.

The stationmaster and the policeman looked through my belongings, fortunately without discovering the party card. Masha, stupidly, refused to reveal her identity and gave a false name. Then they rang the local police headquarters, which was quite near, to send somebody round to collect us. We were marched along our street, and looking up, I could see the light in my sister's room, but could do nothing to let her know what had happened to us. At the police headquarters our names and other details were taken down and then we were made to sit and wait, for what we did not know. I decided it might be wiser to get rid of my party card and asked to go to the lavatory. There I carefully tore it up with all the monthly contribution stamps I had so proudly collected over two years. I flushed the lot down and that was that. Later I had visions of the police retrieving the bits and sticking them together again, but then decided they surely would not go to all that trouble for so little.

Eventually a police car arrived to take us both to the Alexanderplatz, the famous square with the vast Berlin police headquarters. There we had to go through the same questions, and Masha finally decided it was no good hiding her identity. She gave her name and asked for the Soviet consul or ambassador to be informed of her detention. Then we were taken to the women's section and put into separate cells. It was a peculiar feeling to be searched and stripped of all your personal things, and then to be locked in behind a heavy door with only a spy hole as a link with the world outside. The cell was very small with a bare bulb hanging from the ceiling, a bunk bed, a tiny table, a chair and a bucket with a lid. There must have been a small window, but I did not notice it—it was already dark outside.

I was worried that my sister might be worrying about me, but beyond that I was relatively calm. Perhaps I was already conditioned to the possibility of being arrested. Perhaps I even felt slightly romantic, caught in that situation, as nothing serious could have been held against either Masha or myself. I was also trying to steel myself with the thought that Rosa Luxemburg and many other revolutionaries had spent months and years in jail, so surely I could stand it for a little while until the matter was cleared up. I any case, it was no good speculating about it, better get some sleep—which I did.

In the morning I was given a piece of dark, coarse bread and a mug of so-called coffee. I wasn't particularly hungry, but had some of both out of curiosity. At about ten o'clock we were taken down to a large office and then—much to my surprise—told that we could go, that our detention had been a regrettable mistake and there was no case against us. The official returned all our belongings, and all but apologised. So shortly before the election, tempers were getting frayed, he said, and there were people who feared spies or political infiltrators and therefore tended to act somewhat hastily. I thought then that the man in the underground must have been a Nazi sympathiser, or even a member. That was the end of the affair for me. For Masha the consequences were sadder: she was sent back to Russia and I never heard anything from or about her again.

The economic situation in Germany was not good. It had been deteriorating since the Wall Street stock exchange crash in October 1929. Unemployment had risen to six and a half million. This led to a political polarisation, with a staggering increase in the number of supporters of the Nazis—the *National-Sozialistische Deutsche Arbeiter Partei*, or National Socialist German Workers' Party. The election results of the major parties make it clear:

	1928	1930	1932
Nazi Party	800,000	6,400,000	11,750,000
Communist Party	3,290,000	4,590,000	5,980,000
Social Democrats	8,040,000	8,640,000	7,250,000

Between 1930 and 1932 the Nazis had almost doubled their vote. Even so, they had not yet reached the combined number of votes of the German Communist Party and the Social Democrats. If these two parties had stood together against Hitler, the future course of German and world history would have been very different. As it was, the Communist Party, following instructions from the Comintern, rather than uniting against the Nazis, turned against the Social Democrats.

The Comintern, (the Third or Communist International) had been formed in 1919 after the Russian Revolution. It replaced the Second International, which had been dominated by the German Social Democrats and in 1914 had supported war efforts—thus failing the working class of Europe. The Comintern, according to its manifesto, existed 'to mobilise the forces of all genuinely revolutionary parties of the world working class and thereby facilitate and hasten the victory of the communist revolution throughout the world'. In fact, as the revolution was defeated and Stalin assumed greater power, it became a tool in his hand. The decisions of its Executive Committee, which met between congresses, were binding on all affiliated parties, and these were increasingly geared to the changing needs of the USSR as Stalin saw them. It too failed the working class.

By 1923 the revolutionary upheaval in Europe, and particularly in Germany, had come to an end. Both the capitalist countries and the USSR now turned towards building and stabilising industry. Stalin declared that the USSR was building 'socialism in one country'. He was supported by the rapidly spreading party bureaucracy, which, isolated from the depleted working class, and rising above it, took over the state machine. The party became its political instrument. This process of 'Stalinisation' started in 1923 and lasted for five years. During that time Stalin turned his attention towards colonial struggles rather than to Europe, while at home the course was set for super-industrialisation. The first Five-Year Plan was introduced in 1928, based on the forced collectivisation of agriculture and the exploitation of the peasants; its aim was to 'catch up and overtake the USA'.

Internationally Stalin and his supporters now swung sharply to the left, declaring that the 'period of peaceful coexistence' between capitalism and Communism was now at an end. A new period was on hand: one that would bring a sharpening of internal crises and international antagonisms. They decreed a policy of 'class against class'—the so-called 'Third Period'.

A sharpening of the world economic crisis did indeed come in 1929, signalled by the Wall Street Crash in the USA. In Germany the crisis led to increasing political tension: though support for the Communist Party was growing, so too was that for the Nazi Party, as the election figures showed. Yet instead of calling for a united front between the Communist Party and the Social Democrats in order to defeat the Nazis, Stalin's ultra-left policy brought an instruction from the Comintern that Social Democrats should be denounced as 'social fascists'. Stalin called the Social Democratic Party the 'twin-brother' of fascism. Hitler, when he assumed power, threw these so-called 'social fascists' and Communists alike into the prisons and newly opened concentration camps by their thousands. Yet the Comintern declared that the German Communist Party was daily 'strengthening its work' and that Hitler's victory, by destroying illusions about parliamentary democracy, was actually assisting the revolution.

Seven years passed between the sixth congress of the Comintern and its seventh—and last—in 1935. The Comintern became inactive and inert. But as Stalin destroyed the old Bolshevik Party in Russia, culminating in the Moscow Trials of the mid-1930s, so the Comintern politically destroyed the Communist parties abroad, and by the eve of the Second World War Stalin was trying to come to accomodation with Hitler.

It is not surprising that the majority of Communist Party members accepted uncritically the twists and turns in Comintern policy. They believed in a fair and just society and trusted their leaders to take them there, or at any rate to show them the way. The party leaders did not encourage criticism or independent thinking about these policies. There was even an instruction to refrain from delving into party policy, and to turn to oneself and one's comrades for self-criticism, self-accusation and 'vigilance'. In the 1920s there had been criticism and rejection of the party line by some of the German party leaders themselves: from the left by Ruth Fischer and Arkadi Maslow; from the right by Heinrich Brandler and Ernst Thälmann, who had set up the *Kommunistische Partei Opposition*, the Communist Party Opposition. They were all expelled. There had also been some dissenting voices in the early 1930s, in my own time, among the intellectual activists. After Hitler took power they went as refugees to the USSR, where they vanished without trace. The bulk of the membership, including myself, did not know any better and accepted the policy as it was passed down to us, Marx, Engels and Lenin notwithstanding.

In 1930, when I had joined the Communist Party, we had done a lot of propaganda work among the people in our area and especially among the Social Democrats—discussing issues such as unemployment and how to fight the Nazis. We knocked on the doors of the tenement houses with our literature on Sunday mornings, attended meetings in the evenings, and had discussions with Social Democrats on street corners. Sometimes on a Sunday we went out to nearby towns to sell our literature and explain our aims. On one memorable Sunday we went out on bicycles. I went on a borrowed man's cycle, struggling through a wood over branches and roots, with no path to follow. I could just about sit on a bike and eventually I toppled over. My thigh showed a huge bruise in changing colours for several weeks. Every now and then I would spend a Sunday at home, huddled up on my couch, surrounded by papers, journals, pamphlets, books, trying to catch up on party literature, particularly the daily ***Rote Fahne*** and the journals ***Die Kommunistische Internationale*** and ***Inprekor***, which covered foreign affairs. I also studied basic Marxist theory. Stalin was then not yet much of a writer, and Trotsky was taboo, though on occasion we argued passionately and arrogantly against his views, never having read a word by him ourselves.

Occasionally we organised small, local, demonstrations in our district, which the Social Democrats may have joined in. I remember one, probably connected with demands on behalf of women, because Liesel Friedrich and I were leading it with perhaps two hundred women and men following. Suddenly police appeared with their batons drawn and began to charge. What were Liesel and I to do? I was scared and could feel the demonstration behind us disintegrating, the people dispersing on to the pavement or into doorways. But Liesel and I were *leading* the demonstration and could not simply run away at the first provocation. So we marched on. But it was no use. There was no demonstration to lead any more. So we folded up our banner and left. The police did not pursue us and did not beat us up. They had apparently done their duty by dispersing the demonstration.

Once the Social Democrats became 'social fascists' in the eyes of the Comintern, and therefore in the eyes of the Communist Party, the streetcorner arguments sometimes turned into violent clashes between the two parties. There were also clashes between the Communist *Rote Front Kaempfer* (Red Front Fighters) and the *Sturm-Abteilungen*, the Nazi Stormtroopers, or other Nazi thugs.

All the parties held mass rallies, with a lot of flag-waving, banners, slogan-chanting and speech-making. One Communist Party rally in the huge Berlin Sports Palace is particularly memorable, though I no longer recollect the occasion nor the names of the main speakers, or how a Russian delegate got there to say a few words. I only remember that I was suddenly pushed on to the platform to translate his fraternal greeting over a microphone to an audience of several thousand. Another time we were listening, bored stiff, to a lengthy oration by Ernst Thälmann, party leader at the time, who— seemingly under the influence of drink or out of sheer ignorance and arrogance—was getting all his metaphors mixed up, starting with one and finishing with another.

We were spellbound on another occasion by Heinz Neumann, a brilliant speaker and a member of the party's politbureau since 1928. Neumann and a number of his friends began to oppose the Comintern after its change of policy towards the Nazis. Anticipating a possible seizure of power by Hitler after his election success in 1930, Stalin had directed that there should be no more street battles or fighting with the Nazis and their stormtroopers, only verbal argument. Neumann was immediately ordered to Moscow, deprived of all his functions and dispatched to Madrid in late 1932—with strict orders not to interfere with the work of the Comintern representatives there, who were advising the Spanish Communist Party.

But Heinz Neumann urged his old friends in Germany to continue the struggle against Hitler by every means possible. When the Comintern got hold of one of his letters, they ordered him and his wife to Switzerland in 1933 with nothing to do and a false passport, which landed him in prison. Two years later the Soviet authorities declared that they were prepared to grant them asylum. In Moscow they were shunned by almost all their old friends—refugees from Hitler's Germany—but soon noticed that the same reluctance to meet each other prevailed among all the refugees, even those not yet in disgrace. They all lived in an atmosphere of suspicion and fear. During the following two years he was called upon practically every month by one or other authority to 'confess' that because of his opposition to Comintern policy, the German Communist Party had been weakened to such an extent that it was no longer in a position to prevent Hitler taking power. Neumann had already made, while still in Switzerland, various 'declarations' admitting political 'mistakes'. But all his declarations and confessions were to no avail. In 1937 he was arrested and never heard of again.

His wife Margarete, daughter of the well-known Jewish philosopher and Zionist Martin Buber and sister of Babette Gross, Willy Münzenberg's wife, was sent to a Russian prison camp. In 1939, after Russia and Germany agreed the Ribbentrop-Molotov Non-Aggression Pact (named after the two countries' foreign ministers) she and several other German prisoners of the camp were handed over to the German authorities, to be immediately interned in a Nazi camp. It was a truly treacherous act on the part of the Soviet authorities and her account of these events makes depressing reading. Yet my most vivid impressions, on reading her story, were not the equally barbarous conditions in the two camps (perhaps I had by then already read so many descriptions of concentration camps that I had to some extent— deplorably— become inured to them), but the difference betwen them. However tough the Soviet camps were, there was also a certain slap-dash way of dealing with the prisoners, which somehow allowed moments of a more human approach. The way Margarete describes the neatness of the German camp, the precision and military efficiency that ruled there, sent a chill down my spine.

Of all the in-fighting between the Comintern and the individual Communist parties we knew nothing. We followed the instructions that were issued and never realised how near the collapse was. And we all had our private lives to live and problems to solve, everybody in their own way. My problem was once more our brother, who was still without a job. On top of everything else he was stateless. When we lived in Russia we were Soviet citizens, while our mother had acquired German citizenship through her second marriage. When we left Moscow our stepfather had registered us on the exit-permit under his name as his children, to avoid complications. In Germany we registered under our own surname, as stateless, and were given so-called 'Nansen' passports. Then, in the mid-1920s, it became necessary either to opt for Soviet citizenship, or to apply for a full German passport. Since there did not seem any chance of us returning to Moscow at that time, Olya and I applied for German citizenship—but my brother, still under 21, remained stateless. This made it even more difficult for him to get a job.

I don't remember what made him decide to go to Switzerland, but that was what he did. In Basle he got in touch with the small Swiss Communist Party and was given some work on their paper, and was even allowed to sleep on the premises. Andryusha was always very adaptable and quick on the uptake. He could grasp an issue, without necessarily going into great depth, and come up with an article or an argument which gave the impression of a much deeper knowledge than he had. I think we had that in common. It helped us both to tackle jobs that were strictly speaking rather above us, to muddle through and yet succeed. We seem to have both been born under a 'lucky star'. Olya was different. She worked and studied slowly, read more attentively, and the knowledge she acquired was deeper and more lasting.

Andryusha soon made the acquaintance of a very efficient young girl, Frieda, an ardent member of the Swiss party. They fell in love and she offered him a room in her flat in a modern, newly built block of flats. Having entered the country illegally, and not having a residence or work permit, he had to be careful in all his movements. He could not, for example, openly participate in any party activities, though he was active behind the scenes. Then somebody in the block of flats complained about bugs. And the Communist Party took up the case.

The authorities sent their officials to investigate. Whether or not they found any bugs, they did find my brother in Frieda's flat, without papers, without permit, and suspected of being a Communist himself. He was expelled, and chose to go to France as the country nearest to Basle. This was a great blow, but for a while he managed to live half here and half there. In the long run this was not feasible and Frieda and he finally decided to emigrate to Russia, though not till after he had, unsuccessfully, tried his luck in Spain.

In January 1933 Hitler was appointed Chancellor by the elderly von Hindenberg, president of the German Reich and a tool in the hands of the reactionary *Junkers*—the rich Prussian landowning class. There were no protests on the part of the Social Democrats or the Communist Party. Nothing. Everybody was expecting some action, demonstrations, a strike, a united front, difficult as this would have been. But nothing happened. To my knowledge, not a single protest meeting, demonstration or strike took place. The Communist press came out with the slogans 'The worst the better' and 'After Hitler it will be us'—claiming that Hitler and the Nazis would be so discredited that the people would turn to the Communists. It would have been laughable had it not been so tragic.

The signal for the Nazis to turn to ruthless measures was given by the Reichstag fire. On the evening of 27 February 1933 a passer-by noticed a fire in the parliament building. By the time the police and fire brigade arrived, Hitler and his propaganda minister Goebbels had arrived too, but the fire had already engulfed the main chamber. Hitler and Goebbels at once decided that it was the work of the Communist Party, and at dawn the arrests began. First the party's parliamentary chairman Ernst Torgler was detained; a little later the party chairman, Ernst Thälmann. Somewhere in the corridors of the burning Reichstag, a young, mentally unbalanced Dutchman, Martinus van der Lubbe, was discovered wandering around. He too was detained. A fortnight later three Bulgarians were arrested, including an important Comintern functionary, Georgi Dimitrov. The case was brought before the highest German court, but the only evidence seemed to point to the solitary van der Lubbe, who—whether justly or unjustly accused of arson—paid with his life. The Communists, meanwhile, accused the Nazis of starting the fire.

After the fire the Communists, at any rate in my district, became totally inactive. The movement became demoralised. The mass organisations set up by the Communist Party ceased to exist to all intents and purposes. The International Workers' Relief, the Red Trade Unions, the aid organisation for political prisoners, the League Against Imperialism, some of the left-wing theatre groups, all just disappeared.

A nucleus of the party carried on its work on a small scale in a spirit of courageous self-sacrifice, but also rather stupidly and with disastrous consequences. The party was so unprepared for underground work that when the Nazis really got going they managed to round up thousands of party members and sympathisers. Often they found whole lists of names and addresses of party activists and members during their searches.

When the International Workers Relief 'empire' collapsed one person who found himself out of work was Walter Nettlbach. Now he was without a job and without digs, and had to go into hiding. I had, over the previous year or so, run into Walter at public meetings and internal gatherings. He was the photographer on Münzenberg's successful journal ***Arbeiter Illustrierte*** (Workers' Illustrated), and also contributed to other Communist papers. He came from a working-class family in Krefeld, a town in north west Germany near Cologne, well-known for silk-manufacturing. His father had died or left while Walter was still a child, and his mother looked after him and his elder sister on her own. She had a pretty tough time. So, no doubt, did the two children.

As a youngster Walter was apprenticed to a baker. He did not like it, especially the kneading of the dough at night in a huge kind of trough, which they did with their feet! He then became a painter's apprentice, and later worked for some time as a decorator. I remember him criticising the poor workmanship on the doors of our flat. He had been taught to put the paint on so smoothly that no traces of the brush strokes could be seen. And it was as a painter, as he later told me, that he had learnt all those many songs he sang or whistled. When still quite young, he got involved in politics, read a lot, mixed with left-wing people, moved to Berlin, and eventually took up writing and photography. We had occasionally exchanged a few words. He was a good-looking, easy-going chap, well liked by his friends and colleagues. He could also be very persuasive, and somehow had the luck to fall on his feet in difficult situations.

Apart from the banner I had displayed in November 1932, and that brief detention at the Alexanderplatz police headquarters, I could have had no police record and was no more known to them than hundreds and thousands of other Communist Party members or voters. And we had that very small room in our flat, which we did not really use. So, with Olya's consent, I offered it to Walter. It seemed the natural thing to do to help a comrade in those days. We all tried to keep in touch or get together out of sheer animal instinct, searching for closeness and comfort in those stormy and fearsome times, when we never knew what might happen next. We all felt so helpless.

In other circumstances Walter and I might not have been drawn to each other. As it was, a closer relationship and attachment to each other did in time develop, though we also had fierce arguments about many things. Walter was already a convinced Trotskyist and in touch with a few other supporters of the Left Opposition, of whom I met only one, a young Russian trying to set up a group in Berlin. He seemed an intelligent, intense person, with thick dark hair and large, horn-rimmed glasses, who behaved in a conspiratorial way. I only met him once and do not remember his name, but he struck me as typical of a type from before the Russian Revolution: the dedicated student propagandist. Walter and he met often to discuss political and organisational matters, before the young Russian apparently left Germany.

The Left Opposition began in the USSR in the early 1920s, in protest against internal economic policies, increasing bureaucratisation of the party and the pernicious policy imposed on Communist parties abroad through the Comintern. Stalin was already general secretary of the Central Commitee of the Communist Party of the USSR. Lenin, though still alive, was gravely ill. Trotsky led the Opposition.

Stalin's enmity against Trotsky grew when Lenin's 'Testament' was read out to the Central Commitee after his death: Lenin warned the party against re-electing Stalin as general secretary. In spite of this advice, Stalin was re-elected, and Trotsky was too loyal to the party, and too aloof, to fight for his own position. Gradually Stalin took the reins of power more and more into his own hands, supported by some of the old Bolsheviks, primarily Zinoviev and Kamenev. Trotsky was removed from all his posts, expelled from the party in 1927 and exiled, in the depth of a severe winter, with his wife Natalia and elder son Lyova to Alma-Ata in Kazakhstan, in the south-eastern USSR.

This was still not enough for Stalin. In 1929 Trotsky and his family were expelled from the USSR and transported to Istanbul. He was eventually granted asylum by Turkey on the island of Prinkipo, where he remained till 1933, and where, with the help of a succession of secretaries—including Jan Frankel, whom I later met—he could at least read, write and advise supporters in other countries. In 1933 he managed to obtain a visa for France and in 1937 he moved to Norway. At that time the Moscow Show Trials were in full swing, and his name had been mentioned. The Soviet government used this to put pressure on the Norwegian government to expel him. He finally found refuge in Mexico. But even there Stalin's hatred reached him. In August 1940 he was killed, sitting at his desk, when one of Stalin's stooges drove an axe into his head.

But this tragic event was still years ahead. In the winter and spring of 1933 Walter tried to set up a Left Opposition group in and around Berlin. I was, naturally enough, one of his first targets. But although I was deeply disappointed with the German

Communist Party, resentful of its inactivity at that moment of crisis, and doubtful now of its policies, I could not break away from it entirely. It seemed like a renunciation of all I had believed in and had worked for over the past years. Yet there were already quite a few who, like me, felt that the party had left them in the lurch. Somehow a group of old comrades and friends from the International Workers Relief and party, as well as new friends introduced by them, congregated in our flat to discuss all those questions, to take measure of the Hitler regime, and decide on what to do next. Some of them felt that Trotsky's Left Opposition should be considered very seriously. Others disagreed and were more drawn to the right wing, to Brandler's Communist Party Opposition.

To me, Walter's arguments seemed sound, but I still did not want to be pushed or dragged into a new movement without knowing more about it. I wanted to read something by Trotsky himself and then make up my mind in my own good time. Walter's attempts at forcible persuasion did not help—he often carried his arguments into the personal field, calling me a petty-bourgeois, someone who could not make up her mind, and so on. Our membership of the Communist Party—Walter's, mine and that of two or three close friends from the same branch—had quietly lapsed. We no longer attended meetings, if any still took place. And nobody ever called to enquire or to collect subscriptions. As far as we could judge, the movement simply disintegrated in that winter of 1933.

Part Three:
Hitler in power

CHAPTER 5

Left Opposition

ON 5 MARCH 1934 the last democratic elections were held for the Reichstag. The Nazis emerged as the largest single party, with more than the combined vote of the Social Democrats and the Communists, but not yet an overall majority. They received 17,265,000 votes (43.9 per cent) to the Social Democrats' 7,176,505 (18.3 per cent) and the Communists' 4,425,161 (10.9 per cent). The smaller parties made up the rest. (Germany has always had proportional representation).

Hitler wanted more. He wanted unrestricted power. Communists were banned from the Reichstag and on 25 March a reduced and obedient assembly passed an Enabling Bill giving him unrestricted sovereign power. In April and May a number of far-reaching laws were passed. The Social Democratic and Communist parties were outlawed and thousands of known activists imprisoned or sent to newly created concentration camps. All other political parties, except the Nazis themselves, were banned.

A list of banned books was drawn up which included all Marxist and left-wing publications. These were banned from public libraries and bookshops and confiscated during house searches. They were then publicly burnt in the street. A secret police was created, the *Geheime Staatspolizei* or Gestapo, separate and independent from the regular police. One of their duties was the supervision of the press. The death sentence was introduced and draconian anti-Jewish laws were passed. Jews were dismissed from government service and universities. They were banned from the professions. Jewish shops had to display a special notice. A year later marriages between Jews and 'Aryans' were banned, and the Jews lost virtually all their civil rights. Then their property was confiscated, they were confined to ghettos, and finally sent to the extermination camps.

Hitler also turned against the Protestant Church. A new Evangelical Church was created, with a new creed: 'God has made me a German. God wishes that I should fight for my German-ness.'

The Protestant Church protested, while the Catholics founded an association to co-operate with the new Reich. Within the Left Opposition there was some debate about whether to support the churches' struggle, or ignore it.

In May 1933 Hitler announced that labour conscription was to be introduced. The old trade unions were abolished, their most prominent leaders arrested. A new organisation, *Kraft durch Freude* ('Strength through Joy') was created for workers and office employees, organising joint outings on Sundays for the enjoyment of everybody and the development of strength—for the week's labour ahead, presumably. Other regulations were introduced. At work everyone had to prove Aryan parentage, right back to grandparents on both sides. The official form of greeting became the outstretched arm and the words *Heil Hitler*.

Life for ordinary citizens, even those not involved in any anti-Nazi activities, became distinctly unpleasant. In the street marching Stormtroopers had to be hailed with an outstretched arm. Most people tried to avoid this, disappearing into nearby shops or waiting in doorways. I had studiously avoided any such confrontation until one day I was caught totally unawares. As a means of relaxation and to keep up my eurhythmic training, I had joined a keep-fit class. One night we were lined up in a row for some exercise or other when in came the owner of the school—in full Stormtroop regalia and bearing a high-ranking badge. I was thunderstruck. I had no idea that he was a military Nazi. And not only that. He marched into the hall with outstretched arm and a loud *Heil Hitler*. What was I to do? How could I salute a Nazi? Yet how could I not raise my arm and draw attention to myself, when I was already involved in illegal work together with a group of friends? Unwillingness to conform was debating within me with caution. Then I too began to raise my arm, hesitatingly, unwillingly. And suddenly, without being conscious of it, I found my hand not outstretched, but adjusting my hair! Nobody seemed to have noticed it and nobody remarked on it, but I felt a little ashamed at this compromise. And I still do not know what I really should have done.

In June 1934 Hitler had Röhm, the chief of staff of the stormtroopers, assassinated along with his lieutenants. They had advocated the incorporation of the stormtroopers into the army, which was still powerful and independent and the only force that could now resist Hitler. In August a plebiscite confirmed Hitler as *Führer und Reichskanzler*, leader and state chancellor. He now had a completely free hand.

We were spared all that Hitler clap-trap at the DEROP and greatly appreciated it. We carried on as before until, one day in May 1933, there was a raid. The premises suddenly swarmed with stormtroopers. It was totally unexpected. The Russians were quite stunned and for the moment helpless. The Nazis declared the firm closed. Fourteen German employees, obviously known as members of the DEROP branch of the German Communist Party, were arrested. The rest of us were fired, on the spot. I was lucky. When I had started work there the secretary of the DEROP Communist Party branch thought that I was a member of my local party branch (I had in fact left it by then) and no one approached me or collected any contributions from me. That proved to be my luck.

I was not arrested, but I was without a job. I spoke to the firm's Russian chairman, who promised to help. A few weeks later there was an opening for me with the Soviet Trade Delegation, not in Paris as I had hoped, but in Copenhagen. Well, that was better than nothing. I hated the idea of having to look for a job with a German firm, where I would have to *Heil Hitler* every day, and take part in meetings and other activities. And the chances of my getting a job after some years with the International Workers Relief and the DEROP were somewhat slim anyway. So I was glad to accept the offer and glad to leave Germany—though it saddened me greatly to have to part with Olya, and to leave Walter and my other friends and comrades. But none of us expected the Nazis to last very long.

I applied for an exit visa with mixed feelings. The visa was granted, but I delayed my departure for a week or two, planning to spend the long Whitsun weekend with Olya and Walter. On the Saturday before Whit Sunday there was a fierce ringing of the doorbell at about six in the morning: Police! The two men asked a few questions, had a look around Olya's room and mine, without any thorough search, and then, in the small room, discovered Walter. He lived with us illegally, had never registered with our local police station, as required in Germany whether you moved to another town or just to another furnished room or flat around the corner. Then they asked for my passport. I could collect it in a few days' time, they said. They took Walter with them. He returned after a few hours, now properly registered with us. But when I went to collect my passport, I was told it was being withheld on orders from a higher authority. Instead I was given an identity card, for internal use only. That was a blow. It meant I could not leave for Copenhagen. I was now marooned in Germany, and unemployed.

So I decided to apply for a job with the Soviet Trade Delegation in Berlin—and was accepted. This was rather surprising, as according to a new agreement between the Soviet and German authorities no more Germans were to be employed by the Russians in addition to their existing staff. I attributed the exception in my case to my knowledge of Russian. It didn't occur to me until years later that the move may have been deliberate, a chess move by the Nazi authorities, intended to checkmate me at some opportune moment in the future.

The Trade Delegation occupied a huge building, and the atmosphere was very impersonal, quite different from that at the DEROP. I remember very little about it. I sat opposite a young woman whose husband was in a concentration camp or prison, with no prospect of being released in the foreseeable future. Her treasure and joy was her son, a plump little toddler, who, to her despair, suddenly contracted polio and was partly paralysed. But she bore her misfortunes bravely and never complained. I am still reminded of her when using a little rosewood bowl, carved and polished by her father, who made things like that as a hobby. I equally well remember another colleague, sparkling with youth and happiness, telling us about motorbike holidays with her newly-wed husband, both of them ardent Communists.

Trade relations between Germany and Russia gradually became more and more restricted and the Russians cut down their staff. They moved to smaller premises in the west end of Berlin, a very pleasant mansion surrounded by a garden. It was now much more intimate and personal. I worked in the finance section, the head of which was a Comrade Stepanov, who was rather too high up to deal with us on an everyday basis. Our immediate boss was a Comrade Guriev, but both were quite pleasant to work with, especially Guriev.

There were three or four German employees in that section, all, including myself, working in the same room. One of them was a youngish woman whose husband was a refugee in Czechoslovakia. She used to meet him from time to time just across the border and collect illegal Communist literature to bring back to Germany. So there must have still been some activity going on within the Communist Party. There was another, more middle-aged, cheerful woman who kept telling us that she had cured her short-sightedness by refusing to wear glasses when young. Best of all I remember a portly, humorous, rather authoritarian, middle-aged Berliner—a Berlin cockney. In his official capacity he was the chief bookkeeper. Unofficially he was obviously also the secretary of the illegal branch of the Communist Party at the Trade Delegation. I say obviously, because from time to time I could not help overhearing their not too conspiratorial arrangements for some meeting and noticed the collection of money. They seem to have taken it for granted that I was one of them, but they never approached me. In a broad sense, I *was* one of them. But there was no question of my approaching them, now that I no longer considered myself a member of the party. So I sometimes felt slightly awkward towards my German colleagues.

Like everybody else, I appreciated the advantages of working for the Russians in Berlin. The pay was good, but it was the atmosphere itself, without all that *Heil Hitler* business, that I appreciated most. Relations between the Russian and German workers at the delegation were still fairly relaxed: we used the same canteen, often shared a table and were allowed to buy a variety of things at their duty-free shop on the premises. In fact, since there were now fewer Germans working there and we were probably all vetted, the atmosphere was one of friendliness and mutual trust. Up to a point. It did not go as far as allowing personal contact with the German employees outside work.

As business was gradually getting more slack, I sometimes offered my services to the department in the room next to ours. There I was asked to do some typing for a young engineer. Dark-haired, with blue eyes, shy, with very little knowledge of German, he seemed to feel at ease with me. His typing requirements became more frequent and we would exchange a few words. I would have liked to find out more from him about life in the Soviet Union, over a cup of coffee outside the office, but he just sat there, blushing if our fingers accidentally touched when handling the pages of his report, and hinting sadly that they were not supposed to mix with non-Russians. It did not surprise me, but I felt a little sad for him and for the other Russians working abroad. Though for some, exceptions were possible, as I found out later.

Olya was working at the hospital, subjected to the same rules and regulations as everybody else working in a German establishment, including the daily *Heil Hitler* rigmarole. She had to prove her Aryan origin by submitting her own birth certificate, and those of our parents and grandparents. That was complicated, and everything had to be applied for in Riga, now the capital of independent Latvia.

The authorities took their time. In the end she was so fed up that she yielded to Arnold's wooing and married him in the autumn of 1933, as soon as he had qualified as a doctor and taken a job just outside Berlin. She was fond of him, but whether she would have married him without the pressure of life in Nazi Germany, I do not know. He was a very reliable person, a meticulous, better than average, caring doctor, and a devoted husband and father—but a man who was rarely able to show his feelings. He was very sociable, slightly philistine and law-abiding; in other words an average, decent citizen.

Politically, he considered himself a supporter of the right-wing *Deutsch-Nationale Partie*, the German National Party, and for some time after Hitler came to power he still on occasion displayed the party's black, white and red flag. A year or two after marrying Olya, he became assistant to a Jewish doctor in my area. Shortly afterwards the doctor died of old age, before the Nazis had the chance to deprive him of his livelihood or send him to an extermination camp. Under the anti-Jewish laws, Arnold was entitled to take over the practice and the large flat attached to it for no more than nominal compensation to the widow. Arnold was decent enough to pay her the market price, though it took him some time to pay it off.

While Olya and I were still together, and Walter and I engaged in underground work, she never once objected, though it endangered her too. I remember one night I returned home just as two policemen were carrying out a search of our flat. Walter was not in and Olya was sitting in my room, as pale as a sheet. Neither of us thought of asking them for a search warrant. We were too scared and too used to such things . I had already cleared out any incriminating literature, so the police were not likely to find anything of importance. The really 'hot' stuff was dumped in the loft and we just hoped nobody would search up there. They looked through all my books and took quite a few with them: socialist literature of a general kind and some Russian books, including poetry. Then they left without any further demands or any indication what it was all about. What a relief!

Later the Nazis issued an order to clear lofts of unnecessary or inflammable stuff, ostensibly to reduce the danger of fire spreading. It was obvious to everybody that this was a preparation for war and air raids. Now each block of flats and each entrance had to have a warden, usually a Nazi or Nazi sympathiser, appointed by the authorities, who had to check whether the lofts were cleared and in general had to keep an eye on the flats and their tenants. Walter and I surreptitiously carried all our stuff into the cellar. And all was well again.

I had finally decided to join the Left Opposition in the spring of 1933, and for the following two and a half years Walter and I, and a group of old friends and comrades, were active in clandestine work. It was hazardous right from the beginning, but we did it because we felt it to be necessary. The moving spirit behind the budding group in Berlin was Walter, alias Jan Bur—this was his cover name, the name by which he became known throughout the movement in Germany and abroad.

As Jan Bur, Walter met, organised and plotted with former members of the International Workers' Relief and Communist Party, who were sympathetic. Small sub-groups of four or five people were set up on a strictly conspiratorial basis. I never knew how many members there were in Berlin or how many groups in Germany. The principle was simply that the less you knew, the less you could betray. Every member had a cover name (mine was Anna) and only one person in each group knew the name of the leader of another group and how to make contact. This reduced the danger but also made it more difficult to re-establish lost contacts. The German groups eventually adopted the name *Internationale Kommunisten Deutschland* (IKD), the International Communists of Germany.

Jan Bur made contact with the International Secretariat of the Left Opposition in Paris, for guidance and, sometimes, arguments. A supply of literature was organised, brought in by couriers over the Swiss and Czechoslovak borders. This included the German language papers ***Permanente Revolution***, published by the *Auslands Komitee* (the Committee Abroad). This was later replaced by ***Unser Wort*** (Our Word), which was published in Paris and included articles by Trotsky, which he wrote especially for the German groups, translations from the Russian ***Byuleten Oppositsii***, and articles by Jan Bur and other leading members. ***Inprekor*** also arrived this way, I seem to remember. There were pamphlets, such as Trotsky's own **Germany—the Key to the International Situation**, and occasionally a book or two. Another publication—probably produced by anti-Nazi liberals—was a weekly paper which contained nothing but quotations from the official press, speeches, reports and government orders. The selection and arrangement was so revealing and obviously subversive. It was soon banned.

Occasionally subversive books reached us from abroad. During Christmas 1934 Jan Bur attended a conference in Switzerland to discuss the situation in Germany. He brought back a thin, paperback book with a Nazi title. It began with a few pages of Nazi tripe, then, suddenly, without warning, it continued as a treatise on religion, sex and politics by Wilhelm Reich, an Austrian psychiatrist and one-time Communist. He argued that working-class women in particular, exploited and subjugated, finding no satisfaction in their sexual life with an overworked husband, turned to religion, to the organised church, especially the Catholic Church, seeking oblivion and a certain elation and ecstasy in the teaching of Christ and the colourful and intoxicating celebration of the mass. This deflected them from rebellion and active participation in political struggle.

This approach struck a chord with me, remembering how, in my early youth, I had for a while been attracted to the Greek Orthodox Church—the bowing and endless crossing oneself, the kneeling and bowing down right to the floor, the incense and the chanting of the choirs. 'Religion is the sigh of the oppressed creature, the sentiment of a heartless world, and the soul of soulless conditions. It is the opium of the people,' wrote Marx. Reich's book threw a completely new light on the pull of religion and the church on ignorant, worn-out people.

Our activity consisted mainly in passing on information and directives to the members of the other Berlin sub-groups, which often meant stencilling and duplicating material. I often cut the stencils myself, but cannot now remember in detail what they dealt with. And I do not think that we ever had a duplicating machine in our flat, so they must have been duplicated somewhere else. Members who had contact with people who showed interest in our ideas did their best to pass on relevant material and engage them in discussion. I think we also duplicated short anti-Nazi leaflets, which were left around when and where possible.

But such activities were rather restricted and fraught with danger. In certain circumstances even carrying a briefcase or a bag in the underground or bus might arouse suspicion, particularly if you looked anxious. We had to learn to look unconcerned. When we arranged to meet another member in the street to pass on information or literature, we had to be there to the minute. Any loitering could again rouse suspicion. Sometimes a member would already be under observation, and then the Gestapo could easily make another catch. If we felt there was danger in the air, we tried to give the comrade a sign not to stop or approach—if such a sign was ignored or misunderstood, the outcome could be fatal. More than one comrade was caught in this way. Even calling on an active friend could carry a risk if, by chance, the Gestapo was carrying out a search. It needed a degree of ingenuity on both sides to extricate oneself from such a situation. There was just no question of open political work, such as distributing leaflets or having discussions at factory gates.

We also continued our discussions of wider issues: on Germany, particularly Trotsky's analysis; on the theory of permanent revolution; on the nature of the Soviet state (we rejected the view that it was still a workers' state, albeit a degenerated one, and thought it could no longer be reformed from above, but would require a revolution from below); and on the question of a new, or fourth, International (I think most of us thought such a move premature). We also tried to follow events outside Germany. For example we welcomed the armed uprising of the Austrian workers in Vienna against the authoritarian Dolfuss government in February 1934. The rising was smashed after four days. The government that followed facilitated the occupation of Austria by German troops in 1938 and the eventual absorption of Austria into Nazi Germany.

By the mid-1930s the German Communist Party, especially the young Communists, had rallied, but its leaders were very careless about their members' safety. One young Communist, who was wanted by the Gestapo, had escaped to Prague—only to be sent back to Germany by the Communist Party as an illegal courier. In no time he was caught and imprisoned. Apparently he died in prison or one of the camps during the war.

An interesting sideline to this story is that he and his young wife had worked out a complicated code, based on a book obtainable in prison, so that they could communicate if he was arrested. The Gestapo broke the code, and questioned the wife about the Communist Party resistance movement in Germany—but in a way that made it easy for her not to give anything away. Then, when one of the Gestapo officials was left alone in the room with her, he suggested—indirectly—that she should consider emigrating with her four-year-old child. She took this advice and soon afterwards left Germany. The official could hardly have been a Nazi. He interviewed her only once. All other interviews were conducted by other officials, in ways more expected from Nazis.

Our group had a different method for clandestine correspondence. We wrote or typed an ordinary, perfectly harmless letter and between the lines wrote the message we wanted to transmit using invisible ink. The recipient would decipher the message by holding the page over a lighted candle. The heat brought the writing out. It seems unlikely that the Gestapo never discovered this way of communicating, but we never heard of an arrest as a result of it. Of course this didn't work for prisoners. They had no candles.

Frequent visitors to our flat since the spring of 1933 included Liesel Friedrich and her husband Walter. They had both been members of my party branch. He lost his job in that spring, but Liesel still worked somewhere. They were clearly hard up, but never mentioned it. I remember Jan Bur remarking one day, after Walter had categorically refused to share a meal with us, that that was the surest sign that things were not well.

Walter Friedrich became our first casualty. He was arrested and after days of questioning at the Gestapo Headquarters in Berlin was sent to the Brandenburg prison. We were all very depressed by this, and laid low for a while, but then carried on as usual. After six months he was released, and we discovered how near we had been to being arrested too. He had been questioned for hours on end, for days and nights—the Gestapo wanted to know where the typewriter was on which the stencils for the Trotskyist leaflets and information sheets were cut. It was a matter of luck, Walter confessed, that at the very moment he reached breaking point, and was ready to give our names and addresses, the questioning stopped and he was sent to Brandenburg. In prison the treatment was harsh; the food near starvation level, but there were no longer any interrogations. Now, he told us, he would never condemn anybody for 'betraying' comrades or friends. It was a physical matter of how long your nerves would hold out under prolonged and cruelly refined methods of interrogation. After his release he and Liesel could no longer be active, in their own and everybody else's interest. But we still met at our flat privately and discussed matters as eagerly as before.

Then there were Hans Kaufmann and Elfriede Hollos, the wife of Julius, with whom I had worked on those short courses in basic Marxist theory for the International Workers Relief branches, and who had by then already left Germany for Prague, where he worked as a journalist. Hans was an old friend of theirs, the son of an architect, quite well off, with a flat in the west end of Berlin, where our small group continued to meet when it was no longer considered safe to use my flat. Elfriede and Hans became interested in Trotskyism rather late and not all that deeply, but they were both very reliable and ready to take risks.

One day Jan Bur came back from a trip to Magdeburg with a young Trotskyist called Edu. He believed that Edu would be of greater use in Berlin. He was indeed very active—until he was arrested in the street while keeping an appointment with another Trotskyist. As he was a Polish citizen he was released after about a year, but had to become inactive, and soon after escaped to Paris with his wife. There he was active within the German refugee group, which had contact with the French Trotskyists. He later became a successful journalist but in time both he and his wife turned their backs on Trotskyism and Marxism.

There was also Freddy and his sister, both still in their late teens, one a student, the other still at school. They were not in my group, but Jan Bur brought them home once or twice. They were both highly intelligent, enthusiastic and courageous. One day—all to soon—they were caught, and being Jewish had to expect even harsher treatment than other prisoners. Years later I heard that the Gestapo had had no clear evidence against the sister and eventually released her. She subsequently left for the USA. Freddy, however, was kept in prison for several years and eventually died there.

In spite of Jan Bur's gifts of persuasion, he never succeeded in recruiting those who had been more receptive to the ideas of the Brandler opposition group while still members of the Communist Party. But we remained on friendly terms and continued to discuss with each other. There was Willy Best, slim, blond, highly intelligent and somewhat philosophically inclined. When bathing his baby son, he would get lost in contemplation about why water always runs out of the bath anti-clockwise, and similar phenomena. He and his wife had previously been very active in the party, but were now holding back. They both continued to come to us, and she greatly resented having to go home early to feed the baby while Willy would stay on. In those days nobody ever thought of taking the baby with them, wherever they went, whether to visit friends, to a debate or to a lecture at a summer 'Marxism' week. All traces of Willy and his small family vanished during the war. The house they lived in had been razed to the ground by Allied bombs and no one knew anything of their fate.

Willy was one of the three Musketeers, as they were called by their friends. Another of the three was Hans Steinke, who came from a well-to-do Jewish background, and became the economics editor of ***Rote Fahne***. He joined the Communist Party Opposition, I believe, and in 1933 emigrated to England, where he had contact with C L R James among others. In 1937 he was denounced to the British authorities by a former member of the German Communist Party and was deported to New York, where in time he became the editor and publisher of a highly specialised financial journal. I never met him until after the war, but had contacted him previously by letter and he gave me useful introductions to two or three people in England. One was C L R James, whose room in the Bloomsbury district of London was best reached by a fire escape ladder. It was a large room, and it must have had a bed, table and one or two chairs, but all I remember is the piles of books, journals, and newspapers stacked on the floor all over the room.

The third Musketeer was Fritz Neufeld, a skilled worker in the printing trade. Though the German Communist Party was primarily a workers' party, supported by intellectuals and artists of various kinds, the opposition—both Trotskyists and others—were primarily intellectuals with a middle-class background; there were very few workers. Fritz was an exception. But he was arrested very early on and sent to one of the concentration camps in north Germany, where the inmates were made to slave in a swamp cutting peat in the most appalling conditions. They composed the words and the music for a song, *'Wir sind die Moor-Soldaten'* ('We are the soldiers of the swamp'), which became widely known in Germany and among the emigrés abroad.

Many never came back from that camp, but Fritz did. Before the war broke out he managed to get to Norway. When the Germans occupied that country he tried to escape to neutral Sweden. Together with a few Norwegian comrades they went off on foot. They had made it into the mountainous border country and almost to the frontier when Fritz fractured a leg. To carry him would have endangered the whole group, so he was left behind. He stayed with a Norwegian family, marooned in one room for over two years, without leaving it even for a breath of fresh air. He used the time for reading, studying and even some handicraft work. He survived and after the war he left for the USA, where he died relatively soon after.

Through Fritz we got to know a friend of the Musketeers and of many others from the Communist Party Opposition, known by the nickname of *Pfötchen*, 'Gentle paws'—perhaps because of her manner in dealing with people in need. She was the mother of at least five children, all from different fathers. She was very poor, lived on the dole or some small earnings, but nobody ever left her house without being fed or given a corner to spend the night if need be. She was thin and haggard, but she was the kindest person I ever met. She cared for Fritz whilst he was in the camp, collecting money for parcels for him and other camp inmates (there was no refusing to contribute when she asked), and she befriended Fritz when he came out. She not only gave him shelter and food, but shared her bed with him, as she told me, because of all the deprivation he had suffered in those years.

All the while Jan Bur continued his attempts to extend the IKD's influence and activity. He managed to re-establish contact with the *Sozialistische Arbeiter Partei* (SAP), the Socialist Workers Party, originally a break-away group from the Social Democrats whose leader at one time was Paul Frölich, disciple and biographer of Rosa Luxemburg. In 1933 the SAP considered joining our organisation and supported the setting up of a new International. Apparently, however, Trotsky considered them to be too centrist and nothing came of it. Jan Bur now tried to interest them at least in joint actions where and whenever an opportunity arose. They probably still had some contact with industrial workers, which we did not seem to have at all.

Many were the occasions when he came home late in the night after protracted discussions with the SAP. I was always in a terrible state of anxiety, hanging out of the window, listening to the footsteps. Was it him coming? Was it the police? He used to arrive quite unconcerned, countering my reproaches with the announcement that 'Tonight it was a historic meeting!' and that any day now we, the Trotskyists and the SAP, would set up a united front. What could I say? I realised that it was not always possible to break up a meeting, or to let me know, especially as we had no telephone in the flat anyway. But in the atmosphere of that time it was very worrying, to say the least, if someone was late arriving home. I inevitably fared the worst.

Jan Bur was not the most considerate person at the best of times—he was a real bachelor, who did not want to feel tied down. One evening he went to play cards with a few of the former working-class comrades from the local branch, one of whom lived in the street next to ours. He used to go there from time to time and come back rather late. But on that particular occasion he was still not back in the early hours of the morning! I was frantic. I could not even go to the comrades to enquire lest I endangered myself and Olya! Then he arrived, cheerful and quite unrepentant. On the whole he was a merry and easy-going companion, if you knew how to take him.

He also absolutely refused to pull his weight as far as work in the house was concerned, much to my annoyance. I felt that as a socialist he should have a different attitude. Besides, I was working full-time, whereas he was at home a great deal and could at least walk down from the fourth floor (there was no lift) to empty the rubbish bin. Nor would he dream of peeling potatoes or similar chores. There was nothing I could do about it. He would parry all my reproaches with a gay laugh and say, 'Well, let's leave the potatoes for the poor'. He had had too many potatoes in his childhood and did not particularly like them anyway!

All the while he was very active, never afraid of taking reasonable risks, and often getting quite excited about even small successes. Yet he would not let me expose myself too much. It was understandable. I was the goose that laid the golden eggs by having a well-paid job. There would have been little value in endangering myself, Olya, Jan Bur, and the flat, which, in spite of all the coming and going still seemed relatively safe.

It was not all gloom and work and conspiracy, however difficult life was under Hitler. For three years running we went ski-ing in the Isar mountains. There were four of us, as we were always joined by Lieschen and Erich Lange. They knew a tiny village near the Czech border and usually stayed with a farmer's family. It was simple, but comfortable enough without the to- do of well-known resorts. There were no ski-lifts or *pistes* and no entertainment in the evening. All they did on those holidays (the four had previously included Walter's former girl-friend) was to play cards, which I had always hated. However, they insisted on my participating and tried to teach me. I tried, not wanting to be a spoil-sport. Luckily for me, I proved to be so stupid and unskilled that they were glad to get rid of me and leave me to my reading.

My initiation to the actual ski-ing was a bit forceful, but I survived. We arrived at the station on a clear frosty night, at about midnight. From there it was two or three miles up a mountain and down into the valley. I had never before stood on skis. But there was no other way. So we put on our skis, shouldered our ruck-sacks, and, after a brief explanation, off we went into the night, with the full moon shining through the high trees. With the help of the others I somehow scrambled up that mountain. Then I slipped or glided down, miraculously without mishap.

On the following days we were out ski-ing for about eight hours a day, either taking with us a picnic lunch and a hot drink, or stopping at an inn in the forest. It was hilly, wooded country and we went where the mood took us. The snow conditions were far from ideal, the mountain tops rather icy, while down below the snow was often too powdery. After two days I was so stiff that I could hardly lift my arms to put my anorak on. But I enjoyed it enormously and my companions were on the whole very patient with me when, tired, I occasionally got impatient and moody.

Jan Bur was a great lover of outdoor life and in the summer we often used to spend weekends out of town by one of the lakes surrounding Berlin. Then we bought a motorbike and ventured further out to the Parsteiner Lake, a very large, beautifully situated lake in completely deserted surroundings. We used to leave our tent, cooking utensils and belongings with peasants nearby, with whom he had made friends, clamber up to the high plateau overlooking the lake and spend the weekend away from all the strain of life under the Nazis, sun-bathing and swimming in the nude. We were often joined by old friends of his. Together we talked and relaxed and sang folksongs and ballads as well as hit songs, of which 'Alabama' was the most popular at that time—I could never get enough of 'Oh, Susanna...'.

Another singer was Oswald Hafenrichter, who always brought his guitar with him. He too was active in the illegal movement. His girlfriend had at some time been detained by the Gestapo and there were rumours that she had not come out quite clean, though she maintained she had only given the Gestapo names of people she knew had already been arrested. She eventually left for England, where she entered a fictitious marriage with a Trotskyist for the sake of a British passport and the right to work wherever she wanted. Oswald left Germany for Italy shortly before the outbreak of the war, where he became a very successful film editor and enjoyed life until Italy followed Nazi Germany in the persecution of Jews. This began so swiftly that Oswald escaped on the spur of the moment, without returning to his flat or taking anything with him, leaving his car parked in the street. In England, he served in the Pioneer Corps, like so many refugees from the Continent, doing the heaviest and dirtiest work. After the war he eventually got to know Alexander Korda and edited **The Third Man** for him, as well as several other films. Later he worked at the Elstree Studios and bought a house somewhere around there. He was quite content with his life in England, but died relatively young.

One weekend, when collecting our belongings from the village people our idyll was shattered. The stormtroopers had been around and would be back. Sure enough, the Nazis came and we all had to show our papers and explain our reason for being there. This time there was no bathing in the nude. But strangely enough they did not raise any objections to unmarried couples sharing the same tent—as long as both partners were, or at any rate appeared to be, Aryans. They did not particularly molest us but the peace of the place had gone.

Our carefree weekends at the Parsteiner Lake had to come to an end in any case. Jan Bur had worked illegally for over two and a half years, and the International Secretariat decided that he should leave Germany. He was to go to Paris, where there were some leading members of the Left Opposition and closer contact with Trotsky, who was in Norway.

This was quite a blow for us and the separation was not all that easy, in spite of our many arguments and incompatibilities. The time spent together in the atmosphere of Hitler's Germany, the feeling that our illegal work had a certain importance, the shared danger of it, the constant anxiety connected with our activities, the moments of relaxation at weekends and on holidays, all had created a bond between us which we were reluctant to sever. And in France Jan Bur would have to face the precarious existence of a refugee, who had lost his roots and most means of existence. We didn't think he was himself in immediate danger, but so many friends around us had already vanished from the political scene and we felt the noose tightening. The movement obviously considered him too valuable to lose. So in the autumn of 1935 he took the train to Paris—and was gone.

For the Berlin group his departure was a considerable loss. He was a good organiser and a staunch and persuasive supporter of the Left Opposition. Rummaging recently among old letters and papers, I came across a report sent to me in 1977 based on an interview with Friedel Kissin, the leader of the Danzig group of the Left Opposition. (Danzig was a disputed port on the Baltic Sea, in a corridor between Germany and Poland. It is now Gdansk, of Solidarity fame). The report says there were a total of five or more groups in Germany, the leading members of which had all been arrested in the course of 1935 and 1936. Kissin himself left Germany in July 1936, when the Danzig group seems to have been the only one left.

The Trotskyist organisation in Paris was quite strong and Jan Bur was immediately enlisted for work on the monthly bulletin of the Opposition and on ***Unser Wort***. The group there also had good contacts with the French comrades.

I think, by and large, Jan Bur liked it in Paris, even though he did not speak French at first. There was plenty of scope for political activity, for factional discussions and arguments, for writing and studying political literature, and life in Paris was pleasant anyway—as long as one had enough for a cup of coffee in the cafés on the Boulevard St Michel. For the first few months he had the use of a small flat which belonged to one of the French comrades who was abroad. And as long as I was still working for the Soviet Trade Delegation, and the transfer of money from Germany was not restricted, I could of course help.

After Olya's marriage, I had let her room to a young couple with a baby. They were very pleasant and quiet, not interested in politics or our activities. The only noise came from the baby, but even that was not too bad. Now that Jan Bur had left, I decided to let them have my room as well and only keep the small room, formerly his, for my own use. It was very small: long enough for a bed and a narrow, improvised wardrobe, and wide enough for a table, one or two chairs, and a bookcase, though most of the books had long since been taken to the cellar. In one corner there was also a small anthracite stove, which heated the room in no time. But it was sufficient for me. I was out all day, and in the evening I was mostly with comrades, at a meeting at Hans Kaufmann's flat with Elfriede, or visiting the Friedrichs. It was now a much smaller circle, and there were, anyway, no more meetings at our flat, and I no longer had any particular social life. I also spent a great deal of time with Olya, who by now had a charming baby daughter. So life after Jan Bur's departure became much quieter. There was no longer the constant anxiety, although the general atmosphere remained as oppressive as before.

Long before Jan Bur left for Paris, there was some new development in the life of my brother. Early in the summer of 1934, well over a year after he applied, his visa for the USSR came through—on condition that he become a Soviet citizen. I had sponsored him while I still had contact with the Communist Party and the International Workers Relief. It was crazy. By the time the visa came through, I had been a member of the Left Opposition for over a year, and I was still ignorant enough of conditions in Russia (as most of us were) to hope that, whatever the political aberrations there, he would at least be able to get some proper training and a decent job.

As my brother would never have received a transit visa through Germany, Olya and I decided to meet him for a day in Czechoslovakia, somewhere half-way between the frontier and Prague. It was a sad and, in some ways, an abortive meeting. He had arrived in Prague the night before, but with no money for a hotel. He decided to have a stroll and then spend the night in the waiting room at the station. When he returned, the station was closed. There was nothing for it but to go to a park and hopefully get some sleep on a bench. But no luck there either. Eagle-eyed policemen kept a sharp look-out for tramps and vagabonds. So he walked around all night, and was dead tired when we finally met at some pre-arranged spot in the country.

We should have let him sleep for a while, but time was so

short and we had so much to talk about. Yet the talk was sluggish. He was depressed as well, because his Frieda had not as yet been granted her visa, though she had applied together with him. The time came for Andryusha to take the train back to Prague and from there to Moscow. A last embrace, a wave, and that was the last time we ever saw him.

We kept in touch by letter. His life in the USSR was not easy. He first went to Moscow and stayed for a while with Aunt Tori, her husband and their young son: all in one room, with half a share of the kitchen. Yet they were very hospitable. Then we heard that he was working as an electrician in a factory in the Urals. Unfortunately there was a power failure or a short circuit and, whether or not it was his fault, he had to leave. For a while he was a teacher at Kolkhoz, a collective farm, in Central Russia.

All the while he was petitioning the authorities for a visa for Frieda. But she could not believe that it was the Soviet authorities holding it up and thought my brother was prevaricating. When, after a year, he finally told her that the visa had come through, she no longer wanted to go to Russia, having convinced herself that this incomprehensible delay was his doing. It was a sad story. He was really fond of her and she seemed to have had a good influence on him.

Andryusha eventually returned to Moscow and, having accepted the fact that Frieda was not joining him, went to live with a Russian girl, a singer. It began well and they registered their marriage officially. But she was so very different from Frieda. She was not a Communist and interested in nothing except her singing. My brother complained that she was too 'bourgeois' and philistine. Cooped up in one room, with few common interests, they no longer got on, and he decided to divorce her. But first he had to get permission from the party branch, which was granted after lengthy and sorrowful discussions. To obtain the formal divorce after that was not difficult, but to separate physically was quite a different matter. The great housing shortage prevented him from finding a room, or even a corner with a bed. And for a while he continued to live in her room.

How it ended and what he did for his living we either did not know, or I do not remember. We did not hear from him much as correspondence between Soviet Russia and Germany was not advisable at the time, though we corresponded again after I left Germany for Prague.

How often have I thought of him with sorrow, and of the many other sincere and trusting communists, not only prominent activists or intellectuals, but simple men, some of them skilled workers, others unemployed, who felt they might be endangered if Hitler came to power and who, with the help of the International Workers Relief or the German Communist Party, gained visas for the USSR and then were never heard of again. Some may have survived, while others perished in the concentration and labour camps. But none of us could have foreseen developments in the USSR, and those terrible trials were then still years away.

The scene for the Moscow Trials was set in 1934 by the mysterious assassination of Kirov, the head of the party in the Leningrad district. The murder was officially ascribed to enemies of the state. In August 1936 the first trial began. Two others followed in January 1937 and March 1938, all of them involving a staggeringly large number of leading political figures and Red Army and Navy chiefs. The scope of these trials, and the charges of treason and plotting with the Left Opposition brought against the defendants, astounded all observers. But even more bewildering was the fact that all the accused, who were tried in public, pleaded guilty, and did their utmost to get themselves convicted, using the dock to extol the virtues of Stalin and the glories of the regime against which they had allegedly plotted. They included such old and active Bolsheviks as Zinoviev, Kamenev, Pyatakov, Radek, Bukharin, Rykov and many other participants in the October Revolution. Trotsky had already been expelled from the party and the country, but his name was repeatedly mentioned by the accused, as an agent of German and British imperialism as early as 1921 and 1926, as the instigator of the crimes of the accused, and so on. In spite of their 'repentance' most of the defendants were executed. (Some have recently been rehabilitated, including Bukharin, but not Trotsky.) The grim irony was that at least two of the prosecutors and executors were in time themselves accused, and one of them, Yagoda, one-time chief of the GPU, was executed.

Stalin used the trials as an excuse to eliminate the opposition, right and left alike, and to cover up for the malfunctioning of the economy and the inefficiency of the state bureaucracy. Under Gorbachev and his policy of *glasnost* some revealing books have been published about that period. **The Children of the Arbat**, which takes its name from a district in Moscow, was written some thirty years ago but has only recently been published.It has also been translated and published in English. It is the deeply depressing story of a student, an editor of a wall newspaper, who decided in the early 1930s not to publish an editorial in a particular issue, just for a change. This led to an investigation, imprisonment and exile to Siberia for three years.

Suspicion, fear and the desire to ingratiate oneself with the authorities gradually involved more and more people. This was how, during the years of the trials, millions of ordinary people went to the concentration camps, and nobody knows how many of them died there. Could my brother have been sent to one of those camps?

One day, in the early summer of 1935, I received an official letter from the German Ministry of the Interior, informing me that I had been deprived of my German citizenship. The letter said that I was now stateless and would require a labour permit, to be renewed periodically. No reason was given. I protested, for the record, and asked for an explanation, but of course received no reply. So I surmised that it could only have been because of my political connections. This assumption was in a way confirmed by the police and the Authority for Non-German Citizens: when I applied for my new papers they referred to my work with the International Workers Relief and DEROP.

Obviously I felt uneasy, especially as the labour permit could be withdrawn at any time and as a stateless person I had no protection. But for the moment that danger was more potential than real, except that being stateless made journeys abroad and re-entry into Germany more uncertain and troublesome.

Nevertheless, in December 1935 I decided to go to Paris to see Jan Bur. I received the exit and return visa without difficulty and set out via Cologne, where I visited his mother. She was rather concerned about us. I think she would have liked us to stay together. She also presented me with six handkerchiefs embroidered with my initials.

Then I was in Paris—the dream of my youth, and of so many Russians. The cry of Chekhov's **Three Sisters**: 'To Moscow! To Moscow', became among the Russian intelligentsia at the beginning of the 20th century a sigh: 'To Paris! To Paris!'.

Jan Bur met me at the station early in the morning and took me to the flat of a French comrade near the Porte des Lilas. He was living there while the comrade was away. It was in a newly built, modern house in a working-class district. There was one large room with a large triangular-shaped balcony, a tiny kitchen and a shower room. It was pleasantly furnished and had plenty of books. Jan Bur seemed pleased to see me but apologised for not being able to show me round, as on that particular day he had various appointments. That was all right by me, as I knew the language fairly well and was quite capable of going sightseeing on my own. What a day it was for me! I walked and walked, and looked, and absorbed the air, the atmosphere, the light on that fair December day and could not get enough of it. From my reading of Russian classics I was as familiar with Paris as I had been with Moscow: Place de la Concorde, the Tivoli, Place Vendôme, Madeleine, the Opéra, the Boulevards, Champs Elisées, the Tuileries, the Louvre... I knew them all. I had known their names since my childhood and now I was there myself! I was intoxicated.

Eventually I had to think of making my way back to Jan Bur. It was past five o'clock and he must have been wondering what had happened to me. I found the right bus stop and tried to get on the bus. In vain. Every time I made a dash for it I was pushed off the platform with a flood of incomprehensible words from the conductor. Occasionally the passengers chimed in as well. Eventually I noticed that everybody had a little slip of paper in their hands and saw they were tearing them off a machine fixed to the bus stop. That was the secret—the equivalent of a queue! So at last, equipped with my numbered slip, I managed to board the bus. By the time I arrived back Jan Bur had really got worried. He was amused by my enthusiasm.

The following days he took me round other parts of Paris: Montparnasse, Montmartre, Bastille, the Quartier Latin with the Boulevard St Michel—known to us as the *Boul'Mich*—and its numerous cafés. He also introduced me to some of the comrades and told me about their activities, an important part of which was the publication of the Bulletin of the Opposition.

I also met Hilde Robertson, the divorced Jewish wife of a German left-wing intellectual who had remained in Germany. He was quite wealthy and was able to support her and their two children. Hilde had bought a small farm outside Paris, but spent a great deal of time in Paris itself. Though not politically involved, she was extremely helpful to a number of refugees. She spoke French fluently and persuasively when necessary, accompanied refugees to the *Mairie* (the town hall) and the police when they needed an extension of their visas or work permits, knew how and when to put a banknote into their passports or applications, and helped when they were in difficulty with their landladies or *concièrges*. She had helped Jan Bur with his permit to stay.

I spent a week in Paris, and all too soon—and so very unwillingly—I had to take the train back home. My heart sank when I crossed the border and and saw those Nazi uniforms again. The two hours at Cologne, waiting for the train to Berlin, I spent in the famous Gothic cathedral, not sightseeing, but huddled up in a dark corner, crying my eyes out at having to return. When we approached Berlin I had exactly the same impression as I had had fifteen years earlier: a grey town, with large grey buildings that looked so oppressive.

CHAPTER 6

Escape

LIFE IN BERLIN continued to be monotonous and hazardous. I met the four or five comrades of my particular group clandestinely in a safe flat, saw non-committed but reliable friends to exchange information and opinions, or just to relax. A great deal of my free time I spent at my sister's house. Her daughter Nora was just about a year old and very lively and entertaining. I got on well with Arnold, but we no longer discussed politics. His political sympathies had not changed, though by then the German National Party no longer existed. So life was relatively untroubled until, one day in early March 1936, the axe fell.

I received a summons from the Gestapo headquarters, ordering me to appear in three days' time. I read the summons and my heart stopped. I could hardly breathe. It is difficult to describe my feelings. I was scared. Then I began to reason: if they wanted to arrest me, why did they not come, as usual, early in the morning and take me with them. So what do they want? It was strange that I had been summoned to appear at 6pm, after normal working hours. I had no answer to my questions and decided to use the time left to prepare for my possible arrest on the day of my visit. I contacted the Friedrichs. I straightened out everything in my room. I took some of my most precious and valuable books to Olya's in the evening after dark, and then settled down with Trotsky's **My Life**—in a German translation which I must have got either from Walter's stock of books in the cellar or from some other comrade. I was determined to finish it over the weekend, just in case.

Then, with enormous trepidation, I made my way to Prinz Albrecht Strasse and the Gestapo building, with its detention cells and torture basements. The huge building was almost deserted. I was taken by a janitor up a wide staircase, through long corridors, which eerily echoed our steps, into a large office room. A middle-aged man in civilian clothes asked me to sit down and began to leaf through a folder.

My heart was pounding, but I tried to look innocent and calm. Then he started talking: about my being deprived of my German citizenship, of the plans to deport me from Germany, the inconvenience of renewing my labour permit and the restrictions on travel. I replied in the manner of a well-brought-up young woman. Things were inconvenient, I said, but there was no sign of the authorities being willing to return my passport. That was not quite the case, he said. I could get back my German citizenship if I wanted to. Of course I wanted it back, I replied.

What else could I have answered without challenging him? He came to the point. He could promise me the return of my passport if I proved worthy of the Fatherland's trust and rendered it a suitable service. Now I was on my guard, but managed to answer calmly, asking what I, a mere woman, could do. If I were a man I could serve in the armed forces. Well, came the reply, there were other ways of showing gratitude and loyalty—wasn't I working with the Soviet Trade Delegation? I could help them there. They knew of course, all about the work of the delegation, but perhaps I could supplement their knowledge. Nothing special, just a few figures from time to time.

I was stunned but had to carry on. I could do that, I said, if that would help the German Fatherland. But what was there to report? I was only a small employee and had no access to any important material or information, and to the best of my knowledge there wasn't any more to know than that it was an organisation to promote trade between the two countries. That was *his* worry, he said. He would just ask me a few questions from time to time and my answers were all he wanted. I needn't come to the Prinz Albrecht Strasse again. I could meet him in a café, near the Potsdamer Platz, in a week or ten days' time. In the meantime, I wasn't to worry, and now I could go.

Not to worry! I walked out of the building as if in a daze, and walked back home through half Berlin to calm down and gather my thoughts. I knew it was the beginning of the end. My turn had come to leave Germany and join the ranks of political refugees. It was now only a question of when and how and where. It was possible I was under close observation by the Gestapo, and may have been for some time. I immediately had to sever all contact with my political friends, but beyond that I did not want to do anything drastic which would arouse the suspicion of the Gestapo.

I did, however, contact the Friedrichs, who were my best friends, told them the whole story and asked them to pass it on to my group. I continued to maintain some contact with them since, after his release from the Brandenburg prison, Walter Friedrich had had to stop being active and was therefore not endangered as the other comrades would have been. I told Olya that I would have to leave Germany, and in the evenings, under cover of darkness, I carried round to her all my remaining political and valued books and belongings, storing them in large cases in her cellar, unbeknown to Arnold. She was very brave and generous in that respect. During the war, when Arnold was an army doctor on the Russian front, and Olya and the children were evacuated to western Germany, only an old aunt of Arnold's remained in the flat with her daughter and most of the books were used as fuel for the oven in their room. Only a very few survived.

I continued to go to work as usual. I felt it was my duty to inform the administration of the Trade Delegation of the Gestapo's interest in their activities. Although I no longer approved of the Stalinist policy, at home and abroad, those 'degenerated' Communists were still closer to me than the Nazi fascists. Besides they were my employers and had not harmed me personally in any way, and all my German colleagues were socialists (Communist or otherwise); I felt a moral obligation towards them.

My immediate boss, Comrade Guriev, was in Moscow at the time, so I asked to see the head of the financial department, Comrade Stepanov. I was on good terms with him, and when I had to see him to sign some balance sheets or letters, he would ask questions about the situation in Germany. He was a mild man, with soft brown eyes and an attentive expression on his face. He was in his late forties and spent a great deal of time in Moscow. He obviously took me for a member of the German Communist Party and once or twice he had asked me out for a meal (as a high-ranking member of the staff, he could obviously risk such occasional connections). He was a good conversationalist, and quite a well read and interesting person. So when I decided that I had to tell somebody at the Trade Delegation I turned to him. I asked him to arrange for me to see the head of the Trade Delegation himself, normally a totally inaccessible person. The message came back that he was engaged and that I was to speak to Comrade Stepanov, who then sat and listened to my story with a real poker face. I told him I would have to leave Germany and asked if it would be possible for the Trade Delegation to give me a recommendation to their sister organisation in Paris. He would not commit himself and only said he would report the whole thing to the head of the organisation and would let me know.

A day or two before my visit to the Gestapo, Stepanov had

asked me whether I would like to accompany him to a West End cinema, to see the much praised film **Madame Bovary**. I had agreed, but now suggested that he might like to cancel our appointment. He protested and thought there was no reason for that at all. However, having waited in vain at the appointed place for more than half an hour, I rang the Trade Delegation—to be told that he was in conference and could not come to the phone. It was clear to me that after his talk with the head he had obviously got cold feet. I felt rather bitter about it. Not because of the missed film—and probably a meal at a restaurant—but because of the way it was done. He sort of apologised the following day but did not suggest another date. It was really rather pathetic.

The following day I was referred to the personnel manager, a tall and very serious chap whom I hardly knew. Once more I had to tell the whole story, including the precise questions the Gestapo man had put to me and the suggestions he had made. The personnel manager's response was that the conversation was quite harmless, there was nothing to the questions, and surely I could not leave the country anyway without a passport. Why not wait and see whether I might get it back? In other words, the Trade Delegation wanted to use me as a counter-spy. I was to report to the personnel manager after every meeting with the Gestapo. That was like walking on thin ice. I could not even be sure whether, in the circumstances, there might not have been a link somewhere between the Gestapo and the Trade Delegation itself—nothing was impossible at that time. But since nobody other than myself was endangered as yet, I wanted to choose my time for quitting, all the while watching my steps very carefully.

Yet the Russians were obviously alarmed. All sorts of measures were taken by the administration, the meaning of which I could only guess. The German employees no longer had access to the duty-free shop; in the canteen, the Russians avoided sitting at tables with the Germans. These measures were quite incomprehensible to the German staff. In fact they were rather indignant that with the Nazi pressure bearing down outside, the Russian Communists themselves should now turn away from their German colleagues. Any personal contacts, occasional and fleeting as they had always been, were stopped. And all the while the Russians were reducing the trade activity and cutting down both the Russian and German staff.

I met the man from the Gestapo twice more over a brief cup of coffee, and each time reported in detail to the personnel manager. The Gestapo were obviously proceeding cautiously: the questions were mostly about the organisation itself, for example the so-called Special Department. The existence of these in all Russian organisations was common knowledge to everybody who had close dealings with them. Only some of the specially accredited Russian employees had access to them. To my knowledge these departments dealt with highly confidential matters about the business dealings of the respective organisation. (Only years later did we realise that they were also staffed by KGB men, or by genuine members of the staff who were trusted by the KGB.) So in all honesty I could assure the Gestapo representative that there was nothing special about those departments.

I think I was also asked whether there was a branch of the German Communist Party at the delegation, of which, officially, I did not know anything. I was also shown photographs of some Germans and asked whether I knew them. I replied that I had heard their names mentioned but that they were no longer working there. (I don't know whether I was still being tested as to my reliability and willingness to collaborate, but as all new employees had for a long time been agreed with the Nazi authorities, I thought that the dismissals would also have been known to them even better than to me.) He was satisfied with my answers, but for me it was the sign! In future I would no doubt be asked to report on the existing German staff. The time had come to quit.

I put this to the personnel manager, who tried hard to remonstrate with me—how could I leave without a passport, an exit visa, or any valid documents? Why was I in such a hurry? He was sure that in time they could find me some work in Paris. But hundreds if not thousands of Germans had left the country over the previous three years without exit visas, and I would do the same. All I wanted from him was a recommendation for the sister organisation in Paris and my last salary paid in a foreign currency, not in German marks. This was illegal, but I thought they might do that much for me. But, no fear, I did not get either the recommendation or the foreign currency, just a month's salary in lieu of notice. Officially I was pronounced redundant, much to the surprise of my German colleagues, who expected me to be one of the last to have to go on the strength of my knowledge of the Russian language and shorthand.

On my last day at work, I asked Bruno, whom I had always taken to be the Communist Party representative, to walk me home. On the way, in the street, where we could not be overheard by anybody, I told him the whole story about the Gestapo's interest in the Trade Delegation and the German staff. I thought that was the least I could do for my German colleagues: to warn them about any possible danger from the Nazi authorities, and also explain to them the changed behaviour of the Russians. They could expect no help from that quarter. Bruno was speechless; he was grateful and wished me good luck.

The Trade Delegation's refusal to pay my salary in foreign currency was in a way understandable. It was illegal, at any rate, for private individuals to possess any foreign currency. And it was also illegal to take any quantity of German marks out of the country without permission. One of my friends nevertheless managed to change a hundred marks into assorted foreign currencies for me. And Liesel Friedrich, who was working for a small firm of gold and silversmiths, still run by two Jewish brothers, managed to persuade them to separate the handle from the blade of one of my silver-plated table knives, stuff the rolled up bank notes into the empty handle, and solder the two parts together again. It was impossible to detect anything by looking at or using the knife. And no suspicion would be aroused by my carrying it on the 'trip' that I had planned. As a parting gift Liesel also gave me a silver clip, much in fashion at that time, which I still wear occasionally.

There was well-intentioned help from another source. My colleague who used to meet her husband somewhere near the Czech-German border had once asked me whether I knew anybody in Prague. She gave me an address in case I ever found myself there. I memorised the address and then she tore the slip of paper in half, giving me one piece and keeping the other. It was a method of identification that was often used in those days: when the two parts were put together. I was grateful, because I did not know a soul in Prague. But this address was to lead me into great trouble.

I made my last preparations at home and fixed a date for my departure: Saturday 6 April 1936, a suitable day for a ski-ing weekend.

On Thursday night I said goodbye to the Friedrichs. Liesel was in bed complaining about stomach cramps, which seemed to be getting worse. Walter rang the hospital from the nearest telephone booth and was told to rush her to hospital. We hurriedly said goodbye and went our separate ways. Their daughter Vera was born during the night, named after the Russian revolutionary Vera Zasulich. A year or so later they too escaped to Prague. They eventually settled in Sweden, where they gradually succumbed to the lure of Swedish Social Democracy.

Having been lucky with all my preparations so far I did not

want to risk failure on the last night. I packed my rucksack with a few necessities—a spare dress, a jumper, some underwear—and having got my ski-ing gear ready, I left the flat as if I was going to my sister's for the evening, without saying anything to my young lodgers. They would have to face the music after my departure, as I told Olya not to go to the flat any more, and they did not know her address. Olya took me by car to the home of my old friend Lore, from our days at the eurhythmic school. There I spent the last night. Arnold by then knew that I was leaving Germany, though we had not told him the whole story. He was sympathetic and did not stop Olya from accompanying me. It was a long journey, all through the town to the West End, and I kept looking back to see whether we were being followed. So we spent the last evening together, Olya and me, Lore and Gertrud, the painter friend with whom she shared the studio.

Early next morning I set off for the railway station, where I met Elfriede and Hans Kaufmann, who knew about my impending departure and had decided to join me. Elfriede's husband, Julius Hollos, was already in Prague and though they were not yet in danger they thought it was time to leave while the going was good and they had me as a guide. They had got themselves some ski-ing equipment—though I don't think they could actually ski. We arrived safely at the farmer's house where I had previously been with Jan Bur and the Langes, and they welcomed us in their friendly way as always. I told them that 'Walter' would join us for the Easter holidays, but that we now had longer holidays and had therefore come earlier. I don't know whether they believed us or what they thought. It was already rather late in the year and the snow conditions not really suitable for proper ski-ing. So we told them we might go higher up the mountains.

They in turn told us, unasked, of the various changes that had taken place in the area. Their house was only a couple of hundred yards from the shallow river that formed the border between Germany and Czechoslovakia and which one had previously been able to cross unhindered. Now they told us there was barbed wire all along the banks and a constant guard on the bridge. We feigned indifference, but realised that we had a problem. Not only would there be the barbed wire, but in winter the river would have been frozen and one could ski over it. Now we would have to wade through it or balance across over the large stones. There was nothing for it. We simply had to get across. So for the next few days we went out for walks or short ski-ing trips, exploring. Then one morning, leaving behind everything we could spare, plus some money for the farmer, we took the plunge—and managed, without mishap of any kind, to scale the barbed wire, cross the shallow river and make our way up the mountain—on the Czech side!

The relief was indescribable. Sixteen years earlier I had entered Germany reluctantly and in great sorrow, with my family, as refugees from hunger and disease. I was now leaving it with relief and only limited regret, again as a refugee, this time from Nazi oppression and persecution.

The danger was not quite over. We stopped at an inn on the Czech side of the mountain, had some hot soup and made enquiries about trains to Prague. There we were advised not to go to the nearest railway station, but to make our way further down the valley and on to the next one. There was every chance that if the border police found us so close to the border without adequate papers they would dispatch us back to Germany without further ado. This was the Sudetenland, which had never been fully assimilated into the new Czechoslovak state created after the First World War. The predominantly German population hankered after re-unification with Germany, or at least self-rule, and so was to a large extent pro-Hitler. The Czechs in that area, on the other hand, were understandably suspicious of strangers and especially Germans, as they feared Nazi infiltrators.

So we hurried on as quickly as we could. When we reached the station we parted company. Elfriede and Hans were making straight for Prague, while I was going to stop over in Reichenberg, a small town not far from the frontier. I wanted to meet Julik and Käthe Kozlecki, a young Trotskyist couple who were the all-important link between the German groups and the Trotskyists abroad—they distributed the illegal literature and maintained contact with the couriers from Germany. They knew me well, and Jan Bur too, from our clandestine correspondence.

They were very hospitable. I think they received some financial help from the Trotskyist organisation, and perhaps occasionally from the German-Czech group, which enabled them to live extremely frugally in two attic rooms, devoting all their time and energy to the movement and to political study. Käthe was a devoted wife and pupil—Julik's words were gospel to her. He once remarked with slight irritation that she slavishly repeated whatever he said, without ever thinking and reasoning for herself.

For me the fortnight with them was very restful and relaxing. I read a lot, discussed a lot, went for walks in the countryside, and generally recovered from the oppressive atmosphere in Germany and the stress of the past few weeks. I also met the local German-Czech Trotskyist group—whose members were Germans living in the Sudetenland area of Czechoslovakia—although I do not recollect much about them. Then it was time to make my way to Prague, to learn to live the hazardous life of a refugee.

Käthe and Julik managed to escape when Hitler marched into Czechoslovakia in 1938. I think it was then that they split up: Julik went to Mexico, where he started a carpentry business, and Käthe somehow found her way to England, where she slavishly continued to argue the orthodox Trotskyist line.

I hardly remember my arrival in Prague. I had arrived with nothing more than my rucksack, my last salary, part of which was in foreign currency, and that half scrap of paper with an address in Prague—those 'friends' of my colleague Fanny, who 'would be able to help me'. I had never asked who they were or how they might help me—one did not ask too many questions in Germany—but was glad to have this contact. I also had Elfriede's address and one for Berta, an old non-political friend from my days at the eurhythmics school. She was Jewish and had left Germany because of the growing anti-semitism.

I called on Berta first. Together with her friend Lipschitz, also a Jewish emigré from Germany, she lived in a very pleasant studio flat and put me up without any fuss until I could find my feet again. They were a funny couple, Berta shorter than me and Lipschitz exceptionally tall. He forever had a pot of coffee simmering, and their friends made it their habit, much to Berta's annoyance, to call at any time, not so much to see them as to drink a cup of good coffee. Berta had a pleasant voice and played the accordion, and occasionally worked in a club singing folk songs. She had to practise, which was difficult with people milling around. So before long I decided to look for a room of my own.

I went to see Fanny's friends. I found the house, in a street just off the Vaclavski Namesti, a large square right in the centre of Prague. I began to wonder: it did not look like a residential house. Nevertheless I climbed up the stairs higher and higher until I had reached the top floor. I was shown in and, when I showed my scrap of paper, was greeted with exclamations of surprise and relief. I had stepped right into a hornets' nest: this was the Association for the Support of German Emigrés, the refugee committee of the German Communist Party!

I was flabbergasted. Having broken with the party in Germany, I was not anxious to have anything to do with it in Prague. But there I was, and there was no retreating. Information about my intended escape had reached them from Germany three weeks before—which showed their efficiency in such matters—and they had given me a week to reach Prague. They were about to make discreet enquiries through their frontier contacts to find out if I had been arrested. They were relieved that I was safe and sound, but greatly agitated, and kept asking me where I had spent the past fortnight. I could not tell them I had been staying with my Trotskyist contacts, so I simply explained that I had personal friends in Reichenberg, whom I had visited on my way to Prague. They seemed to accept my explanation and recognised me as a *bona fide* refugee from Nazi Germany. They also told me that without recognition by one of the various refugee committees (there was one run by the Social Democrats, another called the Democratic Committee for Non-aligned Refugees, and probably also a Jewish one), the Czech police were not inclined to grant political asylum. They were too nervous about Nazi infiltration.

There was also the matter of financial support, of which I was unaware. When it was offered, I could not refuse without rousing suspicion. The Communist committee at that time paid a small amount each week, not enough to live on, but better than nothing for many. Some refugees lived together to save on the rent, most did occasional menial work. The non-socialist intellectuals seemed on the whole to be better off than the Communists and the small group of Trotskyists. So I collected my allowance, and for a few months that was my only contact with the committee and the Communist Party. I don't remember whether I was assigned to a branch—at any rate I never went to a meeting. For the time being all seemed well, and I set out to organise my life.

First of all I found a furnished room, which seemed most romantic: it was in the attractive old part of Prague, parallel to the Waldstynska—with its famous palace and other beautiful old houses and gardens. What attracted me to my room was that it was in a timber house built around a small courtyard with a gallery running round its four sides. Swallows nested under the roof and flitted here and there. I was captivated by the atmosphere. It was also cheap, but it had drawbacks: one was the big gate which was locked at ten every evening. After that I had to knock up the grumpy old caretaker.

The other drawback was that to reach my room I had to pass through the kitchen, where another lodger slept, and through the landlady's room. She, too, was mostly grumpy. She was getting on, probably not in very good health, certainly not well off, and rather lonely, but on the whole her bark was worse than her bite and she never bothered about me. She told me once that she used to live with a very dear friend who had died some years before, an ardent Social Democrat and the first woman deputy in the new Czech parliament, established after the collapse of the Austro-Hungarian empire in 1918—when it had been split up into its constituent parts, including Hungary and Czechoslovakia. I managed to learn some Czech while there, because the landlady's radio was usually on at full blast, which was useful if at times disturbing.

I felt quite happy in that room. I had a small methylated spirit burner, and Berta had given me a tiny saucepan, sufficient to boil water for tea, or an egg. I had a couple of plates and cups, knives and forks, probably sent to me by my sister, and some clothes. The house was only five minutes' walk from the Vltava, the river that flows through Prague. This is crossed by some beautiful bridges, including a suspension bridge identical to the Chelsea Bridge in London and built by the same architect. There was the famous Karlov Most (Charles Bridge) erected in the mid-14th century, with its baroque statues, and the tall tower with its big gates which led to the old part of Prague. Here the Hradcin, a former castle and now the seat of government, towered over the city on a high hill.

In the evening the lights from the lamps on the bridges and along the embankments were reflected in the water and in a light breeze sparkled like champagne in a glass. In daytime the river was pretty dirty, and I always marvelled how people could bathe in it in the summer. Then, when it got unbearably hot, I too took the plunge and swam every morning from one bridge to the other and back, having a good wash when I got back to my room (there was no running water, only a washstand with a bowl and a jug, and a cold water tap in the kitchen) before sitting down to my breakfast.

In Prague I read a great deal, and studied political literature. And I spent a good deal of time meeting friends. We met mostly at Julich's, a huge café on two or three floors at the upper end of Vaclavski Namesti. There I learned to drink small cups of black coffee, the *mala cava*, the cheapest one could get, which were served with a glass of water. We sat there for hours, discussing, arguing and reading the newspapers supplied by the café and fixed to a pole so that the pages would not become disarranged. We were not the only ones to occupy those tables. Impecunious Czech and German journalists and Czech students also made use of the facilities, the students writing their theses and rehearsing each other. Only at lunchtime did the waiters ask them to move on to make room for more affluent clients. It was quite usual to make use of a café for more than a rest and some refreshment. Later I gave French conversation lessons to a businessman studying French, and we used to meet in a park when it was fine or in a café when it was cold or wet.

Occasionally I went to the Koruna, a small café also on the Vaclavski Namesti, for a cheap, self-service stand-up lunch of a bowl of thick soup, or a dish of *knedliki a zeli*—sauerkraut and dumplings. Cheap as these meals were, there were always people, Czechs, who could not afford even that expense. If somebody left a bowl or plate unfinished, there was always someone who would immediately finish it off before the plates were cleared away. I found this distressing, and so at variance with the official propaganda of Czechoslovakia as a modern, successful democratic country. From my occasional conversations in shops I gathered that there was quite a disparity between wages and the cost of living. Only the relatively new Czech bourgeoisie did not seem to do too badly. There were other features that did not go with the notion of democracy, so boasted of at that time. Letters for abroad, at any rate to Germany, had to be handed in at the Post Office unsealed. But of course, compared with Germany it was almost paradise for us.

Almost, but not quite. We were not allowed to take up any work without a labour permit, and we could not get that without a knowledge of the language, and the necessary skills or training. So most refugees lived rather precariously.

I was better off than many. Even when my foreign currency ran out, I regularly received ten Deutschmarks each month from Olya, the maximum she was allowed to send out of Germany without special permission. It wasn't much, but for a refugee and for Czechoslovakia it was a sizeable sum. And besides, I did not have to pay rent for my next room. I had had to move out of the room with the swallows flying around the courtyard and the Czech radio blaring. Some time towards the end of the summer, my friend Lore had come to visit me. My landlady was kind enough to let Lore share the room—and the large bed—with me. To her horror, Lore discovered that the bed, and no doubt the whole room, was full of bugs! Out of friendship she braved this plague and lasted out through her holidays. But although the bugs had never taken the slightest notice of me, the very knowledge of them sharing my bed made my further stay in that room impossible.

I soon found a room in a respectable residential area, not far from the city centre, in exchange for German and French conversation lessons with a sister and brother. They had grown up in the Sudetenland but after their parents had died they were cared for by relatives in Prague and had forgotten both German and their school French. He was a bookkeeper or accountant and Sonia worked in a government ministry, but she was also a pianist and I much enjoyed her playing. Unfortunately they always kept their rooms locked so I never got a chance to play the piano myself. They were both very pleasant, only he was usually so tired in the evening that he often excused himself from our lessons, which made me feel rather awkward, not 'paying' my full share of the bargain. Sonia was apparently also a very good cook, to judge by the occasional tantalising aromas emanating from the kitchen. But apart from the conversation lessons, we had little personal contact.

A free room and money from Olya and the committee were still not enough for me to live on even remotely comfortably. So I scanned the advertising pages of the ***Prager Mittag***, a German-language newspaper. There were columns and columns of classified advertisements and I was sure to find something. But some ads turned out not to be what they seemed. One sounded very attractive: for a masseuse and assistant for physiotherapy treatment. I sent an application with the requested photograph and discovered that it was some sort of bath establishment, which even to me, with all my ignorance, sounded somewhat suspicious. It was, moreover, in the Sudetenland, where I would not have gone for any job. But I could not get rid of that advertiser, who kept pestering me to accept. Afterwards I was told by more astute friends that all such advertisements—for French lessons, massage and the like—were dubious.

Then I was offered a summer job as a kind of governess or companion to some children, staying up in the High Tatra, a most beautiful mountainous part of Czechoslovakia. I was very tempted, but in the end could not tear myself away from the circle of fellow refugees in Prague, and from our political discussions. Eventually I did find a congenial job as companion for a 15-year-old girl, daughter of a wealthy Czech widow who, after her husband's death, was running their garage and petrol station. They lived in a large house with a large garden in the northern suburbs of Prague, had a housekeeper, and a tutor for her younger son every afternoon. But there was nobody to look after the children after school.

My duties were simple: I had to keep Blanka company while she was doing her homework, accompany her to the hairdresser and dressmaker in town, and above all practise German and French conversation with her. Sometimes, work over, we all had a game of ball in the garden, or Blanka and I would read a German or French book for pleasure. In the afternoon we had tea together with a young aunt of theirs, who spoke only Czech, so that I felt rather out of place. But they were all very pleasant.

Blanka seemed to like me and talking with her was sometimes very interesting. Once she was in a dilemma: the Catholic church considered Jan Hus to have been a heretic and burnt him at the stake, whereas in Czech history he is a national hero. Who should one believe? I knew the family were strict Catholics and very patriotic (as the Czech bourgeoisie was after they had gained independence). I could not upset her feelings one way or the other and was not familiar enough with that particular religious dispute—which took place the end of the 14th century. So I carefully tried to explain to her the conflict between different interests within a state or a nation, and said that one day she would have to find the answer to this and similar contradictions herself. I often wondered what happened to her and her family when Hitler invaded Czechoslovakia.

I also gave lessons to the young businessman, who admired my good knowledge of French. Little did he know that I kept one step ahead of him, carefully preparing my vocabulary on each day's topic from a useful little book.

With all this I could afford a *mala cava* at Julich's or a simple meal at the Koruna. Most important of all, I could afford an occasional concert, of which there were so many in Prague. I was especially drawn to the concerts of 17th and 18th century music given in one of the palatial renaissance buildings in the Old Town. It was always fascinating and somewhat eerie to come out of that beautiful palace, with the sound of music still in my ears, into the dark, narrow, old streets, passing the dark houses with their huge doorways and courtyards, with hardly a light glimmering in the windows. Any minute one expected to see a mysterious figure in black coat and wide-brimmed, high hat furtively crossing the cobbled street.

Never having been to any medieval town in Germany, I was simply fascinated by Prague. Walking back to my room along the wide, well-lit and tree-lined Fochova, it was a delight to watch the play of light and shade in the foliage of the trees. Only once before had I felt such a delight—when I walked in the Tiergarten with Vladimir. But then I was in love. Now it was the sheer relief of no longer living in the oppressive atmosphere of Hitler's

Germany and of having escaped from the clutches of the Gestapo.

The mornings, too, were very pleasant. I now lived quite near a beautiful park overlooking the lower part of Prague. On sunny mornings I used to go there to have my breakfast in a milk bar: sour milk (similar to yoghurt) and a white roll. Then I would sit in the park, reading or writing, and watching. Back in my room, I would cook myself some simple lunch in that tiny saucepan. Then I would go to Julich's to meet some of my friends. There were some interesting people among them, some of whom had been Communists or fellow travellers in Germany, mainly Berlin, and who had worked for the left-wing theatres, such as the Piscator.

My Trotskyist comrades from Berlin and those that I met in Prague were not the types to sit around in cafés. They usually came round to me, as I seem to have had the most convenient room, probably the largest and with no landlady in during the day. We used to read the Left Opposition material and try to write for it too. There was Heinrich, lower middle-class, with no training or qualifications, but a very successful street trader in Berlin. He had been an active member of the German Communist Party and of the Berlin Trotskyist group. He tried hard to write and study but had no training or self-discipline: his room was either too large, or too small; too quiet or too noisy. He eventually lived in London, where he had a small business making electrical equipment. There was also Gerhard from Saxony, quite intelligent but extremely tense, with a sort of crabbed and fanatical expression on his face. He had a very pleasant young wife, Edith, who, though not political herself, devotedly followed him when he had to leave Germany and worked in Prague as a cleaning lady to supplement their meagre subsidy from one of the committees. Gerhard took a fancy to me, though he was some fourteen years younger. He was probably attracted by my interest in politics and tried hard to persuade me to go with him to one of the South American countries. It was really quite pathetic. Edith eventually accepted a job in domestic service in England, near London, hoping he would be able to join her there. Instead she joined him in Belgium, where he somehow or other found refuge and where they survived the war and Nazi occupation. Edith apparently died early, and he occasionally came to London, on business, I was told. But I never heard from him again.

In the spring of 1937 my old friends Liesel and Walter Friedrich left Berlin. Though not particularly active since his release from jail, it nevertheless became too risky for them to remain in Germany. They arrived in Prague with their one-year-old daughter Vera and no means of subsistence. But like other wives, Liesel found some work or other, and they too survived. It was easier for women then for men to find some menial work, though some of the men did find odd jobs to do, such as decorating or moving furniture.

Elfriede, Julius Hollos and Hans Kaufman were on the fringes now. Julius had never joined the Left Opposition while Elfriede and Hans did. In Berlin both were active to a certain degree and were never afraid to take risks; in Prague, all three of them were more of the café set, where they would spend hours on end. Nor did they have the same financial worries as most of our crowd. Julius worked for a German newspaper in Prague, and Hans wrote occasional articles and possibly got money from his father.

Elfriede and Julius managed to escape to London just before the war broke out and Hans eventually left for Hungary, where, as a blond-haired Jew, he survived the German occupation and the war playing in a jazz band in a café. He returned to Germany after the war and then became the first German correspondent in London, on a temporary assignment. He often came to see me. He had this phrase: 'I don't know whether I have betrayed the revolution, or the revolution has betrayed me'. Disillusioned and jilted by a singer he was in love with back in Germany, he literally drank himself to death at an early age.

Julius Hollos, after the war, was appointed by the Allies to run ***Die Welt*** under their supervision, the first post-war German newspaper to be published. Later he worked for the reactionary Spitzer newspaper group, mainly in Israel, and he became rather reactionary and extremely anti-Soviet.

For a while our small circle in Prague was enlivened by the arrival of Georg, a young student from Vienna, tall, lanky, intelligent, and an enthusiastic revolutionary. Later, when I was already in London, he entrusted to me his sister Rose, who had been sent to England by their parents. They were to perish in the gas chambers. Rose was only seventeen when she arrived in London, shortly before the war, very determined and courageous. She began by getting herself a job with an English family; later she worked part-time for a small firm, surviving on very little, and at the same time studying for her A-level examinations and after that for a degree in economics. Eventually she got some research work, and married a fellow student from a Quaker family, who was sent to Berlin after the war with a relief committee. He eventually became a professor and head of German studies at an English university. Now they are grandparents and active supporters of the Campaign for Nuclear Disarmament.

Georg did not stay long in Prague. He returned to Vienna at the end of 1936, was arrested and condemned to two years in prison. He was released in 1938 under a general political amnesty, and visited Prague once more, unaware of the signing of the Munich Pact in September that same year. Under this agreement between Hitler, Neville Chamberlain, the British prime minister, Mussolini, the Italian fascist dictator, and the prime minister of France, the Sudetenland was annexed by Germany. No one was there to represent Czechoslovakia—of which the Sudetenland was of course part. Back in England, Chamberlain declared triumphantly that this agreement was a victory for 'peace in our time'. Hitler's troops marched in to occupy the rest of Czechoslovakia just six months later, in March 1939, and the Second World War started when they marched into Poland the following September. Georg managed to catch the last non-stop plane from Prague to Strasbourg and from there to Paris. He eventually became a writer and political journalist, dividing his time between France and Austria. And he is still a socialist.

By and large, our small group in Prague was stewing in its own juice, with nothing very useful to do politically. We concentrated on discussing important events and political developments, such as the effect of the new policy adopted by the Comintern in the summer of 1935, when the United Front of Social Democrats and Communists gave way to the Popular Front—an attempt to stem the advance of fascism in Europe by an alliance with whatever bourgeois forces could be brought together. This policy was accepted by the Communist parties without a murmur, most seeing it as an extension of the united front policy and a means to gain 'fellow travellers' (people sympathetic to Communist policy in general). Trotsky argued that the popular front policy would render the working class powerless, and would drive the middle classes into the arms of fascism.

In the summer of 1936 it was the outbreak of the Spanish Civil War that stirred us, when the extreme right-wing General Franco led a military revolt against the Spanish Popular Front government. The civil war found an immediate response on the left in England and France and other countries, seen particularly in the formation of the International Brigade, which fought heroically side by side with Spanish anarchists, communists and the POUM—*Partido Obrero da Unificacion Marxista*. For the Hitler government, which supported Franco, the Spanish Civil War was a rehearsal for the Second World War, whilst the Soviet government, through the Comintern, fought against not only Franco, but also persecuted any non-Stalinist communists and Marxists, such as the POUM and their supporters.

Occasionally we had official meetings with Johre and Fischer, two loyal Trotskyist stalwarts of an older generation with whom we had fierce arguments and factional discussions about very little. I am hard pressed to remember what it was all about. Partly, I think, they resented the presence of younger comrades who had minds of their own and who tried to work out new ways to put across the Trotskyist point of view. They were rather rigid and intolerant. There was also old Gryllewicz. But we saw little of him. We resented the fact that although we were the latest refugees from Germany, we had no contact whatever with either the German-Czech Trotskyist group or the Czech group. We were not sure why—though I had an inkling.

I was put in touch with Jan Frankel, leader of the Trotskyist groups in Czechoslovakia, either through the German-Czech group in Reichenberg or by Georg from Austria. Jan introduced me to one or two members of the German-Czech group in Prague. Our separation from them was supposed to be a security measure, and I was not even allowed to mention my brief contact with them to my own group. Socially they were quite different from the majority of our crowd: middle-class professionals and intellectuals, some with business connections, and all apparently quite well off. They were largely responsible for financially supporting the movement and probably Trotsky himself, together with his entourage. That was more or less the explanation for our exclusion, according to Jan Frankel. There were, I believe, six or seven of them, very devoted to Trotsky himself. I was introduced to a few of them, including a woman to whom I gave Russian lessons. She passed on to me a couple of her rather smart and expensive dresses, one of which I continued to wear in England until I was able to buy my own. She was a very pleasant person, but that was about all the contact I had with her or with the group.

With Jan Frankel my contact was different. He was German-Czech by birth, about my age, with short dark hair, well groomed, well dressed, well read, fond of music, witty and amusing—when not plagued by his stomach ulcer. He spoke several languages, including Turkish, and worked part-time for the Turkish Embassy (or Consulate) in Prague. The irony was that Jan Frankel, alias Vérny (the word means loyal or true in both Czech and Russian) had been Trotsky's secretary on the island of Prinkipo and had left Turkey in 1933 when Trotsky obtained a visa for France. The

Embassy in Prague had no knowledge of his previous activity and he was obviously anxious that they should never find out. So he was highly conspiratorial, hiding behind his very respectable bourgeois appearance (which probably suited him anyway). He was totally devoted to Trotsky and the movement. When Hitler occupied Czechoslovakia he left for the USA, as he was in considerable danger. I heard years later that in the States he dropped out of politics, married a wealthy American and went into business, after which all traces of him were lost.

He and I established a very friendly relationship, more personal than political, though based on our common beliefs. He soon confessed to me that he had just emerged, rather battered, from a lengthy and passionate relationship with a married woman, who had decided that she could not after all leave her husband, her child, and her bourgeois way of life. In the circumstances, he said, he could not offer me more than comradeship. I had no inclination to lay any claim on him, but appreciated his company when we were free to meet.

Perhaps because of that void in his personal life he took an interest in me and was a most stimulating guide in our wanderings through the old part of Prague. We would walk up the long steps to the Hradcin and watch the sun set, or stroll in the dark and mysterious streets below on a moonlit night. We walked through the Zlata Ulicka—it means little golden street—where the medieval alchemists had lived and worked in tiny houses built into the wall of the Hradcin hill, trying to convert base metals into gold. He pointed out the splendid baroque churches and the magnificent renaissance palaces. Occasionally we went to a concert, and I particularly remember Mahler's long eighth symphony, to which we listened standing in the gallery.

Of course we also discussed politics and at some stage or other he asked me whether I would be willing to join Trotsky and his entourage in Norway, as my knowledge of Russian and Russian shorthand would be useful. I was staggered and flattered by such a tempting suggestion. On the other hand I would be sorry to leave Prague and all my old and new friends. Jan also warned me of the difficulties of working for Trotsky. He apparently showed little consideration for the personal needs and interests of his co-workers, being no doubt totally engrossed in politics and the difficulties of his own personal life. He was even, so I was told, unwilling to share his bathroom with his staff, which I found rather shocking for a communist. Today, alas, I have more sympathy for such an attitude. However, it was a preliminary enquiry and not yet an offer, and I did not have to make up my mind straight away. And then 'fate' intervened once more.

Since arriving in Prague I had not maintained any contact with the refugee committee, nor attended Communist Party meetings. True, I still received their weekly subsidy, but to renounce that, which I would have been quite willing to do, would have involved explanations and complications in registering with another committee. But it was inevitable that sooner or later somebody who had known me in Berlin would see me in the street or at Julich's in the company of Trotskyists. And so it was. I was stopped in the street by someone who had known me years before, in Berlin—who did not know me well enough even to get my name right. He bluntly asked me why I never came to meetings. I said I had very little time. But he must have set the ball rolling, until in the end my world fell apart.

In December 1936 I had to ask the committee for its signature on a form, which I wanted to submit to an organisation for German refugees with teachers' qualifications. Their signature was needed to testify that I had been recognised as an anti-fascist refugee and was being supported by them. The signature was refused. When I objected, the secretary of the committee told me that they no longer recognised me as a refugee and would no longer pay the subsidy. Asked for reasons, he was evasive: being forced by the Gestapo to do intelligence work was no reason to emigrate; I could have refused this kind of work. He referred me to somebody else. Now I was told that I was supporting 'somebody or something that had to do with the class enemy'; that I had supplied the Gestapo with information to enable them to draw up a plan for a raid on the Trade Delegation, which made me an agent of the Gestapo; and two other weird accusations: that I had contacts with 'some East Asians' and something to do with my 'private affairs'. (I am writing the whole sordid story not from memory but from copies of letters and statements, and the originals of the relevant newspapers, with the names of the people involved, still in my possession.)

I demanded that the secretary either withdraw these accusations and insinuations, or immediately set up an enquiry and produce irrefutable evidence. His reply was that although they could not at that moment give chapter and verse, names and facts, they would be able to produce evidence and photographs. When I insisted that I rejected their accusations and would take appropriate steps, I was openly threatened; 'You do that and we will do the same. But don't say afterwards that we have denounced you'.

And a final threat: 'We shall also testify to your activities here'.

I needed protection and clarification. So I wrote a lengthy letter in mid-December to the head of the Democratic Committee, which looked after all non-Communist refugees, giving him all the details about who I was, where I had come from, where I had worked since before Hitler came to power and afterwards, the Gestapo threats, my emigration and registration with the Communist refugee committee and their accusations, for which they had struck me off their register. I asked for protection and explained I was turning to the Democratic Committee because I had left Germany not because of illegal work for a party, but solely because of my anti-fascist convictions and because I would not have spied for the Gestapo anywhere.

Before the Democratic Committee had time to investigate my case, an article appeared in the national newspaper ***Lidové Noviny***, which in Czechoslovakia was comparable to **The Times** in London, under the heading 'Fierce Fight Between Stalinists and Trotskyists—Suspicious Connections of Trotskyists and Nazis'. Part of the column was devoted to me, although only my initials were used. This was 16 January 1937. Two days later, on 18 January, the German language ***Prager Montagsblatt*** (The Prague Monday Paper) took up the story, remarking that the initials M.W. were easily recognisable to those who knew me, and that so far none of the accused had been arrested. The article expressed surprise that a newspaper claimed to know more than the police. Referring to the Zinoviev-Kamenev trial in Moscow in August 1936, the reporter remarked on the speed, in the struggle of the Stalinists against the Trotskyists, with which a friend of yesterday can become a Nazi-informer today.

On 19 January the Communist paper ***Rote Fahne*** replied, denouncing the ***Prager Montagsblatt*** and threatening that the support of 'bourgeois and certain social-democratic Soviet enemies will not stop the unmasking of the Trotskyists before the Courts of the Soviet Union'.

I was told of the article in ***Lidové Noviny*** by Julius Hollos. I was horrified. He advised me to get in touch immediately with the chief editor of the paper, Dr Hubert Ripka. I explained the matter to him briefly over the telephone and asked for an interview. After I had put my case he was quite taken aback. If my story was true, he had been made an easy prey of unscrupulous people, which could affect his reputation, apart from the harm done to an innocent victim. He immediately suggested a commission of enquiry, with the participation of a representative of the Communist Party committee. They refused to take part. In the meantime, on 26 January, he published a withdrawal of the accusations against me, now giving my full name, and against August Henning, a Trotskyist who had also been mentioned but whom I did not know. On the 27 January **Rote Fahne**, in its second edition, also published my denial of their accusations. To this they added a statement that they were publishing my declaration in order not to deprive me of the chance to clear myself of the 'dreadful suspicion... But we still have to await the outcome of further investigations before we can truly accept her refutation'.

After further submissions and explanations about my interviews with the Gestapo official, the Democratic Committee finally informed me, on 2 February 1937, that after lengthy discussions with the secretary of the Communist committee and four interviews with me, they were prepared to recognise me as a *bona fide* anti-fascist refugee, though they were not in a position to grant me a subsidy.

On 20 February **Lidové Noviny** returned to the subject in a long column, no doubt written by Dr Ripka himself, which once more gave details of my 'contacts' with the Gestapo, my declarations to the investigating commission, and the false accusations on the part of the German Communist Party. He finished his article with a general observation about the Communists and Trotskyists, saying that the dispute between the Prague German refugees was only a small-scale reflection of the tragic conflict of these two tendencies on a world scale.

A few days later, on 24 February, the lawyer appointed by the commission of enquiry requested **Rote Fahne** to withdraw their accusations against me or it would go to court. **Rote Fahne** finally, and rather grudgingly, published a statement on 21 March, referring to the withdrawal of the accusations by the **Lidové Noviny** and adding that their own statement that I was sent to Prague by the Gestapo was based on a 'misunderstanding' and that they 'therefore withdraw the offensive assertions of the article as far as Margarete Watsova was concerned'.

But the damage was done. There is no doubt, I am sure, that the accusations were repeated by other German Communist publications over which I had no control. And these were no doubt read by German refugees from Nazism who were then languishing in Moscow or the concentration camps. As far as I was concerned the matter seemed to be over. But I was mistaken. In fact the Communist press continued to accuse me of associating with the Gestapo. In 1977 Pierre Broué, editor of **Léon Trotsky:**

Oeuvres, the French collection of Leon Trotsky's writings, sent me a hand-written copy of a report in a Czechoslovak police file, which had been based on a further article in ***Rude Pravo*** (Red Flag), dated 13 November 1937. Titled 'Portrait of a Trotskyist', it described me as the 'daughter of a Russian Whitegardist... who towards the end of 1935 had approached the Gestapo and had supplied them with information, but was at the beginning of 1936 dismissed by the Trade Delegation, and who was therefore ordered to go to the Czechoslovakia, where she was supposed to take up contact with the Czech group, which had been interrupted because of the "revelations" of Gryllewicz'. Had I known about this article at the time, I would have protested. But 40 years later... there seemed no point any more.

What was irresponsible on Broué's part was that in an unexpected footnote about me in volume eleven of the ***Oeuvres*** he used this incorrect information. He should have known better. He had come to interview my husband, Hugo Dewar, in April 1980. Hugo was ill in hospital at the time and after the interview Pierre Broué and I talked at home over a cup of tea about his researches for the ***Oeuvres*** and related matters and people. He asked me how I got to England, without a hint of this being an interview, and without taking any notes. It took me many letters of protest, extending over two or three years, until an erratum finally appeared somewhere at the back of volume fifteen.

The reaction of some people around me to the whole affair drove me near to despair. Of course, my personal friends from among our German Trotskyist circle stuck by me and were indignant at the action of the German Communist Party members. Elfriede and Julius Hollos, though they no longer belonged to any Trotskyist group, stood by me too and advised me throughout. But many of the people on the fringes, left-wing intellectuals, ex-Communist Party members who had dropped out of politics, and with whom I had become acquainted at Julich's, would no longer greet me, or sit with me at a table in the café. It was unpleasant for me and undignified for them. It was amazing how rigid people could be in their attitudes, yet how easily they could be swayed at the same time. Sometimes I did not know whether to laugh or to weep.

The worst thing of all, to my mind, was Jan Frankel's attitude. As soon as he got to know about it, he broke off all contact with me. He explained that he could not, for security reasons, expose either himself or the Old Man (as Trotsky was affectionately called) to any contact with somebody who had herself been in contact with the Gestapo, whatever the circumstances. It was not that he did not believe me, or had the slightest suspicion about me. (I must have told him the reason for my having had to leave Germany long before this.) But the very fact that I had had some 'dealings' with the Gestapo, and that the German Communist Party had denounced me as a spy, these were sufficient grounds for no longer considering me as a suitable secretary for Trotsky, and for breaking off all relations with me.

This was the greatest blow of all. Not because of losing the chance of working for Trotsky—I had not yet made up my mind whether I wanted to have that unique chance, though I probably could not have refused it—but I had considered Jan Frankel to be not only my comrade, but also my personal friend. I could not understand at the time how this could affect Trotsky, who was anyway hundreds of miles away, or how Jan Frankel could act in such a cold way, guided by nothing but political expediency. I do not remember whether he expressed any indignation at the local Communists' behaviour, or any regret at having to break off contact with me, though I can see the reasons now and am surprised by my own violent reaction at the time.

I felt shattered. It seemed that everything around me was breaking up and I was going to pieces. It was worse than the weeks before leaving Germany, when I could at least make decisions for myself and recognised the necessity for my actions. But the strain of the Nazi years, the emigration, the uncertainties of life as a refugee, the tension gradually building up in Czechoslovakia, all took their toll. I don't know how long that state lasted, but I remember days, and especially evenings, when I would pace up and down in my room, void of any clear thought or desire.

Neither I, nor apparently Jan Frankel, nor any of my old comrades, connected the attack against me with the Moscow trials, the second of which had started in January 1937, at exactly the same time as the Communist denunciation of me and the two others. None of us considered me to be an important enough person to be used as a pawn in Stalin's pursuit of Trotsky and his old comrades, whether of the Left Opposition or not.

I was also worried about my brother. I kept wondering how all this might affect him, whether he still had contact with German anti-fascist refugees, whether he read the German Communist publications. I had no idea how he would interpret the denunciation. I could not write and explain. I could only hope that if he read the later accusations and statements about our father having been a 'Whiteguardist', he would realise and not believe the rest of the story either. I would not have liked him to doubt my real political beliefs.

Worst of all was the possibility that since becoming a Soviet citizen he may have been arrested and sent to a concentration camp, without ever knowing anything about the denunciations against me. There had been one ominous incident. We did not often correspond, but some time during that winter of 1936-37 I sent him, upon his request, some ink, talcum powder and other small items. All harmless things, unobtainable in the shops; but my small parcel was returned by the customs officials, marked that these objects were not admitted into the USSR. The parcel was returned to the cover address I had given my brother—the address that turned out to be that of German-Czech Communists, which had been given to me as 'safe'. Whether or not this had something to do with the return of the parcel I do not know.

After the denunciation articles I wrote once more to my brother, trying to make it clear to him that there are times when it is better not to know each other—by which I meant that he should deny me completely if questioned about me. That was my last ever contact with my brother. I received no reply to that letter, and he never knew that I left Prague for London a few months later. He could not write to Olya in Germany. So we lost contact with him. After the war we sometimes wondered whether to try to trace him, but hesitated after all those years, hardly able to help him in any way. When we did try through the British Red Cross, as advised by the Soviet Embassy in London, the answer came back a year later that there were no traces of him, and no files about him could be found at that late stage. I doubted this, but there was nothing we could do. All that is left of him are a few snapshots, and a tiny teddy-bear, which somebody gave him when he was three years old and I have kept as a kind of mascot. Most of its fur has worn away, but its eyes are still bright.

So I had good reason to be distressed. But everything passes, and this acute state of despair also passed. I picked up the threads of my life and carried on as before. And there were still some enjoyable moments.

Dr Hubert Ripka, for example, kept in touch once the whole affair had been cleared up. Perhaps he felt guilty for having landed me in that mess. Or perhaps, being a journalist, he genuinely enjoyed our lively political and philosophical discussions at his office. I think I expounded Marxism to him in a rather idealistic way and firmly believed that though there were inadequate, unintelligent and downright objectionable people in the world, mankind as such had positive features and abilities and was bound to find the right way to a genuinely socialist society. He was sceptical about 'mankind', but had great respect and admiration for outstanding individuals. He thought I should read Francis Bacon and David Hume to broaden my ideas.

Hubert Ripka had started his career as a lecturer on the History of International Politics and a journalist, and eventually became foreign editor of the ***Lidové Noviny***. He was apparently a member of the Czech National Socialist Party, a liberal rather than a nationalist party. After Hitler marched into Prague in 1938 he fled first to Paris and then to London, where he was appointed State Secretary for Foreign Affairs by the Czech government in exile. He returned to Prague in 1945 but left again after the Communist coup in February 1948, again first for Paris and then for London. He played an important political role in exile and died in 1958.

He introduced me to his French wife, a lecturer at the French Institute in Prague and later in London, and his two charming little boys. And once he invited me, together with a friend of his, a Professor of Political Economy at the University in Prague, to a sumptuous dinner at a very smart restaurant overlooking the river Vltava at Baranov, a well-known villa resort on the outskirts of Prague. For me it was a real treat: the dinner no less than the illustrious company and the conversation. The journey to Baranov led through a very beautiful built-up area, with large, well-kept private gardens and villas built in the most modern and attractive styles—the abode of the rich Czech upper classes. Their architects seemed to me very avant-garde, without indulging in architectural excesses.

One really enjoyable event in the summer of 1937 was a visit from Olya and Nora, who was now two and a half. My landlady was kind enough to put a second bed in my room and I managed to borrow a cot. The cooking on a small primus cooker was less convenient, but we managed that too. We often went to the nearby park where there was a special playground for small children. Nora was puzzled. She kept wanting to play with the other children, but always came back to us, evidently wondering why they could not understand each other. She was also used to walking around naked at their little summer house with its large garden, which Olya and Arnold had acquired outside Berlin. So every now and then she would take all her clothes off, and then pull on her playsuit again, seeing the other children wearing them.

These strange surroundings must have bothered her, unknown to us, or at any rate to me. One day she lost her temper and threw my alarm clock on the floor. I could ill afford a new one, or even a repair, so without checking whether the clock was broken, I lost my temper too: I grabbed Nora and dumped her in her cot, where she cried loudly for an hour while I furiously insisted that she would have to stay there until she stopped wailing. Olya never interfered or said a word about my educational methods, though she must have felt strongly for the child. How much Nora must have missed her familiar surroundings was clear from what Olya wrote to me of her reaction when they returned home: 'There is Nora's little bed,' she called out happily when she entered her room. That was quite a lesson for me.

But on the whole it was a happy meeting, and Nora was usually very good. We didn't meet again until after the war, when I visited them in the summer of 1947. Arnold was then still a prisoner of war in Russia, having been captured on the last but one day of the war, and Olya and the children were nearly starving, like so many people in Germany at that time.

In Prague in the summer of 1937 I somehow felt the noose was tightening again. The growth of Nazism in Austria, the increasing possibility of war—we knew we would be trapped in Czechoslovakia, and more and more thought of the possibilities of seeking refuge somewhere else. Edith, the wife of Gerhard Schild, one of our group in Prague, had a domestic job in England, at Stanmore near London, and she put me in touch with a family that was in need of help and willing to take a refugee from Germany—as many families were. That was the only way for refugees from Nazi Germany to be accepted in England, unless you could prove you had sufficient means to support yourself. I agreed to go and work for them for thirteen shillings a week, with one afternoon a week and every other Sunday off. I was to start on 1 October.

The family, whose name I do not remember, except that their little boy was called Derek, turned out to be rather suburban middle-class—the husband was the local bank manager in Stanmore. But they were quite pleasant. I did not have to overwork: I learned English vocabulary while hoovering, and was free in the evening. But I felt isolated there in that London suburb, which was dead at night. And, my goodness, didn't I freeze in that small unheated bedroom of mine in winter! It had no plug for an electric fire, and a hot-water bottle (a new idea to me) did not help. The cold seemed to rise from the bed and creep all over me at night.

I had received the visa for England in good time and decided to stop over in Paris, secretly hoping to find a foothold there. I spent my last days in Prague saying goodbye to comrades, friends and acquaintances, and felt sorry to leave, in spite of everything. I was particularly reluctant to go to that unknown country across the Channel, hidden behind its fog, so far off the mainstream of events and revolutionary political life, with its morose and conventional inhabitants. But I remember being in Julich's with Willy Schramm, a German refugee and a journalist with leftish views, who tried to cheer me up and thought it was a good thing to get away for a time from doing nothing much, and to absorb new ideas and views. It was good advice.

So at the end of August 1937 I took the night train from Prague through Austria and into a new life once more. This time I was laden with two suitcases instead of a rucksack, though one contained little more than my typewriter and my pillow. I was not leaving much behind, but had no idea what to expect ahead. Yet I was considered lucky by many to be able to get out at all.

It was a long and tiring night on those hard benches in the third-class carriage, with the feeling of uncertainty about the outcome of this new adventure. I would have liked to visit Vienna on my way, but could not afford it. So I took the shorter route via Salzburg. I had to change trains there and had two or three hours' spare time. I went sightseeing, up to the castle on the hill overlooking the town, past the concert hall where all the famous Salzburg festivals are held and Wagner operas performed. I found the whole town rather unnatural, a pretty picture postcard, with all those pretty little houses in the old style. Most preposterous of all were the women: in the streets and the cafés, bank clerks and shop assistants, young and old, slim or fat, all dressed in those pretty *Dirndl* dresses with gathered, flower-patterned skirts, white blouses with short, puffed sleeves, ridiculous little aprons and some sort of cummerbund. I found it all very folksy and silly. Perhaps it was because I was sleepy, disgruntled and apprehensive. At the station I had struggled with my two cases and refused the help of a porter because, as I explained to him, I had no Austrian money to pay him; he insisted on carrying the case, but was really angry when I offered him my remaining Czech coins. As if I hadn't warned him!

From Salzburg the train went southwards, skirting the German frontier, then westwards towards Switzerland. That part of the journey was fascinating. I could not take my eyes off those craggy rocks and snow-clad summits as we passed the alps of the Tirol. The train was crowded and next to me sat a very healthy, young German-speaking man, who seemed to have done quite a bit of mountaineering. Where he was going I did not know, perhaps on holidays, perhaps he lived in Austria, but he kept pestering me to break the journey so that he could show me the mountains at close quarters for a few days. Why was I in such a hurry to get to Paris, he wanted to know. I became quite scared, wondering whether he might be a Gestapo agent who suspected I might not be the holidaymaker I pretended to be. But then he got off and I could relax and continue the journey unmolested.

I have no recollection of my arrival in Paris, whether Jan Bur met me at the station or how I spent the first few days. While I was still in Prague, Jan Bur and I had of course corresponded and I already knew that he was now helping Hilde to run her farm just outside Paris and had also assumed the role of husband and stepfather to her two young children. He felt very bad about it but asked me to understand: having arrived in Paris in 1935 with practically no knowledge of the language, he felt very lonely, with no personal contacts, only political ones. The tiny flat where I stayed with him in 1935 had had to be vacated, so there was the question of where to live. And my escape from Germany had also meant a financial setback for him, as I could no longer send him any money. Hilde, on the other hand, found it difficult to run the farm on her own. So she befriended Walter. She was probably a little older than him and though there was probably no particular love between them, there had in fact not been much more than attachment and friendship between him and me either. So although I had been disappointed by his revelation—mainly because it seemed to make the possibility of establishing myself in France more difficult—I had not been shattered by this development and in Paris we met again like good old friends.

I quickly found out how difficult the refugees' position was in France. If you were lucky enough to find a room or a small flat somewhere, you were constantly watched (like the Parisians themselves) by the *concièrge*, and there was no question of anybody offering you a bed for a few nights. In Prague you could always have counted on being put up by somebody for a while. In Paris everybody was much too scared. It was equally difficult to find work: there were just no casual or occasional jobs available, either for men or women. If you were lucky enough to find one, it often involved bribing the authorities to get a work permit, or bribing the police to have your visa extended.

I had too little money to go to a decent hotel but eventually found a room in a cheap working-class hotel, near the Porte des

Lilas, the sort which poor people make their permanent home. My room was on the ground floor. It was long enough for a bed and washstand, and wide enough for a table and a chair by the side of the bed, and the table was big enough to write a letter on or to have a meal of bread and cheese or a ready-made salad from a *charcuterie*. There was a small window at the end, opposite the door and high up near the ceiling, like in a prison cell. In daytime it gave just enough light to read a few pages. In the evening the bulb fixed to the ceiling was not sufficient even for that. Access to the room was either through the noisy, smoke-filled bar or through a side door on to a passage full of the stench from the toilets. But I was not unhappy there. I took the whole thing with good humour and, after all, the room was very cheap. I spent most of the days and evenings with friends, either in their rooms or their favourite café on the Boulevard St Michel, arguing and talking about the conference of the German Trostskyist organisation, the IKD, which was being held in Paris that August. I also walked around on my own, visited museums and galleries, and enjoyed Paris to the full, in spite of everything.

The atmosphere and morale among the refugees was in general not very good; not half as good as in Prague. Life was much harder in Paris and the factional struggles much sharper. I had come to Paris as a member of the Prague group, originally the old Berlin group that Jan Bur had organised. On the other hand, I was also somehow an outsider: newly arrived and just about to leave again. So I was not quite drawn into the discussions that were going on.

I also spent a few days outside Paris on Hilde's farm. It was a simple but pleasant house, in pleasing surroundings. Jan Bur had very enterprisingly gone in for sheep breeding and, much to the surprise and indignation of the local farmers, let his imported sheep stay out in the open all night long—quite unheard of! Hilde's two children went to the local school and spoke fluent German and French. About twice a week Jan Bur used to drive into Paris to meet the comrades, have discussions and organise the publication of the Bulletin.

When the German army invaded France, Jan Bur escaped to the south but was interned in a camp in Montpelier, then caught and imprisoned by the Germans. After Germany's surrender he made his way back to his home town of Krefeld, near Cologne, and began to organise help for former victims of the Nazi regime. He joined the Social Democrats, got married and eventually became a town councillor and honoured citizen of the town. He died some time in the 1970s. Hilde came to England after the war, where she started an agency for holiday exchanges between European children.

Whilst in Paris I also spent a few days with my old Russian friends the Pruzhans, in Tresnaux, where it was very peaceful. The garden was full of flowers and the orchard full of fruit. Insects hummed in the air. When it was time for me to return to Paris, Margarita Dmitriyevna walked down the footpath with me. She stopped half way. I kept turning round and waving to her, and can still see her in that sunny field with her big apron and kerchief on her head, waving back. When I next saw them, in 1947, they had not quite recovered from the terrible experience of the war, their failed escape to the south and life under German occupation.

I also visited her daughter Lyolya, a painter and writer, in her luxury flat in Paris. Her husband, also a Russian, was some sort of industrial consultant and they both travelled extensively. She greatly cheered me up by telling me how much she liked London and the English, who, contrary to general belief on the Continent, she found very pleasant and not at all morose and formal.

The day of my departure drew closer. One of the last things I did was attend the conference of the German group, or, more correctly I believe, of Jan Bur's faction. There I met Georg Jungclas, a comrade from Hamburg who had remained active under Hitler, but who eventually had to escape to Denmark. Later, after the Nazis marched into Denmark in 1939, the Gestapo caught up with him, he was sent back to Germany, imprisoned and sentenced to death. He escaped execution when the Allies, in the nick of time, invaded Germany in May 1945. When I met Georg, in 1937, he was a very round-looking person with a round face, a round body, and a cheerful disposition. After one of our meetings he asked me whether I would like to accompany him to the offices of the French Trotskyist paper ***Lutte Ouvrière***. I had nothing to do, so I went along with him. And there was Hugo.

He was sitting astride a wooden bench by a large trestle table stacked with papers, the walls of the room decorated with posters, his head raised towards a French comrade standing in front of him, as the two discussed something very heatedly—or should I say as Hugo held forth with a persuasive voice, first in French and then, when matters got too complicated, in English. It struck me that here was a real, ardent agitator.

Somebody introduced us and told him that I was a comrade and a refugee from Germany on my way to London. He introduced me to his friend Michael Colman, a young student, and they gave me their names and addresses in London. That greatly surprised me. Since 1933 nobody in the movement in Germany had lightly given their name and address to anybody.

Hugo was due to leave for London in a day or two, but Michael was leaving a few days later and we arranged to travel together. At the last moment, however, there was a hitch. My money had dwindled to practically nothing. After paying for my room and some odds and ends, and putting something by for the journey across the Channel, I had only a few francs left. These I loaned to Jan Bur, who found he had to make some unexpected payments in Paris. We arranged to meet at midday on the day of my departure, at the usual café, after I had given up my room and deposited my luggage at the station. But at midday there was no Jan Bur, nor at 12.30, nor at 1pm. Lunch time came and went. I did not know what to do. I could not leave for fear of missing him, and I could not order endless coffees, let alone a meal. Nor could I leave without those few francs, the only 'capital' I had—worth about £2. Then a Frenchman joined me. He must have been watching me for some time, wondering what I was doing. My tale about waiting for a friend seemed to sound a bit improbable, so in the end I left.

I walked around until 6pm and then went back to the café, hoping to run into one of the comrades. One or two turned up early and so—at last—did Jan Bur. He was very apologetic, but by no means distressed! On the way to town he had run over a chicken in a small village, and the farmer and neighbours were up in arms. Even the local policeman was called to the scene. That was why he had not turned up on time.

But now I had missed my train. Where was I to spend the night? I could not go back to my old hotel. Nor could I afford a room in another. None, but none, of the comrades could put me up. And nobody had sufficient money to offer me something for a hotel, even if it had occurred to them. Then, as we were passing yet another café, Willy Joseph, a former member of the German Communist Party who had fought in the Spanish Civil War, spotted two old friends, Claire and Pavel Thalmann. We did not know each other, but when Willy explained the situation they offered to put me up. They were a remarkable couple. They had been founder members of the German-Swiss Communist Party in their youth, after which Pavel spent three years as a student in Moscow (probably at the Lenin Institute). in 1936 they both went to Spain as journalists, got caught up in the Civil War and fought with the POUM and the Anarchists, who greatly influenced them.

They were eventually arrested by the GPU, which operated in Spain during the civil war, and spent a year in jail in Valencia, partly in solitary confinement. They were eventually released by the Spanish Republican authorities and had arrived, penniless, in Paris shortly before I met them. Somebody had given them temporary use of a small flat and that is where I stayed for my last night in France, on a mattress on the floor.

Being Swiss, Claire and Pavel survived the war in Paris, though not without danger since they were active in helping and hiding people, mainly Jews, and guarding their belongings. When Hugo and I visited them after the war, they were running a small news agency and kept open house for whoever turned up. We visited them every time we were in Paris. Later they moved to the south and grew carnations on a small property in the hills above Nice, which Claire then sold in the local market. For the rest of their days they lived a rather bohemian life, and welcomed numerous young left-wing people from Switzerland, Germany and France. Together they wrote a book about their experiences. Pavel died in 1980 and Claire in 1987. Her obituary notice must have been her own. It was in four languages and read: 'I am going to make the revolution in heaven.' It was typical of her.

The next day I boarded the train for Dieppe and took the night boat to Newhaven—a new haven indeed. I had never been on a sea journey before, except as a small child on that ship in the north of Russia, so even this short journey was an event for me. Having stowed my luggage, I went on deck to watch the harbour lights and buildings gradually vanish into the darkness of night. But the sky was clear, the moon was out, and the sea was very calm. I stood at the railings for a long time and watched the sea and the sky, listening to the soft splashing of the water against the keel, reflecting on everything that lay behind me, and wondering about the new life before me.

A great calm came over me and I suddenly had a feeling of great confidence in the unknown future, in the new life to come, in a new land. This confidence has proved to have been fully justified.

Epilogue

SOON AFTER my arrival in England I contacted Hugo and we used to meet on my free afternoons and on Sundays. Hugo introduced me to Daisy and Reg Groves, with whom he shared a house in Balham, as well as to other comrades who had once been members of the by then defunct Marxist League. He also took me once or twice to meetings of his trade union branch, of which he was chairman and delegate to the Wandsworth or Battersea trades council. Over Christmas I had a few days off and spent them with him. I had my first English Christmas dinner with him, his mother and his sister Roma. In the afternoon he took me for a stroll over Clapham Common—my first introduction to London's thick pea-soup fog.

By that time I had already decided to change my job, in spite of the protests of the family in Stanmore. A German comrade had given me an introduction to Freda Utley, at that time a well-known journalist and writer, who needed somebody to look after the house and her five-year-old son, John. Freda, an ex-Communist, was an interesting person and we three soon became friends. In the 1920s she had met Arkadi, a Soviet Russian who was working in London (probably with the Anglo-Russian Committee). When Arkadi was transferred to China and, at the beginning of the 1930s, back to Russia, Freda went with him. In 1937 he was arrested. Not till years later did she learn that he had died within a year of being deported to a labour camp in the far north to build the White Sea Canal. In Freda's house I worked twice as hard as in Stanmore, but I did not mind. Occasionally I even typed her manuscripts, which helped me greatly with my English.

Through her I also had the opportunity to meet and to learn something about the left-wing intellectuals and writers of the 1930s: Bertrand Russell, H N Brailsford, the poet Stephen Spender, the publisher Warburg and his somewhat eccentrically dressed wife, whom I met at one of Freda's parties. At the same party I had to give up my bed to Bertrand Russell—I must have slept on the floor in the boy John's room. So right from the beginning I was drawn into aspects of English life, without, however, entirely losing contact with German refugees.

Shortly after Christmas Hugo suggested that we get married. I hesitated, wondering whether he was just trying to be helpful, as a British passport would free me to take a more congenial job. But Hugo convinced me that he was quite sincere and as I, too, had grown fond of him, we were married at the end of January. But I could not leave Freda in the lurch and join my 'lovely' husband—which is how, in my faulty English, I had repeated the word 'lawful' in the marriage vow! So Hugo had to be content with visiting his 'lawfully' wedded wife and ringing me every day: 'Has Freda found somebody yet?' he would ask. Not till April could I join Hugo in his two upstairs rooms.

Hugo came home from work more than once to find me crying because I had no job and because I did not want to be dependent on him. He then used to soothe me by reciting poetry, which he did extremely well—he was the son of actor parents. I remember in particular the threats and incantations of 'The Congo—A Study of the Negro Race' by Vachel Lindsey, an American poet of the beginning of the century: 'Boomly, boomly, boomly, boom' and 'Mumbo-jumbo, will hoo-do-you'. As for Freda, she wrote her autobiography, **The Lost Illusions**, and later supported every wrong cause: Chiang Kai-shek, Nasser in Egypt, and she even had a good word to say about some aspects of Hitler's policy after a post-war visit to Germany.

In the summer of 1938 Hugo's mother moved out of London and we took over her flat facing Clapham Common. Hugo and the other comrades spent most Sunday mornings speaking to the crowds that gathered there. In August they launched the Socialist Anti-War Front, of which Hugo became the organising secretary, using as a base the nearby William Morris House, which belonged to the Independent Labour Party (ILP). They distributed leaflets, issued a pamphlet and a manifesto on the outbreak of the war. But it soon faded out.

Towards the autumn I managed to get a job as a shorthand typist with a company promoting Austrian steel. I did not like it very much, especially as the boss and his two youngish assistants seemed to have fascist leanings. But I stuck it out until the company was liquidated soon after the start of the war. Almost immediately I found work with the British branch of a Czechoslovak firm, also dealing in steel. It was a large business, with more interesting work and pleasant bosses and colleagues. By that time we had moved again, into a more spacious and sunny flat at the far end of Battersea Park, where we lived for the next 33 years. The start of the war saw a succession of refugees from Prague passing through that flat, some trying to establish themselves in London, others in transit to Sweden or the United States. The flat was also used for our political meetings till after the war. A young English friend of ours once said: 'That was not a flat, that was an institution.'

After a year and a half with the steel company I went to work as a radio monitor for the British branch of the United Press of America, which was then setting up a monitoring station in competition with Reuters, the BBC and other news agencies. They had rented a large two-storey house in High Barnet, a suburb to the north of London. We were a motley crowd of eight or nine women and men, all refugees from Europe, all with different backgrounds, all with a knowledge of languages and a grasp of international relations and the course of the war. We worked eight-hour shifts, but had to be on the premises for 24 hours, eating and sleeping there, followed by 24 hours off. We sat glued to our special radio sets, following the transmission times round the world, in English, German, Russian, French, and even in Rumanian for some of the time, taking the news down on paper, slightly sub-editing it, and then telephoning or teleprinting it to our head office in London.

It was hectic work at the best of times and the competition with other news agencies and the BBC was fierce. We had to be on the alert for special announcements or speeches by Hitler or Stalin. Or for war communiqués, usually introduced by a few brief bars of martial music. English announcements from Germany were often made by their star announcer and English renegade, nicknamed in England Lord Haw-Haw. Special news from Russia was read by an actor. Moscow Radio specialised in breaking the news of victories at any hour of the night, so one could never relax. How hectic this work was can be gauged from a letter a colleague and I received from head office congratulating us on an 'elegant scoop'—we had beaten Reuters by one second!

It was a well-paid job and the work was not routine, but after almost two and a half years of listening to the news—so many planes shot down, cruisers sunk and crew drowned, battles won or lost, so many men killed, wounded, taken prisoner, I could not take any more. In December 1943 I left. For a short time towards the end of the war I went once a week to replace a friend of mine who worked for another news agency, to give him a break. I remember the heart-breaking appeals for help one night from Prague radio, when the town was being bombarded by the Nazis and the Soviet Army, on the other side of town, was standing idly by, without firing a single shot.

At the beginning of 1943 Hugo was called up, after his application to be a conscientious objector on political grounds was rejected. After some tough initial training, mostly on the sloshy fields in Warwickshire, the new recruits could go on to do further specialised training. Hugo chose a six-month course in shorthand and typing—in London! Afterwards he worked in army offices, mostly in the Home Counties, near enough to be able to take part in the meetings in our flat. More than once he had to cycle back to barracks at the crack of dawn.

These meetings involved a group of old comrades and a few new ones, who were working as a Trotskyist group within the ILP—the Independent Labour Party—trying to stop it from rejoining the Labour Party and bring it nearer to Trotskyism. We continued this work right through the war, with me acting as go-between when Hugo was posted abroad. I used to send him reports of the meetings and he would, whenever possible, give advice or instructions, or send articles for the ILP paper **New Leader**, or for our own duplicated journal **Free Expression**, as well as the Scottish **Forward**.

Hugo's impressions of the war made him write verses and poems, which were published by **New Leader** and **Forward** and later as two booklets. In the army offices he had access to his own file, where he found the remark: 'Not considered officer material'. It amused him, and he much preferred the company of the other rank and file 'material', with whom he got on well, keeping up their spirits with his sense of humour and political discussions. But they could not keep a good man down for ever, and they eventually promoted him to the rank of corporal.

Early in 1945 Hugo was posted to a prisoner of war camp near Brussels where they had to sort out the belongings of the prisoners and dead German soldiers. It was distressing work, reading the letters from wives and sweethearts hoping for the end of the war and a speedy reunion. Equally disturbing was the fact that they were not allowed to socialise with any of the German soldiers, not even those who were cleaning their barracks and offices. That continued for quite a while after the end of the war. Not even a cigarette could be offered to a prisoner of war. All they could do was throw half-smoked cigarettes on the floor or leave them in ashtrays to be picked up.

At that time the army ran its own courses and discussion meetings for the British men, under the auspices of the Army Bureau of Current Affairs. The education officer in charge noticed Hugo's great skill in initiating discussions, and handed over the courses to him, after an initial two-week training. That suited Hugo very well, especially as he was given time off and a separate room for his preparation work. In his free time he made the acquaintance of some Belgians and made contact with the Trotskyists in Brussels.

In 1946, while he was still in Belgium, Hugo was nominated as the ILP candidate in a by-election held in Battersea. His nomination was accepted by the ILP leaders Fenner Brockway and John McNair, though probably somewhat half-heartedly, and the campaign was run on a Trotskyist programme, with the slogan 'Demand Socialist Action! Vote Socialist'. I will never forget that sweltering summer, the canvassing up and down the stairs of the tenement houses, knocking on the doors of the crammed terrace houses, the endless tea-making in our flat which served as an election office and a refuge for our exhausted comrades. Hugo received 250 votes—which was not surprising in the wake of the 1945 Labour landlside—and a letter of thanks from the ILP national committee, which had given him precious little support.

Then he was demobbed and had to decide what to do next. After a half-hearted attempt at a second-hand book business, which he thought would give him plenty of time to write, he became a teacher of English as a foreign language for the London County Council. In time he became the instructor in charge at one of its colleges.

In the meantime, before the war ended, I had taken over the job of a friend of mine who was expecting a baby. This was in the office of the Association for Education in Citizenship, an organisation founded by Mrs Eva M Hubback, who had been a friend of Ellen Wilkinson, Labour's first woman MP, and a group of like-minded liberals. They had branches in many parts of the country, published a monthly newsletter, pamphlets, and once a year ran a mock-parliament for senior school pupils which met in Westminster Central Hall, London. I was greatly impressed by the ease with which those young people made speeches from the rostrum or participated in discussion from the floor. Mrs Hubback, the honorary secretary, only visited the office to give instructions and answer the correspondence, by dictating letters to me. Once I had got the hang of the establishment I was mostly on my own, except for an occasional voluntary helper and the German bombs—

which shook that old building opposite St James's Park Underground Station and had me hiding in the corner to avoid splinters of flying glass.

I learned a great deal about English institutions and organisations while I worked there, but soon had to think about better-paid work, since Hugo's army pay was rather small. I found a job as personal secretary and bookkeeper to the owner of a chemical laboratory. I had hardly anything to do with the small crew of research chemists, except write the cheques for their salaries. The atmosphere was pleasant and friendly and much of the running of the office was left entirely to me. But when I received an offer to join the staff of the Royal Institute of Foreign Affairs, known more familiarly as Chatham House, I could not resist, even though it meant a cut in wages.

At that time Chatham House existed mainly on membership fees and contributions for specific research projects from various organisations, such as the Rockefeller Foundation. To some extent it was considered a privilege to work there, rather than just working for the money. I began on a part-time basis (combining it with my work at the laboratory), studying work practices in the Soviet Union. This had been initiated by a group of company directors based in Manchester, who turned to Chatham House for a study of the methods used by the Soviet opposite numbers to make their workers work, while here in England, they said, workers whose fathers and brothers were fighting at the front would still go on strike over a ten-minute tea break. I undertook the work with some amusement at the difficulty those directors were in! It was not easy to get the relevant material at that time, but I was able to produce a 130-page monograph on 'Industrial Management in the USSR', which was published in duplicated form in 1945.

After that I was offered a full-time job as assistant to Jane Degras, who was compiling and translating a comprehensive selection of foreign documents of the USSR, followed by three volumes of documents of the Communist International. Jane was an ex-Communist and a friend of Freda Utley, who had worked in Moscow for three years at the Marx-Engels-Lenin Institute. The arrangement didn't quite work out, and after a while she continued on her own, while I was moved to information and research, where I read the daily Soviet press and Soviet economic and political periodicals, providing members with such information as they required. Sometimes a trade union official would ring for information for a meeting or conference that night. Or I would have to interpret a Soviet move, such as the annual budget, for the monthly publication **The World Today**. I produced a study on 'Foreign Trade with Eastern Europe, 1945-1949' which was published in 1951.

Eventually it was suggested that I do some research on 'Soviet Labour Policy from 1917 to 1928'. I think it must have been requested by Professor E H Carr, who had already started on his **History of the Bolshevik Revolution**. But before I had finished my study, which had already developed into a substantial book with an appendix summarising all the relevant Soviet decrees, the funds from the Rockefeller Foundation ran out and Chatham House could not afford me any more. So I finished the book in my own time and it was eventually published in 1956. (A second edition came out in the United States some years later.)

I then followed Hugo into teaching and applied to take evening classes in German or Russian. But I was persuaded to teach English instead because, it was explained to me, I knew from experience all the difficulties of mastering English and understanding the English way of life. I accepted and, with some initial prompting from Hugo, taught successfully and greatly enjoyed it for twelve years. But for both of us this involved a split working day and mainly work in the evening, which really cut out active political work.

This was during the political downturn of the 1950s and early 1960s, and we were also probably tired of the many splits, fusions, and further splits in the various groups of the Left Opposition. But Hugo did manage to write, in particular a study, in crime-story style, of the persecutions and assassinations by the Soviet Secret Police of their former intelligence agents who had tried to defect. He also wrote an analysis of the Moscow Trials and the trials in Eastern Europe which followed. And a book on the Hungarian Rising of 1956.

Another book, with the title 'Communism in Great Britain', reached page-proof stage. but the 1959 printers' strike made his publisher bankrupt and the book never appeared. It was eventually published in a shortened version by Pluto Press in 1976—some chapters on the British Communist Party's fellow-travellers and Stalin's sympathisers among intellectuals and prominent Labour Party members having been cut—and now with the title **Communist Politics in Britain**. By that time Hugo had taken up writing poetry again, most of which appeared in **Socialist Worker** and some in **Socialist Challenge**. A small collection of his poems was eventually published by Bookmarks with the title **Arsy-Versy World**.

In the meantime we had acquired a rather dilapidated bungalow in the country which, by doing really pioneering work in both house and garden, we converted into a home to retire to. But we kept in touch with old and young friends in London, never quite integrating with the local population in this predominantly conservative area—though lately I have come across some pockets of dissent. Two or three years ago an elderly road sweeper remarked to me, 'What we need is a revolution!' I was so surprised that, regrettably, I did not stop long enough to ask what kind of revolution he meant.

In conclusion I should like to quote one of Hugo's poems:

If I should grow so old and wise
I look no longer with joyful surprise
at sunset and sunrise
—let me forever close my eyes.

If there is nothing left to know,
if the blood runs so cold and slow
I yearn not for all tyrants' overthrow
—then let me go.

If I forget the seed that lies
beneath the snow will someday rise;
if at the sight
of workers arming for the fight
my heart leaps not with delight
—then bury me tight.

For he that his whole youth denies
is surely dead before he dies

Hugo died in 1980, as convinced a Marxist and revolutionary socialist as he had been throughout his adult life—as, I hope, will I. Obviously I am disappointed that it is taking so long for the revolution to materialise. But come it must, if exploitation of man by man is to end and mankind is to survive. It is now up to the younger generation to give a lead.

Lindfield, December l988

Bibliography

Babette Gross, ***Willy Münzenberg: Eine Politische Biographie*** *mit einem Vorwort von Arthur Koestler* (Deutsche Verlagsanstalt, Stuttgart, *2te Auflage* 1968).

Tony Cliff, **Lenin: All power to the soviets! 1914-17** (Bookmarks, London 1985).

Tony Cliff, **Lenin: Revolution Besieged 1917-23** (Bookmarks, London 1987).

Chris Harman, **The Lost Revolution: Germany 1918-23** (Bookmarks, London 1982).

Margarete Buber-Neumann, ***Als Gefangene bei Stalin und Hitler*** (Seewald Verlag, Stuttgart, *2te Auflage* 1978). Published in English as **Under Two Dictators** (Gollancz, London 1949).

Pierre Broué (editor), ***Léon Trotsky: Oeuvres*** (23 volumes, Institut Leon Trotsky, Grenoble).

Duncan Hallas, **The Comintern** (Bookmarks, London 1985).

Hugo Dewar, **Communist Politics in Britain** (Pluto Press, London 1976).

Pierre Frank, ***Histoire de l'Internationale Communist 1919-43*** (two volumes, Editions de la Breche, Paris 1979).

Bookmarks
publishes many books on the revolutionary struggle for socialism.
Write for our current catalogue to: Bookmarks
265 Seven Sisters Road, Finsbury Park, London N4 2DE, England.
PO Box 16085, Chicago, Illinois 60616, USA.
GPO Box 1473N, Melbourne 3001, Australia.

Bookmarks bookshop in London also runs a large socialist mail order service. We have stocks of books and pamphlets from many publishers on socialism, internationalism, trade union struggle, women's issues, economics, the Marxist clasics, working-class history and much, much more. We will send books anywhere in the world.
Write for our latest booklists to:
BOOKMARKS
265 Seven Sisters Road, Finsbury Park, London N4 2DE, England.